SUCCESSFUL GRANT WRITING FOR SCHOOL LEADERS

10 EASY STEPS

Kenneth T. Henson
The Citadel

PEARSON

Boston   Columbus   Indianapolis   New York   San Francisco   Upper Saddle River
Amsterdam   Cape Town   Dubai   London   Madrid   Milan   Munich   Paris   Montreal   Toronto
Delhi   Mexico City   São Paulo   Sydney   Hong Kong   Seoul   Singapore   Taipei   Tokyo

Vice President and Editorial Director: Jeffery W. Johnston
Senior Acquisitions Editor: Meredith D. Fossel
Editorial Assistant: Nancy Holstein
Vice President, Director of Marketing: Margaret Waples
Senior Marketing Manager: Christopher Barry
Senior Managing Editor: Pamela D. Bennett
Project Manager: Kerry Rubadue
Production Manager: Laura Messerly
Senior Art Director: Jayne Conte
Cover Designer: Suzanne Behnke
Cover Art: James Randall Henson
Full-Service Project Management: Munesh Kumar/Aptara®, Inc.
Composition: Aptara®, Inc.
Printer/Binder: BindRite Graphics
Cover Printer: Lehigh-Phoenix Color Corp.
Text Font: ITC Garamond Std

Library of Congress Cataloging-in-Publication Data
Henson, Kenneth T.
  Successful grant writing for school leaders : 10 easy steps / Kenneth T. Henson.
    p. cm.
  Includes index.
  ISBN-10: 0-13-707272-4
  ISBN-13: 978-0-13-707272-9
  1. Educational fund raising—United States—Handbooks, manuals, etc. 2. Proposal writing for grants—United States—Handbooks, manuals, etc. 3. Proposal writing in education--United States—Handbooks, manuals, etc. I. Title.
  LC243.A1H46 2012
  379.1'10973—dc23

                                                                              2011023928

10 9 8 7 6 5 4 3 2 1

PEARSON

ISBN 10:   0-13-707272–4
ISBN 13: 978-0-13-707272-9

This book is dedicated to my wife Sharon (Worley) Henson,
my best critic and support.

CONTENTS

Introduction ix
Preface x

Chapter 1 GETTING THE RIGHT ATTITUDE 1

Introduction 1

Getting Focused and Knowing the Myths 2

MYTH NUMBER ONE: THERE IS NO MONEY AVAILABLE 2

MYTH NUMBER TWO: THE AVAILABLE MONEY GOES TO THE BIGGEST AND BETTER-KNOWN SCHOOL DISTRICTS 3

MYTH NUMBER THREE: SUCCESSFUL GRANT WRITING REQUIRES CONNECTIONS, AND I DON'T HAVE ANY 3

MYTH NUMBER FOUR: I DON'T HAVE TIME TO WRITE GRANTS 3

MYTH NUMBER FIVE: GETTING FUNDED JUST REQUIRES PREPARING SEVERAL GRANT PROPOSALS, AND LUCK DOES THE REST 4

MYTH NUMBER SIX: MEETING THE DEADLINE IS EVERYTHING 5

MYTH NUMBER SEVEN: I NEED TO FIND SOME EXPERTS TO COLLABORATE WITH ME. IT WILL FILL THE GAPS IN MY MISSING SKILLS, AND COLLABORATION WILL SAVE ME TIME BY DISTRIBUTING THE GRANT-WRITING WORKLOAD 6

MYTH NUMBER EIGHT: ALL I NEED TO DO TO GET MY PROPOSAL ACCEPTED IS TO CONVINCE THE EVALUATORS THAT MY DISTRICT HAS THE GREATEST NEEDS 6

Summary 7 • Recap of Major Ideas 8

Chapter 2 MOVING BEYOND THE MYTHS 9

Introduction 9

Tips for Handling Discouragement 9

Tips to Overcome the "Less Fortunate Us" Syndrome 10

Tips for Making Connections 11

Tips for Having More Time to Write Grants 13

Tips for Handling Deadlines 16

Tips for Collaborating with Others 18

*Summary 20 • Recap of Major Ideas 21
• List of Tips 21*

Chapter 3 USING THE RIGHT VOCABULARY AND TOOLS 22

Introduction 22

Getting the Language 22

Getting a Personal Library 24

Books 24

Journals 24

Cataloging 25

Three-Ring Binder 25

Mission Statement   26

Rating Forms   27

*Summary   31   •   Recap of Major Ideas   31
•   List of Tips   31*

Chapter 4   CHOOSING YOUR PATH   32

Introduction   32

Mapping Your Source   33

Targeted Audience/Block Grants   33

Range   33

Check the Amount   34

Taboo Topics   34

Matching Your Strengths with the Funding
Agency's Goals   34

The Triangular Model   35

The Funding Agency's Mission Statement   36

Using Your Three-Ring Binder   37

Your School and School District's Mission Statement   38

Sustainability   39

Facilities and Space   39

Human Resources   39

Awards   39

*Summary   42   •   Recap of Major Ideas   42
•   List of Tips   42*

Chapter 5   INCLUDING ALL THE RIGHT PARTS   43

Introduction   43

Transmittal Letter   44

Title Page   45

Abstract   47

Table of Contents   47

Purposes, Goals, and Objectives   48

Timetables, Timelines, and Flowcharts   49

Sustainability   50

Evaluation   50

Budget   51

Checklist   51

*Summary   52   •   Recap of Major Ideas   53
•   List of Tips   53*

Chapter 6   PREPARING THE BUDGET   54

Introduction   54

Clarity   55

Brevity   55

Personnel 56

Fringe Benefits 57

Indirect Costs 57

A Look at Sample Budget Parts 58

Personnel Expenses 58

Be Reasonable 59

Make In-Kind Contributions 61

Other Expenses 61

Evaluation and Sustainability 63

Project Sustainability 63

Giving the Mirror Test 65

*Summary 66 • Recap of Major Ideas 66
• List of Tips 66*

Chapter 7   DEVELOPING A SUCCINCT WRITING STYLE 67

Introduction 67

Write Simply/Avoid Unnecessary Jargon 68

Use Simple Structure 70

Replace Phrases with Single Words 70

Write Forcefully 70

Formula for Writing a Powerful Sentence 72

Write Correctly 74

Write Positively 74

Treat Genders Fairly 76

Use Graphics 76

NUMBERS 76

TABLES 77

GRAPHS 77

TABLES OF SPECIFICATION 77

*Summary 80 • Recap of Major Ideas 80
• List of Tips 80 • Reference 80*

Chapter 8   FINDING FUNDING SOURCES 81

Introduction 81

Part I: Funding Sources to Improve Classrooms 82

Funding Source: Credit Union of America 86

Parents: An Important Source 89

**Another Excellent Source: Professional Association
Grants** 90

Funding Source: Kappa Delta Pi 91

Funding Source: Phi Delta Kappa International 91

Small/Individual Grant Summary 91

**Part II: Funding Sources to Improve Schools
and School Districts** 94

A Principal's Proven Strategy for Identifying Grant Sources 94

Additional Excellent Funding Sources for School Districts   96

Funding Source: New England Dairy & Food Council   96

Funding Source: Ronald McDonald House Charities (RMHC)   96

Funding Source: Your Local College   98

Collaborating with Other School Districts   99

FOUNDATIONS GRANTS   99

NATIONAL ASSOCIATIONS   99

SPECIALTY PROFESSIONAL ASSOCIATIONS   103

Special Education   104

*Summary   111   •   Recap of Major Ideas   111
•   List of Tips   111*

Chapter 9   FORMING PARTNERSHIPS   113

Introduction   113

Proposal 1: Emergency Response and Crisis Management   114

Application Checklist   114

Table of Contents   115

Proposal Abstract   115

Budget Narrative   116

Executive Summary Performance Report   118

Lessons Learned from the Emergency Response and Crisis Management Grant   118

Proposal 2: Classrooms for the Future   121

Proposal 3: Project Elementary and Secondary Competency Approach to Performance Education (ESCAPE)   123

Purpose of the Proposal   124

A REJUVENATION PROGRAM   125

SETTING GROUND RULES   125

CURRENT ISSUES   127

DISSEMINATION   127

Lessons Learned from Project ESCAPE   128

Proposal 4: The Summer Physics Institute   129

TALKING THE TALK   130

UNIQUE FEATURES   130

A SPECIAL COURSE   131

A WEEKLY SEMINAR   131

Lessons Learned from the Summer Physics Institute Grant   132

Proposal 5: A Million-Dollar Technology Proposal   133

Results   135

Lessons Learned from the Technology Grant   135

*Summary   136   •   Recap of Major Ideas   136
•   List of Tips   136   •   Reference   136*

Chapter 10 GOING TO THE STARS   137

Introduction   137

Keeping Your Grant   137

Documenting Your Grant   138

Using Action Research   139

Developing Questionnaires   142

Selecting a Topic   142

LENGTH OF QUESTIONNAIRE   143

Types of Questions   143

ARRANGING THE QUESTIONS   143

Administering the Questionnaire   144

Testing the Questionnaire   144

Sending the Questionnaire   144

Preparing a Cover Letter   145

Summary   147

Workshops   147

Summary   148   •   Recap of Major Ideas   148   •   List of Tips   148   •   Reference   148

Appendices   149

3.1   Extended Glossary   149

6.1   Enhancing Education Through Technology Grants   151

6.2   Kathy Haven's TWI Bilingual Grant   165

7.1   Grammar Exercises   169

7.2   Grammar Exercises   174

8.1   List of Kappa Delta Pi Awards by State   181

8.2   Phi Delta Kappa International Regional Project Application   183

8.3   Beating to a Different Drum   188

8.4   Reach for the Stars   194

8.5   Ronald McDonald House Charities Grant Application Form   198

9.1   Cullman's Community Awareness Emergency Response Grant Project Narrative   201

9.2   Classrooms for the Future   213

9.3   A Module on Modules   237

9.4   Project ESCAPE Module List   240

Book Overview (Summary)   243

Index   246

INTRODUCTION

This book is written as a tool to help leaders improve their own grant-writing skills and to instruct others on how to write successful grants. The author has written more than 30 funded grants on a variety of topics—from art to physics, ranging from a few thousand dollars to several million. Altogether, the author has written and contributed to proposals earning over one hundred million dollars.

PREFACE

This book helps educational leaders give first-time grant writers the skills they need to write highly competitive grants. It helps leaders of experienced grant-writing teams prepare even more competitive proposals, large ones designed to substantially improve schools. Pennsylvania grant writer Joe Ziegler gives this advice to beginning grant writers: "Make the format simple and the message powerful." That's what I wanted to do for this book. Too often, grant writing is clothed in acronyms and jargon that make the process mysterious and unnecessarily difficult. Grant writing even has its own special language, a foreign language that challenges experienced grant writers and often confuses and overwhelms beginners. But you can help your teachers cut through this wasteland of strange terminology by examining the most frequently used terms, found in Figure 3.1 in Chapter 3, and by using the more comprehensive glossary found in Appendix 3.1. Experienced grant writers will probably choose to bypass these glossaries.

Those who have some grant-writing experience under their belts know the satisfaction of being empowered by grant writing. You probably want to get more big grants for your school and district, and you know you must engage your teachers in this pursuit as you continue to sharpen your own grant-writing skills. If you are one of the many leaders who has been given responsibility for directing your school or school district's grants, and you have never written a funded grant, or, if you have voluntarily taken on this responsibility to improve your administrative unit, and you feel like you are building a plane while flying it, relax; this book is designed to help you do both. If you already head a successful grant-writing program, this book increases your grant-writing knowledge base by giving you many powerful tips to enrich every proposal that comes through your office. The big bucks are out there waiting for you to take your schools to new levels. Those who have yet to write their first funded grant will be surprised to find how easy and rewarding grant writing can be. Many will learn to enjoy it.

This book breaks down grant writing into 10 easy steps. *Chapter 1* helps school leaders get their teachers' brains wrapped around this rather unnatural process—unnatural because it is clothed in unfamiliar terms, and its potentially straightforward and easy process is hidden beneath a sea of jargon and myths. Chapter 1 introduces several of these myths. *Chapter 2* provides tips for dispelling the myths. This chapter, and the remaining chapters, end with a list of concrete tips.

The best way to approach any job is to find an accommodating place to work and then equip it with the correct tools. *Chapter 3* helps you do just that: Set up your own grant-writing library and equip it with the right tools. Having gathered the necessary tools, your next step is to decide whether you will write your grants, search for funding sources or opportunities, and then craft each proposal to meet the needs of the funding sources. *Chapter 4* makes this decision easy.

Now it is time to decide what parts to include in each proposal. *Chapter 5* helps you decide this and shows you how to design each part to sell your proposal. Because the budget is such a critical determiner of a proposal's fate, a full chapter (*Chapter 6*) helps you prepare an irresistible budget. Here, you find several clearly stated practical tips accompanied by examples taken from many successful proposals written by Pre-K–12 educational leaders throughout the United States. Effective grant writing requires the use of a special writing style. Nothing turns off proposal evaluators faster than a poorly written proposal. *Chapter 7* is designed to help you develop your own grant-writing style.

Having learned all the steps required to write a highly competitive proposal, you are ready to "go fishing." The best angling skills and the best tackle and bait are of little use unless you know where to find the fish. *Chapter 8* directs you to good grant sources for educators, providing many Web sites. Here, you get grant-finding tips from successful grant writers across the country. Because *grant funders favor collaboratively written partnership proposals, Chapter 9* shares five partnership grants. Listen to these authors as they tell us why they wrote each grant, the grant's strengths, and what they learned from the experience: *Tips you and your colleagues can use in your next grant*. Once you learn that your proposal has been accepted, what's next? Then it's time to shift gears and make the grant work. It's also time to ensure that it will be refunded. These are the purposes of *Chapter 10*.

Throughout the book, you find examples of real grants, most written by Pre-K–12 educators located throughout the country, from Boston to Florida and Pennsylvania to California, in a mix of urban, suburban, and rural schools. You see the actual grants and hear the authors explain, in their own words, how they learned about these opportunities, why they wrote their grants, how each one helped their schools, and what they learned from writing the grants.

The appendices store the backup tools, including a glossary of grant terms, several full-blown grants, and some grammar exercises to help you develop a crisp writing style and avoid the most common grammatical mistakes.

WARNING! JUMPING AROUND IN THIS BOOK MAY BE HAZARDOUS TO YOUR HEALTH!

Not really, of course, but I wanted to get your attention.

This book has been very carefully designed to help you teach your grant writers to reach for the stars and beyond, to achieve goals they never thought possible. That's why it's done in 10 steps. You wouldn't ascend a staircase that offered to take you to your wildest dreams and try to skip a few steps, would you? You'll be amazed at how much you can accomplish if you take it one step at a time. Isn't that the advice you give when asked about a difficult task? Take it one step at a time. Isn't that how you got where you are today?

I am certain that if you follow these steps faithfully, and in order, you will accomplish so much more than you imagined. And you'll be making all kinds of money for your schools. Isn't that worth being a little patient? I think so.

Obviously, some of you have already been successful with small grants, or maybe a few bigger ones, but you wouldn't be reading this book if you weren't looking to improve your team's performance. And it's been my experience that even the most elementary facts, which you will find in the early chapters, are often overlooked by the most experienced grant writers.

No one can really make you do this, but as an experienced—and successful—grant writer, I'm here to offer you the keys to the kingdom. Don't let them slip through your fingers because you didn't take the first opportunity!

Let me know. And I mean that. Following is an Invitation to Provide Feedback where you can give me your honest opinion.

INVITATION TO PROVIDE FEEDBACK

To make future editions of this book better serve its audience, your comments are encouraged. If you have experiences and/or sample grants that you would like to share, your input will be carefully reviewed and considered for use in future editions. Meanwhile, I wish you success with all your present and future proposals.

Ken Henson
henson.kennetht@gmail.com

ACKNOWLEDGMENTS

I want to thank the reviewers of this book, whose input made the book better: M. Sabriya Dempsey, Philadelphia School District; Mary Henderson, Monmouth University; Roy Morris, Oconee County High School; Scott Roberts, Laredo Independent School District; Regina M. Taylor, Allen Independent School District; Marilyn Underwood, Marion County Schools; and Karen W. Ward, Centennial Middle School.

Appreciation is given to those who contributed to this book by sharing their grants and their expertise on grant writing. For giving their time so generously, a special thanks is given to elementary teacher and grant writer Christine File of Charleston County Schools (SC); teacher Cindy Brown, Lake Tahoe Unified School District (CA); teacher Brenda Mescher, St. Joseph Middle School (MI); Dr. Emily King and the Natrona School District (WY); teacher and grant writer Ryan Cumback of Charleston County Schools (SC); grant director Dr. Isaias Rodriguez of LaJoya Independent School District (TX); Dr. Fancheon Funk, retired Professor of Education at Florida State University; Dr. Patricia Williams, grant writer and retired Professor of Education at Sam Houston State University (TX); grant writer and former principal Connie Phelps of Emporia (KS); grant writer and former principal Dr. Karen Hayes of Omaha (NE); parent and volunteer grant writer Kathy Haven of Bijou Community School (CA); Paul McKenzie of Lancaster School District (SC); Victoria Spear, Secondary Curriculum Coordinator and Special Projects grant writer of Cullman County Schools (AL); grant writer and former high school principal Dr. John Ziegler of Greenville Area School District (PA); grant director Dr. Julie Cadwallader-Staub of Burlington School District (VT); former teacher Christie McWilliams (MI); and special educator and grant writer Wendy Wingard-Gay of the York School District (SC).

For his expertise in foundations, thanks go to Dr. John Beineke, formerly of the W.K. Kellogg Foundation and currently Professor of Education at Arkansas State University. For his expertise on partnerships with other districts, my thanks to Steve Zadravec, Assistant Superintendent of Portsmouth School District (NH), and for his expertise on partnering with colleges and universities, my thanks to Eastern Kentucky University's Dean of Education, Dr. Bill Phillips. My appreciation also to Peter Drescher and Peter Brownell, Vermont Department of Education; Pam McIntyre, Salina Education Foundation (KS); Heidi Walker, Cullman County Schools (AL); Susan Gehlmann, Berkley County Schools (SC); Alicia Korkinis, Charleston County Schools (SC); Phyllis Ledbetter, Dorchester School District (SC); project managers Kerry Rubadue at Pearson Higher Education and Munesh Kumar at Aptara; and copyeditor Gloria Paternostro.

Getting the Right Attitude

INTRODUCTION

Grant writing is all about power. As a leader, you understand power. Without it, you can do nothing. With it, there's no stopping. Successful grant writers have expert power. Your job is far too demanding for you to just dabble with grant writing. You know the old cliché: "Anything worth doing is worth doing right." You also know it is usually true, and because of the huge rewards and strong competition, it's never truer than when applied to today's grant writing. On the critical economic landscape, grant writing can turn a struggling school into a top performer. Done right, it will serve your school, your students, and your teachers. Those teachers just beginning to write grants will be surprised at the number of ways grant writing can enrich their classrooms.

Becoming a highly successful grant writer requires knowledge, skills, and work. But there is good news. It is within every dedicated teacher's reach. Teachers can take their grant-writing success to the level at which they are willing to work. I base this conclusion on the large number of first-time successes among my workshop participants. Furthermore, when they get some of these skills under their belts, grant writing can become easy and fun. All beginning grant writers need encouragement. Don't expect all your teachers to like grant writing, especially those who haven't tried it. Nobody is born with a drive for writing grants. In fact, even for those who come to embrace it, grant writing is definitely an acquired taste. But once they taste the success that comes from their first acceptance and once they feel the victory of serving their school and their students, most teachers never give it up. Department chairs will want to share the success stories scattered throughout this book with their teachers, such as the one written by Christine File, who had this to say about her first grant: "I spent 30 minutes writing and submitting a fully funded grant." Christine shares her grant source and walks us through this quick and easy process later in this book. Actually, much of the knowledge

Teachers can take their grant writing to the level they are willing to work.

"I spent 30 minutes writing and submitting a fully funded grant."

and skills required to succeed at grant writing is already in your teachers' heads. This book provides the key to help them unlock these skills.

Successful grant writing requires casting away some previous attitudes and reeling in some new ones. Some, but not all your teachers already have the self-confidence required to succeed at grant writing. But don't forget that it can be confusing and intimidating to inexperienced grant writers who do not realize how much potential they have to take total control and produce proposals that will be selected over all the competition. So the next step is to forge ahead.

GETTING FOCUSED AND KNOWING THE MYTHS

For those who embrace it, grant writing is a clear pathway to improving their classrooms.

Competence requires focus. Although the 30-plus funded proposals I have written and contributed to have earned over one hundred million dollars, I still learn from every grant I write. I realize there are tons of insights to be gained, if only I can remain focused and determined. For those who embrace it, grant writing is a clear pathway to improving their classrooms. For those who are willing to collaborate, it is the best hope for transforming their school and district to a level they, otherwise, could only dream about.

Being aware of the obstacles they will face on their grant-writing paths will enable them to turn frustrating and discouraging roadblocks into small bumps, letting them cruise by the many myths that defeat less confident and unsuspecting writers.

Myths are not strangers to educators. In our schools, we hear many myths. "I didn't do as well on that test as I could have because I over prepared." Or "I simply overstudied." And I'll bet you have heard this one: "You are wasting your time preparing for the GRE and MAT. Studying for standardized tests doesn't help." We never seem to outgrow these myths. In fact, they follow us right through graduate school. Regardless of where you went to school, you probably recognized these all-too-familiar statements. But you know better; these are myths, and they are wrong. What does overstudied mean? Certainly not that the material became overly clear. This is the voice of the inexperienced. It probably means I waited until the night before taking the test and pulled an all-nighter.

After three decades of conducting workshops from coast to coast, I have learned that most myths are created by people who haven't taken time to learn how to write competitive grant proposals, who do not plan to develop such skills, and some who, either consciously or subconsciously, would prefer their colleagues do not develop these skills. By spreading these myths, their either purposeful or subconscious strategy is to discourage others from successfully developing proposals that will be funded, knowing their colleagues' grant successes would raise the bar for them.

By spreading these myths, their purpose is to discourage others from writing grants and raising the bar for them.

Following are some myths that trip, discourage, and defeat many aspiring grant writers. Your teachers don't have to fall victim to these snares. Alert them to these and similar discouraging myths. Once they recognize these myths, they can dismiss them and get on with their grant writing.

MYTH NUMBER ONE: THERE IS NO MONEY AVAILABLE.   The message embedded in this myth is that because of the current economic disaster, we are wasting our time trying to get money that isn't there. Although the economy waxes and wanes, and although it is currently in a state of critical disrepair, at any time during any year, millions of dollars—no, not millions, but *billions* of dollars—have been set aside and are waiting for us to come and take them. There's even better news; the people who work in the government and private foundations and agencies making this money available are just as eager to find the right person to give the money to as we are eager to receive it. A former Kellogg Foundation director said giving away money is easy, but giving it away well is difficult. Obviously, grant funders get excited when they find the right recipients for their money. I feel their energy every time one of my grants is approved. You can assure your teachers the grant-writing money pot has never been empty, and it isn't likely to run dry any time soon.

MYTH NUMBER TWO: THE AVAILABLE MONEY GOES TO THE BIGGEST AND BETTER-KNOWN SCHOOL DISTRICTS.
I've heard it again and again, "My district is poor and relatively unknown. Ironically, that's why we need the money. We are critically underfunded. It seems like a catch-22. Those who have, get. And those who don't, don't."

Actually, some grants are earmarked to help lesser-known, disadvantaged schools. But even if you work in an unknown, needy district, don't depend on these monies. Perhaps better said, target these funders, but don't target your grants *only* to requests for proposals (RFP) designed to help impoverished districts.

Your suspicion that some districts seem to get far more than their share of the grant monies is warranted; some districts definitely do get more than their "fair share." This is because someone (or perhaps a group of individuals) in those districts knows how to write really good proposals, and once funded, these experts do an excellent job managing the money. Naturally, their long track records of delivering in full on their promises build serious credibility as the funding agency workers become familiar with the work of these dedicated and skilled grant writers. The funders will be predisposed to give careful consideration to those grant writers who have earned this trust. If your district struggles financially and does not have a polished grant-writing program, it is definitely disadvantaged. But relax; this is no cause for worry. This book shows you how to build and improve your own grant-writing machine.

MYTH NUMBER THREE: SUCCESSFUL GRANT WRITING REQUIRES CONNECTIONS, AND I DON'T HAVE ANY.
To be sure, when used effectively, knowing people in the funding agencies can be a valuable asset. If you have colleagues or friends in one of these offices, or even if you have friends who know people in the funding agencies, you should use these contacts; let them know about your application. But the old saw, "It's who you know, not what you know or what you can do that matters," is dull from overuse. All you have to do to dispel this myth in your own mind is to step back and think, "If I were trusted with the responsibility of handing over someone else's money, would I look to friends or would I ask what the owner (my boss) wanted to get from this money and try to find the proposal that would get the most return for the dollar?" The bottom line is that although good connections can help, successful grant writing does not require them. In case your teachers don't find these words convincing, and they still believe connections are necessary, Chapter 2 offers three effective strategies for making connections.

MYTH NUMBER FOUR: I DON'T HAVE TIME TO WRITE GRANTS.
The pace in today's schools is such that most educators are scurrying to get through the tasks that must be completed by the end of each day. When

Funders are just as eager to find the right people to give the money to as we are eager to get it.

The grant-writing money pot has never run dry, and it isn't likely to do so any time soon.

The old saw, "It's who you know, not what you know or what you can do that matters," is dull from overuse.

the day is over, they hit the freeways, where almost everyone finds 70 miles an hour uncomfortably slow. In recent years, to accommodate this lightning-fast lifestyle, yield signs have been replaced by merge signs, where disaster awaits anyone who doesn't take time to look for oncoming vehicles. If we do take time to notice our own behaviors and the behavior of others, we realize it is, indeed, a mad world; no wonder we conclude that we don't have time to write grants. Yet we have the same number of hours in the week as everyone else, and we are all challenged daily to meet accountability standards and keep up with the demands of advancing technology. Most school districts are not fortunate enough to have employees whose only responsibility is to write grants. Having a designated grants office can facilitate the development of a well-oiled grant-writing machine, but even these offices are seriously pressed for time. The rest of us will have to learn how to work grant writing into our overcrowded schedules. Chapter 2 shows you exactly how to help your teachers do just that.

Only a few schools are fortunate enough to have employees whose only responsibility is to write grants.

MYTH NUMBER FIVE: GETTING FUNDED JUST REQUIRES PREPARING SEVERAL GRANT PROPOSALS, AND LUCK DOES THE REST. Many

unsuccessful, would-be grant writers lean on Lady Luck for help. Incidentally, they also blame Lady Luck for their failures. Actually, sometimes luck does play a role in determining whether a proposal will be funded. For example, you might prepare an excellent proposal but it just happens that this RFP brought in the largest number of well-prepared proposals ever received. Now, that's bad luck, and you just have to live with it. At this point, some grant writers throw up their hands and quit. Others respond to rejection by cranking up their grant-writing activities, attempting to even the odds by rapidly producing a lot of proposals. But sadly, just writing a lot of grant proposals is not likely to produce the level of success you and your teachers are capable of reaching. A sustained program of successful grant writing requires producing *top-quality* proposals. A few excellently crafted proposals, targeted to the appropriate markets and chosen to meet your district's most pressing needs are likely to succeed at a level far beyond the success that comes from writing a flurry of mediocre proposals. If, indeed, your district's grant-writing team is to use grant writing to substantially improve the performance of your schools, each proposal must be nothing short of *the best it can be*.

Each proposal must be nothing short of the best it can be.

Sometimes we can clear our vision by putting ourselves in someone else's place. It is now time to put your teachers in the shoes of those people who read and evaluate grant proposals. Sometimes called reviewers, in this book these people will be called evaluators. What would impress your teachers the most if they were responsible for selecting one grant proposal over another? First, they would consider the funding agency's mission. What kinds of jobs does the agency want to get done? What evidence is there that the writer of Proposal A will do a better job than the writer of Proposal B, or vice versa? Most grants exist because there is a job to be done. So if you are an evaluator, the first thing you would look for in the proposal is assurance that this proposal writer would do a better job than all the competitors.

Next, if you were hired to evaluate proposals, you would want to get your boss's money's worth, a high rate of return on each dollar. So you would examine the budget carefully to be sure it is economically responsible. Suppose you find three or four proposals whose authors have convinced you that, if given the job, they would do high-quality work. Then, from these best proposals, you probably would select the one with the lowest budget, but only if you believed the budget was big enough to provide a quality job.

In summary, luck plays a major role in determining the grant writer's success *only* if the grant writer lets it. Effective grant writing shadows and diminishes the role that luck plays in determining success. Strong leaders don't put their future and the future of their schools in the hands of Lady Luck. Neither do strong grant writers. They don't have to. All they need to do is learn how to outperform their competitors by preparing stronger grant proposals. This book provides the guidance needed to prepare a highly competitive grant proposal, including a convincing budget.

Luck plays a major role in determining a grant writer's success only when the grant writer lets it.

MYTH NUMBER SIX: MEETING THE DEADLINE IS EVERYTHING.   By itself, meeting the deadline is nothing. The only time meeting the deadline is important is when you submit a *high-quality* proposal on time. Consider the following example; you might call it the eleventh-hour proposal (see Box 1.1).

BOX 1.1   The Eleventh-Hour Proposal

Monday morning had lived up to its reputation. It was one of those mornings when everything goes wrong. No major disaster, but all morning long, little fires had broken out everywhere. The second hand on grant director Bonnie Shaw's office clock slowly jumped and skipped until it finally reached 12:00. Desperately needing a break, Bonnie began closing her office door and reaching for her brown paper lunch bag. Finally, she could catch her breath and have a little peace and quiet with her lunch. But then she heard a familiar voice address her secretary, who also had lunch on her mind and was closing the door on the opposite side of her office.

"Wait! Wait! Wait! Before you close that door, please, I need Dr. Shaw's signature on this grant proposal. It must be delivered to the state capitol building before closing time today."

Because of the enormous amount of paperwork that flowed through her office daily, Bonnie had a rule that all papers requiring her signature had to be left overnight. This was a good policy because it gave her time to read and reflect on each document. Yet because this was one of the district's outstanding teachers and a seasoned grant writer whose previous grants had brought the school tens of thousands of dollars, Bonnie made an exception and agreed to read this proposal during her lunch hour. Because this was only one of the many pieces of mail awaiting her attention, and the noon hour was the only time she had during the day to go through her mail, Bonnie quickly scanned and signed this large proposal. After all, this teacher was always careful to dot her *i*'s and cross her *t*'s. At 1 P.M. the secretary called the anxious teacher, and the signed proposal was on its way to the state capitol.

About a month passed before Bonnie learned about her oversight, a big mistake for which she would pay with her own reputation for being careful about details. Somewhere within the 30 pages of this proposal was a plan for introducing a few advanced placement (AP) college courses scheduled to be offered at a local university the coming fall. Proposals for any new courses have to pass through the university's academic committees, a process that usually takes several months. How embarrassing! But Bonnie knew she had only herself to blame.

Other grant directors may not use the term "eleventh-hour proposals," but they know the concept, and most are aware of the damage that rushing to meet a short deadline often causes. Donald Orlich, a grant-writing expert in the state of Washington, said he considered this habit of rushing to meet deadlines one of the greatest weaknesses of most grant writers. He set a minimum time of 20 working days for writers to have available before a proposal is due, warning that the writing of proposals for complex projects or for projects to which writers have not already given considerable thought, will require even more than 20 days. In summary, *there is no prize for meeting deadlines, only penalties for missing them.* Chapter 2 shows you how to avoid these penalties.

There is no prize for meeting deadlines, only penalties for missing them.

MYTH NUMBER SEVEN: I NEED TO FIND SOME EXPERTS TO COLLABORATE WITH ME. IT WILL FILL THE GAPS IN MY MISSING SKILLS, AND COLLABORATION WILL SAVE ME TIME BY DISTRIBUTING THE GRANT-WRITING WORKLOAD.

At some point, a teacher is going to ask you whether collaborating with colleagues is a good practice and whether it will reduce the workload and the time required to craft a quality proposal. These are good questions. Collaboration has both advantages and disadvantages. When the right people collaborate, the quality of the proposal and the quality of the experience can be enriched. Also, the really big grants needed to bring systemic improvement to schools are almost always written by teams of colleagues and other members of the community who are passionately committed to reaching the same district-wide goal. This makes the decision to collaborate on large proposals a good choice. But collaborating will not reduce the workload, and it can become a crutch for those who depend on the expertise of more experienced grant writers; therefore, you may want to encourage those teachers who have never written a proposal to begin by writing a small proposal by themselves. They must realize that if their goal is to write a small classroom improvement grant, *they don't need anyone else's help. This is something they can do by themselves.* For a confidence builder, see the Kathy Haven's story in Appendix 8.4.

For writing small classroom-improvement grants, teachers don't need anyone's help.

MYTH NUMBER EIGHT: ALL I NEED TO DO TO GET MY PROPOSAL ACCEPTED IS TO CONVINCE THE EVALUATORS THAT MY DISTRICT HAS THE GREATEST NEEDS.

For education grants, especially those funded at the state level, and for grants funded by philanthropic agencies, this belief may have some validity; however, for most other funding agencies—including state and federal agencies—it totally misses the mark. This could be called the Uncle Daniel approach, named after the kind old gentleman in Eudora Welty's book, *The Ponder Heart.* Uncle Daniel's favorite pastime was going downtown on Saturday morning and looking for strangers. When he saw an unfamiliar face, he introduced himself and gave the stranger a lot of money—just to make his new acquaintance happy. Unfortunately, there are few Uncle Daniels in the grant-writing world. So don't spend all your time and energy trying to convince the grant readers your needs are the greatest; spend your time designing a proposal that will convince the readers you will do the best job meeting, not your own needs, but *the funder's needs.* Chapter 2 is written to prepare you to do just that.

Most grants go not to those with the greatest needs but to those with the strongest proposals.

Summary

Because people's attitudes inevitably shape their behavior, the most important factor that determines the degree of success people experience when writing grant proposals is their attitudes. Many would-be grant writers who have the talents to become outstanding grant writers are prevented from reaching their goals by several misconceptions about the process. The most important attitude a grant writer can have is a sense of efficacy: "I *can* and I *will* develop the necessary skills, and I will succeed at the level I choose to succeed." As a leader, you must take this attitude one step further: "I can and I will lead my faculty in successful grant writing and in the development of grant-writing skills."

This attitude reflects an internal locus of control: "I am in charge of my world." I won't trust my grant-writing future to Lady Luck or even to my more experienced colleagues. Most effective leaders, and some teachers who are not in leadership positions, have this take-charge attitude. Most people who don't have an "I can do it" attitude don't succeed at much of anything, and they build their lives on excuses. Many people who choose to take the low road, avoiding anything requiring additional work, don't particularly want the people around them to succeed either, especially their own co-workers or colleagues, because it would make the less industrious look bad. So people who consider themselves incapable of grant writing often initiate and promote false beliefs (or myths), and are always all too willing to share these beliefs. For example, they may say that the grant money sources have been emptied by the failing economy; that the grant money always goes to larger, better-known districts; that successful grant writing requires connections; or that they just don't have time to write grants. These conclusions are simply wrong. Billions of dollars await the arrival of well-written proposals. Connections are great, and if you have any, you should use them. But they certainly aren't necessary. All that is required to establish or improve the grant-writing program in your school is to help your teachers master the tips given in this book, help them determine the needs of potential funders (more help is coming on this one), and help them craft each proposal to match the requirements of the potential funders.

Grant-writing success will not come from rushing to produce a lot of quickly thrown-together proposals just to meet the deadlines. Success will come from learning how to produce excellent proposals, each targeted to a specific funding source, and from taking the time required to make each proposal better than the other competing proposals.

Because of the economic crisis and the pressure to improve high-stakes test scores, there's never been a more *critical* time for educators to write grants. But to succeed at grant writing, you must help all members of your learning community recognize several myths that provide roadblocks to unsuspecting writers. Regardless of the size or location of your schools, if you are determined to make each proposal *the best it can be*, well-crafted grant proposals, coupled with the skills laid out in the coming chapters, will provide you and your teachers an excellent chance of getting each proposal funded.

The rapid pace in today's schools leaves us feeling we don't have time to write grants. But, in fact, we have the same number of hours in the week as our counterparts across the country, many who are using grant writing to turn around their failing schools or to take their already successful schools to even higher levels.

Feeling a little unsure of their ability, some beginning grant writers believe they need to form or join a team. But, in fact, your teachers don't need a team, at least not until they have first developed some essential basic grant-writing skills. As many district grant directors testify throughout this book, there is no substitute for a well-oiled, grant-writing team. However, for beginners who are not willing to work hard to develop their skills, a team can become a crutch. All you need is to learn how to help your teachers craft excellent proposals, which the following chapters are designed to prepare you to do. If you need a little more assistance as you work to help your teachers deal with the myths you have just confronted, Chapter 2 (Moving Beyond the Myths) provides some specific nuts-and-bolts tips you can use to help your teachers overcome these obstacles.

RECAP OF MAJOR IDEAS

- Attitudes shape your behavior; therefore, your grant-writing success cannot exceed your belief in your own abilities.
- Successful grant writing doesn't require luck; it just requires crafting excellent proposals.
- Money is always available and waiting for those who prepare well-written proposals.
- The major goal for grant writers is to produce proposals that convince readers they and their district will do a better job than any of the competing writers will do at meeting the funder's goals.
- Adequate time is available for those who assign grant writing a high priority.
- Meeting the deadline has no rewards unless coupled with a very well-crafted proposal.
- Collaboration can become a crutch; it never replaces the need to develop basic grant-writing skills.

Moving Beyond the Myths

INTRODUCTION

This book is full of hard nuts-and-bolts tips, each of which will increase the probability of your proposals being accepted. The tips offered in this chapter will help you get your teachers beyond the myths discussed in Chapter 1. As you read this chapter, put your teachers and yourself on alert and, at all times, *watch out for the many obstacles that defeat less aware, would-be grant writers*. Although you probably would like to fire all the naysayers you meet (and perhaps the world would be greatly improved if you could), you know you can't do that. The next best option is to *focus on the winners, not the losers*. Here's my next tip, which you should share with your teachers. *Any time you hear a discouraging comment about grant writing, it's time for some critical thinking, so distance yourself from the speaker and think it through.*

TIPS FOR HANDLING DISCOURAGEMENT

When naysayers tell you the grant money well has dried up or you are wasting your time writing grants because you don't have the right connections, how do you convince them their thinking is wrong? You don't. Why would you discuss grant writing with anyone who doesn't write grants? For every reason you give them for writing grants, these naysayers can give you three reasons why they should not. Warn your teachers about the naysayers. Tell them that when overhearing such discouraging comments, the best response is to say nothing and just walk away. No doubt you have had plenty of contact with people who are against anything coming down the pike, especially anything that could cause more work for them. The naysayers you will face in your grant-writing world are no different from the ones you already know. Nothing can be gained from focusing your attention on them.

For every reason you give naysayers to write grants, they can give you three reasons why they should not.

Fortunately, you probably have several teachers who are the exact opposite of the naysayers; teachers who are upbeat and positive. Use your time and energy to help them.

TIPS TO OVERCOME THE "LESS FORTUNATE US" SYNDROME

For most grants, the time between the release of the request for proposals (RFPs) and the proposal due date is, to say the least, uncomfortably short. What can you do about the fact that some school districts have an inside track on grant writing? They even learn about the upcoming grants long before the RFPs are released, and they are usually able to get grant approvals to come their way. What can you do about their high levels of success? Nothing, except maybe borrow some of their strategies.

You might label this sort of thinking the "Less Fortunate Us" syndrome—the idea that other districts are favored to get the money, and we are the orphan school district that always gets left out. Or you might even admit that the idea of grant writing frightens you. That's understandable because some teachers are appointed to the position of grants director simply because they have English degrees. Or you might even admit that this whole grant-writing business is just not your cup of tea. So why not leave it to those who love it?

Paul McKenzie, Director of Research and Development in the Lancaster School District in South Carolina, shares all these feelings. He hates being the underdog. He hates being located in a state that doesn't get its fair share of grants. He even admits he hates grant writing. But guess what? Over the last 10 years he and his partners have written grants that have collectively earned over 50 million dollars, and they have no plans to stop writing grants. Box 2.1 shares his explanation.

Tip: Rather than envying successful school districts, *start developing or improving your own grant-writing program now*. Once you have developed the necessary grant-writing skills, you may need a small grant-writing team that will become experts at this game. Vermont's Burlington School District Grants Director Julie Cadwallader-Staub offers a good tip for all individuals who are thinking about writing grants: Always work with your district office and with your principals and teachers. A major reason for your teachers to contact the district office at the onset of a new proposal is that the district office can give helpful advice and support. Another reason to encourage your teachers to inform their administrators is to avoid

Always work with your district office, principals, and teachers.

BOX 2.1 We Hate Grant Writing

Pressured deadlines, confusing bureaucratic constraints, way too many acronyms. In 10 years we've authored over $50 million dollars in funded state, federal, and foundation grants. And we hated every single minute.

We've received funds for after-school programming, health and fitness activities, arts education, substance abuse prevention, college preparation, mentoring, and teen pregnancy prevention. We've authored grants to fund an annual conference that has drawn participants from over 20 states and Canada.

We've used grant funds to support preschool education, home visitation models, and an initiative to address the minority achievement gap. We hated every minute of it. But in the end, we're still doing it and would do it all over again.

the situation where a member of your team asks a potential donor for money without first making sure someone else in your district is not already asking them for support." Here's a worst-case scenario example of why every grant writer should always check with the district office. How would you feel if you learned a local bank was about to honor a request from your district for $50,000 to install SMART Boards until a teacher tapped the same donor for $2,000 to buy calculators for her math classes, and then another teacher asked them for money to buy books for his reading classes? Now, it appears the donor may start getting monthly requests from your district, so the donor decides to withdraw the $50,000 gift and have nothing else to do with your district. The point here is to encourage teachers who decide to write small grants for their classrooms to always inform the principal's and superintendent's offices when they begin considering developing a new proposal.

TIPS FOR MAKING CONNECTIONS

You told your teachers they don't have to know anyone in the funding office, although such connections can be helpful, but if you have any connections, you should use them. You also told them connections are not required to get their proposals funded. But suppose some of your teachers still believe that inside connections are necessary. Now, what can you do? Here's what you can and should do. Help them make some connections. Following are three easy ways to do this.

Connections are not essential, but they can help, and you can make your own.

First, take them on a trip. If at all possible, arrange for them to meet with the funding agent. If it's a state-level grant you are seeking, make an appointment to talk to a member of the grant committee and drive to the capitol. If you live in Alaska or Texas, the distance to the state capitol may prohibit a personal visit. In such cases, the telephone is a good option. Be familiar with the RFP. As you talk to the grant officers, listen to see if you can identify any agency needs not discussed in the proposal. Be ready to tell the agent all the unique features (strengths) of your proposal. But, suppose this is a federal grant and your travel budget is nonexistent or depleted, or your district needs you and you can't afford to be away, even for a day. What then? When I posed this question to Patricia Williams, a grant-writing friend who lives in Houston, Texas, she immediately said: "Pick up the phone and call the agency." I've never known Patricia to be wrong. **Tip:** *Pick up the phone and call the agency.* Patricia's grant-writing success speaks for itself. So listen to her advice. But before you do, let me give you my own tip. **Tip:** *Before making your call, carefully read the RFP, making a bulleted list of the donor's needs.* Perhaps the most important fact a grant writer can know and remember is *the needs and desires of potential funders always trump the grant writer's needs.*

The needs of potential funders always trump the writer's needs.

Now take a sheet of paper such as the one shown in Figure 2.1. Notice that the top half of the page is to be used to gather additional information from the potential donor. More exactly, the top half is used to gather some of the funder's wants that are not expressed in the RFP. Leave a few bulleted spaces at the top to write in any unannounced, new wants of the funder. Think about this for a moment, and you will realize just how important this tip really is. The odds are overwhelming (probably 99%) that none of the

I. Funder's wants beyond those discussed in the RFP:

-
-
-
-

II. Additional information about the proposal to further whet the agent's interest:

-
-
-
-

FIGURE 2.1   Phoning the Agencies

Use phone calls to whet the funder's interest in your proposal and to gather information that is not in the RFP.

other grant writers who apply for this grant will phone the agency. This means your competitors know only what is in the RFP.

Now, notice that the bottom half of this page will have some short, bulleted statements. Each statement informs the funder about one of your proposal's strengths. (Incidentally, I use bullets because they remind me to keep my responses short. Funding agents appreciate brevity. Furthermore, this bulleted list forces me to include each proposal strength.) Funders also appreciate clarity. When you begin writing or rewriting and embellishing your proposal, you will want to *use each bulleted statement to whet the agent's appetite*. Your phone call has two purposes: To gather some funder wants not mentioned in the RFP and to cause the agent to look forward with much anticipation to receiving your proposal. When you hang up the phone, while these additional funders' needs remain clear in your mind, you must carefully work each bulleted need into your proposal.

So these are two good tips for making connections. But I believe I promised to give three; so, just in case you are counting, here's my third tip. **Tip:** *Offer your service, and encourage your teachers to let you offer their services as proposal evaluators*. Most of the national funding agencies, such as the National Institutes of Health or the National Science Foundation, receive dozens, and sometimes hundreds, of responses to each RFP—far too many for their limited staff to read; therefore, they frequently find they need help. With your superintendent's permission, send your curriculum vitae and those of your volunteer faculty members, along with a cover letter explaining everyone's area(s) of interest and expertise, and let these funders know that as the needs arise, you would like your teachers to serve as proposal evaluators. For a look at some sample volunteers, check the list that Buffalo Colorado School District uses in its proposals (see Figure 4.5).

Serving as a proposal evaluator lets you see others' mistakes and how other readers react to each mistake.

At least two reasons make volunteering your teachers' services an invaluable experience. First, your teachers will get to see some very effective proposal-writing strategies they can use in their own future proposals. Second, and this is an especially important advantage, you get to see other grant writers' mistakes. Seeing how the other evaluators react to these mistakes will remind your teachers to avoid them. If your schedule permits you to take this third option, my advice is to go for it. It will shape and improve all your future proposals. In effect, it will give your grant-writing team's foundation for writing grant proposals a dimension that could never be attained from books or workshops.

TIPS FOR HAVING MORE TIME TO WRITE GRANTS

We spend much of our time sleeping and working. Incidentally, we may not need quite the number of hours of sleep that we think we do. When Thomas Edison was working on his light bulb theory, two other teams of scientists in other countries (England and France) were working on the same theory. For many months, all three of these teams knew the light bulb was about to be invented and, furthermore, they knew the prize would not be shared among these teams; it would go to the first team to construct a workable product. It was winner take all. How right they were! Today, everybody knows the winner's name, but few people know the names of members of the other teams. In fact, few people even know the race ever happened.

Choosing topics of passion can give you more time for grant writing.

During the final months before the discovery, young Mr. Edison seldom went home at the end of the day; instead, he curled up on his lab tables and took short power naps. For months, these teams worked around the clock, testing every kind of filament imaginable, trying to discover a material that would light up without immediately burning out. Like inventors, successful grant writers must have passion and persistence.

Successful fiction writer Kurt Vonnegut was giving a writing lecture when a member of the audience asked him why he continued to write. He said the only reason to write is because you cannot keep yourself from doing it. Think about that. That's the kind of passion all successful writers require, including grant writers. Box 2.2 shows the importance of passion.

The good news for aspiring grant writers is that extreme sacrifices are not required. All that is required to find the time needed to become a highly successful grant writer is to put yourself in the position of that motorist who is approaching a merge sign—slow down for just a moment and monitor your own lifestyle. Most of us will be surprised to learn how many hours we waste daily, engaged in nonproductive activities. For example, consider the time we spend watching poor entertainment on television. Let's face it: the quality of most shows isn't that high. The reason most of us are willing to tolerate the mediocrity is that after a hard day's work, we are so desperate to escape the daily frustrations, rushing, and tension, and just relax, that we will tolerate almost anything. Ironically, this type of entertainment is not relaxing. **Tip:** *Write grants only on topics for which you have a passion.*

BOX 2.2   A True Story About Passion

People who can't dance, and don't want to put forth the effort to learn how, seldom admit they lack the passion for it. Instead, they say they "have two left feet," implying they are incapable of learning how to dance. That's the dumbest thing I've ever heard. Here's a true story. At a monthly dinner dance, my wife and I share the table with Tom and Daisy. Tom is teaching Daisy how to dance several American and Latin dances. Daisy's favorite is the East Coast swing. Throughout the evening, this couple hardly misses a dance, and Daisy literally skips to the dance floor. More passion for dancing is seldom seen; yet Tom is 93 years old and Daisy is 98.

Those of us who grab a bite of dinner and either wolf it down while turning on the television or, even worse, take it to the television to eat without even attempting to taste the food, totally miss the point. We tell ourselves we are too tired to go another moment, but the truth is we are not tired, at least not physically. Most contemporary jobs don't require enough physical labor to rest us, let alone to make us tired. Unfortunately, today's lifestyle leaves most of us emotionally drained. We turn on the television to relax, yet unless we see a really good show, we discover that watching television doesn't relax us. Five or six hours later, when it is time for bed, we realize we are just as tired as ever. To put grant writing into perspective, see Box 2.3.

BOX 2.3 The Cincinnati Story

It was Saturday morning. Three universities in Cincinnati had pooled their resources to offer a weekend workshop. Saturday morning began with a delicious on-site breakfast. Now it was time to get down to work. The large room was completely filled with people who wanted to sharpen their writing skills, although from the outset at least one person, who was sitting up front, was skeptical about whether the workshop would work for him. Chris had delivered the workshop so many times to so many audiences that, not only did she anticipate the question that followed the raised arm, but before the arm went up she knew the point at which this question would come. The skeptic was careful to phrase his question just right.

"I hear you write a lot of articles and grants."

"Two or three a year," Chris replied.

"I also hear you oversee a large, N-12 grade school."

"That's right."

"Then, how do you find time to write?"

Realizing this was a legitimate question, and, furthermore, a very good one, Chris welcomed it and responded calmly and kindly.

"This is an excellent question, and it deserves an honest and complete answer, but first let me tell all of you when I do NOT engage in grant writing or in writing for publication. I do not write between the hours of 7 a.m. and 7 p.m. on Monday through Friday. During these times, I am either driving to or from work or I am at work, usually sitting in a meeting worrying about the enormous amount of incoming mail, both hard copies and email, and worrying about the number of phone calls collecting on my answering machine and the number of people who will be waiting at my door the moment I return to my office. I also do not write on Sunday morning because I am usually in church. I never write on Saturday night, because I am somewhere on a dance floor highly engaged in American and Latin ballroom dancing. Because I am more than a little crazy over sports, I don't get many grant proposals written on Saturday afternoons in the fall or at night during the winter months. I have shared these details to assure you that even the busiest schedules leave time for writing grants. I do have a routine. Being an early riser, when the weather permits, I enjoy getting up early on Saturday morning, walking 2 or 3 miles over some steep hills, and driving to my favorite fast food restaurant for a slow breakfast, where I sit, sip my coffee, and write for the next 5 or 6 hours.

You are going to like this next tip. **Tip:** *Do not give up those activities that you enjoy most.* This includes golfing, tennis, running, and watching sports and other shows you really enjoy, including sitcoms.

In a workshop in Texas, a participant raised an unexpected question, and the speaker, Bob Baker, responded with an equally unanticipated answer. The participant asked, "You said that to be productive, you need large blocks of time to write. During these long writing periods, when do you take breaks?" Bob was stunned by this question because he realized for the first time that he had never thought about that question. Furthermore, until now he wasn't aware that he never took breaks. Bob admitted that there were many times when he had gotten so intense and so excited over a piece of research he was doing, or a grant proposal or article he was writing, that he stayed up all night working on it, knowing he had to be at work at 8:00 the next morning. So, Bob answered the workshop participant's question about when he takes breaks: "I suppose when I am writing I never think of taking breaks because I enjoy writing so much that when I am writing, I consider myself to already be on break."

If you do not find yourself or your teachers so exhilarated over grant writing, check your topic. Encourage your teachers who plan to write individual grants to acquire materials for their classrooms to write grants only about topics in which they are profoundly interested, and encourage them to continuously research these topics. Never write a grant just to get money. Each grant should enable you or your students to do something you otherwise could not do—something very important to you. For example, you might choose to write grants to help others. Help your teachers understand that grants written on well-chosen topics can improve the quality of their work. Teachers enjoy their work more when they know they are doing a good job. In fact, knowing you are doing an excellent job is very satisfying, whereas getting a pay raise or more fringe benefits may remove some dissatisfaction, but don't bring satisfaction. Whether you are writing a grant to buy your teachers and students new computers, help teachers improve their teaching skills, improve your students' reading skills, create a learning community, improve the safety level in your schools, or improve your schools' test scores, *grant writing will bring you a lot of satisfaction*. With such goals, regardless of how heavy your schedule becomes, how could you *not* have the time it takes to write these grants? The next time we are tempted to complain about our workloads, we should remember the writer found in Box 2.4.

Never write a grant just to get money; always write your grants to fulfill your dreams.

Now that you have seen Mr. Trollope's time-finding strategies, what about *your* schedule and your faculty's schedules? In a 7-day week, how many uninterrupted daytime and nighttime hours can you find in your

BOX 2.4   The Mystery of a Mystery Writer

During his lifetime, Anthony Trollope was Britain's most prolific mystery writer. Yet he was England's national postmaster. His secret? For many years, he had a 2-hour commuter train ride to work, and he wrote dozens of novels on his way to and from work. Later, even when his job moved him to Ireland, his writing did not suffer. The point here is that once we assign grant writing a high priority in our professional lives, somehow we always seem to develop strategies to find the necessary time to make it happen.

| Monday |
| Tuesday |
| Wednesday |
| Thursday |
| Friday |
| Saturday |
| Sunday |

FIGURE 2.2   Finding the Best Time

schedule? Encourage your teachers to jot down these times and develop routines that take advantage of these interruption-free times.

Don't give up those activities you find most important.

Using the form found in Figure 2.2, you might want to map out some times that work for you. But *don't give up those activities you find most important.* Becoming a successful grant writer may require a slight change in lifestyle, but it does not require giving up those activities you enjoy most. Tell your teachers the important thing to remember is to earmark times they can protect themselves from disruptions and then honor these times just like they honor their hours at work.

TIPS FOR HANDLING DEADLINES

Always put quality over quantity.

When you notice that an RFP has an uncomfortably short deadline, and yet this is a topic you like, go ahead and draft your proposal, but don't rush to meet the deadline. Most federal funding agencies, and many other agencies as well, work on annual cycles. This means most grants will be offered again. Many are offered exactly 1 year later. This means you will have completed your proposal and, as you discover additional critical information and data (percentages, graphs, etc.), you will have time to enrich your proposal with these data. If the grant is not offered again next year, you always have the option to submit it to another funding source. **Tip:** Always *put quality over quantity.* Remember that a few well-thought out and well-written proposals targeted to appropriate potential funding sources will produce far more success than a pile of quickly thrown-together, half-baked proposals.

Both you and I know that some teachers are highly skilled organizers and time managers. Others appreciate some help figuring out how to fit this additional work into their crowded schedules. Chapter 1 promises some help. For these writers, a grant-writing timeline such as the one shown in Box 2.5 should help. Stress the fact that the time allowed for each part on this timeline is a general suggestion. Should one of the steps require a few extra days, it should not matter. Should a step be accomplished more quickly than the suggested

BOX 2.5   Grant-Writing Timeline

Single-Authored Proposals

Week 1 Design and send a questionnaire to support your needs statement. If you do not work in the superintendent's office, share your intentions with the district's senior grant writer. If your district has no designated grant writer, inform your superintendent's office of your plans to write this grant.

Week 2 Using the RFP, your district's mission statement, and the data in your three-ring binder, write a rough draft. At this stage, don't worry about grammar and typographical errors; just get your ideas on paper and address each item mentioned in the RFP. Ask one or two colleagues to read your draft, not for grammatical errors, but for suggestions about parts that are unclear and any specific suggestions about ways to improve the proposal. (You are not seeking compliments; you are looking for weaknesses and ways to improve this document.)

Week 3 Using your colleagues' feedback, improve your proposal. Make those changes you believe will improve your proposal.

Week 4 After you put your proposal into running condition, it is time to give it a polishing and make it look really good. Look for opportunities to add graphs, charts, and tables. Begin this search by returning to those parts your colleagues noted to be a little unclear. Especially here, you will want to consider adding visuals and examples to clarify your meanings.

Week 5 Proof, proof, proof. Using your checklist, make sure you haven't omitted anything. Send or deliver your proposal.

Collaborative Proposals

Week 1 Design and send a questionnaire to gather data to support your needs. If you do not work in the superintendent's office, share your intentions with the district's senior grant writer. If your district has no designated grant writer, inform your superintendent's office of your plans to write this grant.

Week 2 Using the RFP, your district's mission statement, and the data in your three-ring binder, write a rough draft. At this stage, don't worry about grammar and typographical errors; just get your ideas on paper and address each item mentioned in the RFP. Ask one or two colleagues to read your draft, not for grammatical errors, but for suggestions about parts that are unclear and any specific suggestions about ways to improve the proposal. (You are not seeking compliments; you are looking for weaknesses and ways to improve this document.)

Week 3 Schedule meetings with your grant-writing team. Share this draft and ask for input. Using this input, revise the proposal to include suggestions from everyone.

Week 4 Take your proposal to the community. Arrange a meeting with the school or district parent organization. Solicit teacher input, and use it to revise your draft.

Week 5 Share your proposal with all your partners. Be sure to include those agencies and institutions from whom you will be asking for support letters. Try to include at least one suggested change made by each partner institution.

Week 6 Collect all necessary signatures. Using your checklist, be sure you do not accidentally omit any item required in the RFP.

Week 7 Add charts, graphs, tables, or examples you believe will increase the level of clarity of your proposal.

Week 8 Proof, proof, proof. Mail or deliver your proposal.

time, the writer should go right ahead to the next step. In Box 2.5, the proposals in both groups—those individually written and those written collaboratively—begin with a survey questionnaire to gather data to support the school district's need for this grant. Questionnaires are powerful instruments. For small grants, the questionnaire should be only one page long. Suggestions for designing and administering questionnaires are found in Chapter 10.

Notice also in Box 2.5 that time is allotted for authors of collaborative grants to gather input from each group represented. This includes not only all members of the grant-writing team but also all members of the learning community, especially parent representatives. Input should also be gathered from all partner institutions and businesses, and these suggestions should be worked into the grant. More exactly, the best collaborative proposals contain some wishes from all groups involved, giving all partners ownership.

TIPS FOR COLLABORATING WITH OTHERS

Tip: *Encourage your teachers never to base their decision to collaborate on the hope it will save them time or on the hope that collaboration will alleviate their need to develop their own grant-writing skills.* It will do neither.

But collaboration has some advantages. Perhaps the most important one is that collaborative, team-written grants can improve their schools far more than can an individually written grant.

Remind your beginning grant writers that *they don't need anyone else's help* unless they are applying for an enormously large grant. But just in case they do decide to collaborate, here are some good tips.

The commonly asked question, "Should I collaborate?" is a good one, but two far better ones are, "If I decide to collaborate, how many partners should I have, and how should I choose them?" Unless the project is a multi-million dollar proposal with many varied facets, a grade-level team should not exceed three or four members, and preferably three, because the larger the team, the greater the time needed to complete the project. Of course, school-wide and district-wide grant-writing teams are likely to require more members so that all vested parties will have their voices heard.

Choose grant-writing partners who have reputations for getting things done.

When participants ask for help in choosing the right partners, they are usually referring to their colleagues' subject-matter expertise: How can I ensure that I choose colleagues with the right combination of content expertise? I can tell by the way the question is worded that the participant is using the word "expertise" to mean the colleagues' academic subject-matter fields of expertise. For most proposals, the only expertise whose consideration is critical is not content expertise at all, but rather the skills needed to collect and treat data and the skills required to draft and refine the proposal. Far more important than these skills are the work habits of the partners. **Tip:** *Base your selection of grant-writing partners not on their knowledge but on their work habits.* You don't want someone on your team who just talks a lot and never manages to get things done. You don't want a member who is uncooperative and unwilling to concede to the majority. You don't want someone who has a knack for upsetting other people. Grant writing should be fun, and it should be productive. Psychologists have never been able to devise a test that predicts success as well as former behavior. That's why when used to predict college success, the ACT, SAT, GRE, MAT, GMAT, and all the other standardized tests fall short of the students' high school grades.

BOX 2.6   Collaboration: The Right Way

Three colleagues, who happened to be good friends, decided to write a massive grant proposal. One was a seasoned author, one the editor of a national journal, and the third the head of a research department in their college. This combination of experience and expertise made a good team. The fact that one was a writer, one a researcher, and the other an editor was a definite plus, but only because of the way they used their experience. From the outset, they decided what jobs were to be done, who was the best fit to do each one, when the meetings would be held, and what would be accomplished at each meeting. They immediately began developing a huge questionnaire to gather the data they needed to write the grant. They decided that developing the questionnaire would be the only task that would require all three members' efforts. Then their individual work assignments began to get real specialized.

The writer was a proactive thinker who volunteered to sequence the questions and formulate an outline because she envisioned the articles eventually emerging from the findings of the study. In other words, she wanted each section of the proposal to concentrate on related information that would be meaningful to certain people. She also wanted a similar, separate section of questions to gather data for each of several additional audiences. In essence, her plan was to write several articles from the data gathered by this single questionnaire.

The editor accepted responsibility for physically mailing the questionnaires and communicating with the respondents to ensure a high rate of return. When the data arrived, the researcher fed the data into the computer and interpreted the results. With the results in hand, the author drafted the articles. A large project can provide the substance for several articles, and articles are needed to establish a successful track record that the collaborators can use as fodder for sequential or related future grant proposals. Adhering to the cliché that "there is no such thing as good writing, only good rewriting," the author and editor edited and rewrote each article several times.

All the forewarnings about the many collaborating pitfalls would be misleading without an acknowledgment that *collaborative grant writing can be highly enjoyable and highly productive*, as shown in Box 2.6.

A key to the success of the collaborators discussed in Box 2.6 was their willingness to begin dividing the responsibilities equally among the members. An even greater factor in producing a successful project was the fact that all three collaborators were self-motivated. In addition to considering their levels of congeniality, the selection of grant-writing partners should consider people's work habits. *Choose grant-writing partners who are self-motivated and who have good track records in getting things done.* Avoid mixing personality types. When a Type A personality collaborates with a Type B personality, the Type A personality is driven crazy from having to wait for the Type B to show up at meetings and from Type B's failure to meet deadlines. The Type B personality thinks a deadline is an indicator that it is time to start working on the project. If you are a Type A personality, whatever you do, avoid the Type B personality. I jokingly tell my workshop participants that if they have a Type B personality, it doesn't matter what type partners they choose because all they are going to do anyway is just talk about it. Actually, this may be a slight exaggeration because the Type B personalities suffer equally from a mismatch because they can't enjoy the ride; their Type A partner is always rushing them and pushing them to work faster.

Grant writing should be both productive and fun.

Personal Goals:

1.

2.

3.

Professional Goals:

1.

2.

3.

FIGURE 2.3   Personal and Professional Grant-Writing Goals

How about your own preferences? Are you willing to risk your success because of a colleague? Whom do you know who, you are confident, will get the job done and be an asset more than a liability to your grant-writing program? What parts of the job would you want to do yourself, and what parts would you want your collaborator(s) to do?

The original question, "Should you collaborate?" is very personal and one every grant writer must answer. Using Figure 2.3, refer to your personal and professional goals, and then make a list of advantages you might gain from collaborating on grant proposals. Make a similar list of disadvantages. These might include the fact that collaboration takes more time. If you choose partners who are not proactive and self-motivated, you would be entrusting the future of your grant writing to others who are less productive.

If you have teachers who choose to write grants by themselves over joining a team, they should not be dissuaded. Some people simply work better by themselves than when assigned to a team. Make a list of your teachers whom you know to be self-starting, task oriented, and congenial. Invite but do not force them to serve on the team. You might also wish to identify the roles each prefers to play on the grant-writing team so you will have this information available in advance each time you begin a new proposal. This will be helpful because *the turnaround time between the release of the RFP and the deadline for proposal submission is usually uncomfortably short.*

Summary

This chapter has been about attitudes that generally affect people's levels of success when they write grant proposals. The tips discussed in this chapter have worked successfully again and again. But what about your faculty's attitudes? It is their attitudes that will determine their success. So ask your teachers to take a moment to assess their own thinking.

On a scale of 0 to 10, what score would they give themselves? Like many of us, did they grow up being taught to be modest? Were they taught to never evaluate themselves generously? Do they associate a high level of self-confidence with bragging or vanity? After all, nobody likes a bragger. But we need to build on our strengths, and to do this, we must first acknowledge them. Your teachers have the ability to succeed at grant writing at the level they choose to succeed but only to the degree they believe this and are willing to work to make it happen.

Finding time to write grants is a challenge to everyone and it is accomplished by prioritizing. Successful grant writers don't make excuses; they find ways to overcome obstacles. They don't panic over deadlines. Instead, they put quality first.

Collaboration is invaluable to education grant writers because a collaborative team's proposals can acquire resources far beyond those acquired by single-authored proposals. But teachers should realize that joining a grant-writing team does not save time and that it does not replace their need to improve their own grant-writing skills.

RECAP OF MAJOR IDEAS

- Everybody is pressed for time. Grant writers have to prioritize and commit time to write grants.
- Connections are important but not essential.
- Collaborative grant writing can raise a school district's performance level, but it does not replace the need for individual teachers to improve their grant-writing skills.
- Grant-writing team member selection should be based on teachers' good work habits and success records.
- Producing excellent proposals should never be sacrificed to meet deadlines.
- Most federal funding agencies operate on annual cycles.
- Knowing how to choose partners is more important than knowing whether to collaborate with others.
- Some grant-writing groups are highly productive. Others just like to talk about the grants they never write.
- Collaborating can be advantageous, but it always takes more time from its members' schedules.

LIST OF TIPS (SLIGHTLY ALTERED)

1. When you hear a discouraging comment about grant writing, it's time to run for the hills.

2. Start developing your personal grant-writing program now.

3. Identify one or two goals you want to get from writing grants.

4. Buy a three-ring binder and start looking for some "beans" for the proposal evaluators to count. In other words, begin collecting numerical data to use to support your programs. Remember that good data can be used in more than one proposal.

5. When writing any grant, keep a finger on the RFP, and don't move it downward until you have responded to every sentence.

6. Pick up the phone and call the funding agency. Use the call to get information the competitors won't have and to whet the agent's appetite toward seeing your proposal.

7. Write grants only on topics for which you have some passion.

8. When you find an attractive RFP with a short deadline, draft your proposal and sit on it, improving it as you discover new data. Submit it during the following funding cycle.

9. Always put quality over quantity.

10. Do not collaborate to reduce the workload. It will backfire, increasing the work.

11. Choose partners who actually get things done.

12. Choose partners who get along with other people.

13. Instead of belaboring your needs, convince the readers you will do a better job than any of your competitors in meeting the intent of the grant.

14. Submit some proposals to local funding agencies.

15. Make a list of professional goals you might wish your unit to reach through grant writing.

16. Advise your faculty that they will not need to give up their favorite activities to write grants.

17. Reassure your teachers that successful grant writing does not require connections but it does require producing high-quality proposals.

18. Know and use your strengths and those of your school district.

Using the Right Vocabulary and Tools

INTRODUCTION

All workers can do a better job if they have the right tools. Essential tools for grant writers include a grant-writing vocabulary and a loaded toolbox. This chapter uses a glossary to help the reader become familiar with those words and phrases that often confuse beginning grant writers. A personal library is essential, although the library may be nothing grander than a well-organized briefcase and a three-ring binder. This chapter equips beginning grant writers with these basic tools and shows experienced grant writers new ways to use them to organize their grant-writing programs.

Too often, grant writing is thought of as a mysterious, otherworldly activity, or something that others do. But grant writing is perfect for practitioners, from the individual teacher who needs travel money or classroom supplies, to district office managers, principals, and department chairs who want to improve their departments and schools. You can begin unraveling the mystery of grant writing by becoming familiar with its many otherworldly terms. Then you can build your own grant-writing world by pulling together a few materials and forming a specialized grant-writing library. Remember that your grant office can simply be contained in a briefcase and a three-ring binder. You will need the following tools.

GETTING THE LANGUAGE

One thing that discourages prospective grant writers is the tendency of the grant world to clothe itself in a language of its own. Words and acronyms abound: grant versus proposal; cover letter versus query letter; letter of intent versus letter of support; block grant versus category grant; input goals versus output goals; corporate grant versus government grant versus foundation grant; project narrative, sustainability statement, in-kind contributions; indirect costs, and requests for proposal (RFPs). Perhaps the jargon is there because most of the funding sources are organizations in specialized fields and government agencies. But such terms can confuse and discourage novice writers. And yet grant writing can and should be fun, once you get a handle on the language. A quick glance at the glossary in Figure 3.1 should help. A more complete glossary appears in Appendix 3.1. If you are an experienced grant writer, then you will probably choose to bypass both glossaries.

Abstract: Brief summary of the entire proposal.

Block grant: Federal funds given to a state, city, or county for broad purposes, the amount based on population.

CEO: Chief executive officer. The top officer.

Collaboration: Two or more individuals or groups working together to achieve a mutual goal.

Dollar-for-dollar match: Cost sharing on an equal basis between the grantor and grantee.

DUNS Number: A number assigned to organizations that apply for grants. The federal government and an increasing number of other government funders require organizations to provide a data universal numbering system (DUNS) number as part of their grant applications and proposals.

Federal Register: A government document that contains the requests for proposal (RFPs) for all government-funded grants in a given year.

Foundation: A private or public charitable funding source.

Funder: Source of grant funds.

Funding cycle: The period in which foundations make grants (annual, semi-annual, etc.)

Funding guidelines: Descriptions of forthcoming grants, including eligibility requirements, announcements, and directions for applying.

Grant: A gift for performing a job.

Grantee: Institution or individual who is awarded a grant.

Grantor: Organization that awards a grant.

Grants administrator: Individual charged with directing or overseeing a funded program.

In-kind contributions: Noncash donations to a funded program, including salaries, space, heating, and electricity.

Jargon-free proposal: A proposal that avoids the use of unfamiliar or unintelligible language.

Letter of support: A letter of testimony from an individual, sometimes representing a group, that offers support for the proposed program.

Mission statement: A brief statement of an organization's purpose.

Needs statement: A written description of an organization's problems and shortcomings that the proposal author purports to overcome through the grant.

Partnerships: The collaboration of a combination of two or more individuals, schools, school districts, or universities to achieve a common goal benefiting all parties.

Principal investigator: The senior member of a proposal writing team.

FIGURE 3.1   Glossary of Common Terms (*continues*)

Proposal rating form: A form that assigns a specific number of points to each part of a grant proposal.

Quotable quote: A short quote that expresses an important idea with unusual clarity.

Request for Proposal (RFP): An invitation sent to prospective organizations encouraging them to submit a proposal to secure the funds they need to procure a product or service.

Review of literature: A review to determine what is currently known about a field of study under investigation.

Smokestack theory: The premise that funding agencies are partial to proposals that are developed locally (within the shadows of their smokestacks).

Source map: A form used to identify funders appropriate for a proposal.

Sustainability plan: A written strategy to ensure continuation of a project beyond the funding period.

Timeline: A schedule showing when major steps in a program will be accomplished.

Triangular model: A grant proposal writing model that puts the funding agency's goals first and uses the grantee's individual, school, and school district's strengths to convince the grantor that the grantee will do a better job than the competition in reaching the funder's goals.

Weighted rating form: A guideline for proposal evaluators to use that gives varying points to its items.

FIGURE 3.1   Glossary of Common Terms

GETTING A PERSONAL LIBRARY

Grant writing can and should be one of your most enjoyable activities. Some grant writers have a room at home that they use exclusively for grant writing. Having your own library room can offer much-needed solitude, away from your perpetually hectic and interrupted school life. If you are among the lucky few who do have a home office or spare room you can use for a library, then consider equipping your library with your favorite books and journals. If you do not have a home library, then an inexpensive bookcase will work fine.

Books

Every educator has a few books near and dear to the heart. These may include old college textbooks, textbooks from current courses, teacher yearbooks, or books bought at bookstores and library sales. Inside these books are valuable facts, charts, tables, and graphs—all items that are useful, from time to time, when grant writers want a memory refresher. Textbooks and other books such as dictionaries, style manuals, and grant-writing books are indispensable.

Daily journal reading keeps grant writers on the cutting edge of their fields.

Journals

Many leaders in education subscribe to journals or have access to them through their departments. Others receive quarterly or monthly journals through their association memberships. These journals help to keep these leaders informed of the latest developments in their fields. Unlike much of the questionable information on the Internet, the reliability of these journals makes them indispensable; however, there is a problem—an often missing link—that must not be overlooked. The problem has already been addressed and, because of its handicapping ability, is addressed several times throughout this book. Put simply, all the information in these journals is worthless unless, somehow, it gets into the leader's head. As you already know, today's teachers, especially lead teachers, don't have the time to read journals from cover to cover. As a very busy leader, you will need a streamlined process that will let you absorb not all the information in these journals, but that which is most important to you. Furthermore, as you know, the teachers you work with are fighting the clock. You must help them streamline their own process for getting the most from their journals in the least time. You can do this by mastering the following steps and then helping them do likewise. Following is a method that has proven effective, again and again.

CATALOGING

To sift out and capture the journal information that means the most to you, carefully follow this simple, straightforward process.

Step 1: When a journal arrives, scan the table of contents, and, using thin (1/8") sticky notes, write two or three words on each note, capturing each topic that you find especially meaningful. For example, you might look for terms such as "action research," "learning community," "school safety," "improving test scores," "grant writing," "teenage literacy," or "child obesity."

Step 2: Affix each labeled tab to the edge of the first page of each article, making a journal index.

This five-step process will reduce your workload by 80–90%.

Step 3: Shelve the issue *backward*, with the open side of the journal and the tabs facing outward.

Step 4: Place the current, tabbed issue in front of all other journals on the shelf. The positioning is important because grant writers need ready access to *current* data. Now, when you have a few minutes, from time to time, you can quickly pull these issues and peruse these tabbed articles, always returning them to their current positions on the shelf.

Step 5: When you begin writing your next grant, you can quickly pull the journals relevant to your grant topic and put them on a table, leaving the remaining 80–90% of the journals on the shelves. You have just reduced your workload by 80–90%. More important, you have put the information needed for your next proposal at your fingertips, ready for immediate use.

As you write your grant proposal, ignore the rest of the journals around you, even the untabbed articles. This streamlines the job.

THREE-RING BINDER

You know it's true. Whether you are adding a room onto your house or preparing a multicourse meal, the job is much easier if you have the right tools. Furthermore, to avoid spending a lot of time searching for these tools each time you begin a job, you must have a common place to put them. Robert Louis

Grant evaluators love exactness and brevity. Data and quotable quotes make your grants exact and brief.

Stevenson advised his readers to carry a pencil and paper at all times so they could write down their ideas because, said Stevenson, "the best ideas often come at the least expected times and may never return." Perhaps the most valuable tools a grant writer can have are a briefcase and a three-ring binder. Also drop a handheld, hole-punch tool into your briefcase. Now, the multipurpose binder will capture those good ideas by allowing you to collect valuable data and quotable quotes. A *quotable quote* is a short, one-sentence statement that captures an important idea and passes it along to others, with unusual and unforgettable clarity. Ben Franklin's many short quips are excellent examples of quotable quotes ("A penny saved is a penny earned." "Be not first on whom the new is tried or last to lay the old aside." "A stitch in time saves nine.").

Most grant evaluators love numbers, graphs, and percentages.

As you read your professional journals and books, watch for percentages and graphs. Many grant evaluators are *bean counters*; they have an unusually strong affinity for numbers and percentages. These number lovers also like tables (which may contain lines or columns of numbers) and graphs showing trends and predictions. So, any time you find percentages, numbers, and graphs showing important changes in your field of study, photocopy them, being sure to include the volume, issue, page numbers, and the names of the author(s) and the source (journal, magazine, newspaper, or book). Put these retrieved sources in your three-ring binder. If your proposal has these items in abundance, then the probability of its being accepted is significantly increased.

You can use the same data again and again and if you do, they become part of the best library of all—your brain.

There's more good news; you can use these items repeatedly in grant after grant. Many grant writers shortchange themselves by purposefully refusing to use a concept or statistic more than once. They believe that using the same material in more than one proposal is somehow unprofessional or unethical. This is nonsense. Think how such a practice would handicap an engineer, who would have to reinvent the wheel for each new project. The more you use a concept or statistic, the more it becomes retrievable and ready for fast assessment. This is the best part of all; as you use these data and quotes over and over, they become part of the best library of all, your brain.

Suppose you are determined to help your department, grade level, school, or entire district raise your students' scores on the state's standardized test. And suppose you see a list of concepts covered on that exam. You must capture these terms in your notebook. Or, suppose you read in a school report or in the local newspaper that last year your school district performed the second lowest in your state on reading. Ouch! This seems like a damning statement. You might find it too embarrassing to report, but look again. This is a strong statement, and, correctly used, it can become an effective tool for convincing potential funding sources that your school needs help. It may be time for a literacy grant. You might choose to follow the model shown in Box 3.1, which was successfully used to garner a much-desired literacy grant.

MISSION STATEMENT

Another tool you should include in your binder is a copy of your school district's mission statement. Knowing this can position you to capture the attention of potential funding agents when you are in informal situations. Referring to this statement in your proposals is a way to convince every potential funding source that your school district is the perfect partner to help meet this common mission.

BOX 3.1   Amy's Literacy Grant

For the past ten years, Bob Wright, a reading professor at a local university, had been giving half his time to coordinate a program he had developed to help children in the schools downtown who were reading 2 or more years below their grade levels. This outstanding program had produced excellent results, and the district's test scores were reflecting the progress. When the downtown superintendent, Amy Molly, read of Bob's forthcoming retirement, she found the news disturbing. Realizing the loss this change would bring to her district, she began looking for ways to continue the summer program. First, she would search locally for the needed support. If all local attempts failed, she would expand her search. She would search through the *Federal Register* and see what sources are funding literacy grants. But first she would check all the local businesses. When she consulted the manager of a bank that had just opened in town, the agent saw this as an opportunity to build strong bonds with the community and asked her to write a two- or three-page proposal explaining the need just as she had orally explained it to him. The following day, she gathered data on the reading scores from prior summer program participants and used those data to write a short proposal. She edited the proposal, reducing its length to exactly three pages. Voila! The program was funded for the next 5 years. The strategy paid off for Amy, and it will pay off for you.

RATING FORMS

Successful grant writing requires following the RFP guidelines to a T and crafting an excellent proposal that meets all the expectations of the targeted funding agency. Indeed, most grant proposals are evaluated by a team of readers, and each team member is provided a rating form, such as the one shown in Figure 3.2.

Notice that this sample form has a space for totaling the points for each criterion. When teams of readers are used to evaluate proposals, the process is simple mathematics; after all proposals have been evaluated, the grant is awarded to the proposal receiving the most points. Often, by checking the RFP or by contacting the prospective funding agency's secretary, you can obtain a copy of the rating form. Do not be embarrassed to ask for a copy of the rating instrument. This is a fair and wise move on the part of expert grant writers.

When requested, most grant offices provide copies of a grant's rating form.

The creators of some rating forms assign more points to some items than to others. Such weighted ratings indicate the relative values the funding agents expect the evaluators to place on the different proposal parts. By looking closer, you can extend the advantages the rating form is capable of giving you over those less fortunate competitors who do not have this tool. For example, notice that the particular rating form in Figure 3.2 begins with a set of instructions to the evaluators, telling them to "Study [the] entire proposal before beginning the rating process because information relevant to a single rating criterion may be found in several sections of the proposal." This tells us the reviewers will be looking for strengths and weaknesses. *Never assume the readers will automatically notice and appreciate all the strengths of your proposal.* To ensure they don't overlook some of your proposal's strengths, highlight your proposal's strengths.

Although the reviewers are given these explicit instructions, there is no guarantee they will follow them. We know that, faced with a big job of evaluating many proposals, some evaluators will be tempted to jump right in

Mathematics and Science
Improvement Program

INSTRUCTION TO THE REVIEWER: Study entire proposal before beginning the rating process because information relevant to a single rating criterion may be found in several sections of the proposal. Respond to each item on the rating form by (1) commenting on the strengths or weaknesses of the proposed project and (2) indicating the earned point-value on the scale, 0 through 5. The highest composite scores will identify the meritorious proposals. It may be helpful to note in your comments where in the proposal you found the significant data.

Indicate the total number of points awarded to the proposal at the bottom of page 3. On page 4 suggest any revisions that would better meet the overall objective of improving statewide teacher qualification in mathematics, chemistry, and physics.

Complete the reviewer identification section below. Send two copies of each review, one signed and one unsigned, to _____

_____

Reviewer Name: _____

Address: _____

_____

Office Telephone: _____   Hours: _____   Home Telephone: _____
Reviewer Signature: _____
Date Signed: _____

A. Are the objectives to be achieved in the institute precisely stated and reasonable?
   Comment(s): _____

   _____

   Points earned: _____   _____   _____   _____   _____   _____
                      (0)   (1)   (2)   (3)   (4)   (5)

B. Are the recruiting and selection procedures appropriate?
   Comment(s): _____

   _____

   Points earned: _____   _____   _____   _____   _____   _____
                      (0)   (1)   (2)   (3)   (4)   (5)

C. Do the proposed courses give reasonable assurance of achieving the objectives of the institute?
   Comment(s): _____

   _____

   Points earned: _____   _____   _____   _____   _____   _____
                      (0)   (1)   (2)   (3)   (4)   (5)

D. Is the instructional staff appropriate to the successful implementation of the institute?
   Comment(s): _____

   _____

   Points earned: _____   _____   _____   _____   _____   _____
                      (0)   (1)   (2)   (3)   (4)   (5)

FIGURE 3.2   Sample Proposal Rating Form (*continues*)

E. Have adequate provisions been made for management and support personnel?

Comment(s): _____

_____

Points earned: _____ _____ _____ _____ _____ _____
                  (0)   (1)   (2)   (3)   (4)   (5)

F. Are sound evaluation procedures included that will assure obtaining usable information about the degree of attainment of project objectives?

Comment(s): _____

_____

Points earned: _____ _____ _____ _____ _____ _____
                  (0)   (1)   (2)   (3)   (4)   (5)

G. Has the sponsoring institution committed the necessary facilities, including instructional equipment, to the institute?

Comment(s): _____

_____

Points earned: _____ _____ _____ _____ _____ _____
                  (0)   (1)   (2)   (3)   (4)   (5)

H. Does the proposal indicate an adequate level of fiscal and in-kind support from the sponsoring institution?

Comment(s): _____

_____

Points earned: _____ _____ _____ _____ _____ _____
                  (0)   (1)   (2)   (3)   (4)   (5)

I. Is the proposed budget consistent with the size and scope of the proposed institute?

Comment(s): _____

Points earned: _____ _____ _____ _____ _____ _____
                  (0)   (1)   (2)   (3)   (4)   (5)

TOTAL POINTS AWARDED _____

FIGURE 3.2   Sample Proposal Rating Form

and begin assigning points to the various parts. (These are the same people who jump in and put bicycles together without first reading the directions, and, when the job is done, usually have a few parts left over!) To ensure that those evaluators who ignore the instructions will notice all the strengths in your proposals, make certain each strength is included in an appropriate proposal part.

A familiar hymn says, "And to my *listening* ears all nature sings." Again, examine the rating form shown in Figure 3.2. This rating form continues to talk to those who know how to listen. "Also, suggest any revisions that would better meet the overall objective of improving statewide teacher qualification in mathematics, chemistry, and physics." This particular proposal form was designed to evaluate proposals written to improve statewide teacher qualifications in high school math, chemistry, and physics. It reminds the evaluators to keep their eyes focused on the proposal's purpose and to reward those investigators who have convinced them that they would do the best job of reaching this goal. We can strengthen our proposals by responding to *all* advice given to the evaluators and by keeping the overall purpose or mission of the funding source in mind when developing each part of the proposal.

Tip: *Help your teachers identify one or two goals that they want to reach through grant writing.* For example, suppose you or your teachers are serious about creating or expanding a learning community. Make sure these goals serve that purpose. In other words, if you intend to use grant writing to develop a learning community (or for any other purpose), each goal you set should relate to improving the learning climate in your school.

The glossary in Figure 3.1 defines an RFP as "An invitation sent to prospective organizations encouraging them to submit a proposal to secure the funds they need to procure a product or service." RFPs often ask for an abstract explaining why your district should be chosen for this grant. *Exactly* how would your

---

BOX 3.2 Classrooms for the Future RFP Outline

1. **Abstract**—What are your (1) expectations for this program's impact on how teachers and students will work in your high school (including changes in instructional strategies and practices and in student performance and learning) and (2) anticipated successes and challenges at the teacher and student levels?

2. What are your expectations for organizational changes (such as the way you manage staff and administrative and communications tasks) and your proposed activities to promote best practices and incorporate lessons learned?

3. **Needs Assessment**—Describe how technology is currently being used in instruction, communication, and administration (or current plans for technology integration in these areas).

4. Describe your school's participation in programs that use teachers to help coach other teachers on technology use in instruction. This may include the Keystones Program of the Pennsylvania Department of Education (see http://www.portal.state.pa.us/portal/server.pt/community/keystones/8956 for a description of this program). Enter N/A if not applicable.

5. Describe any other current programs that train and/or assist your teachers in technology skills. Enter N/A if not applicable.

6. **Project Plan**—Provide goals from your current district strategic plan. Goals should reflect an overarching purpose and desired end result of action or ability. Create aligned research-based strategies for all aspects of Classrooms for the Future implementation.

7. **Sustainability**—Provide a detailed plan to sustain the proposed project beyond the initial grant-funding period. The plan should address maintenance and growth for all project-related resources and activities, including technology refreshment, upgrades, and enhancements, as well as ongoing professional development.

8. **Assurances**—26 listed directives must be met by the administrators and teachers.

9. **Budget Narrative**—Grant award amounts will be based upon technology costs established through a statewide contract, which is currently in the bid process, etc., etc.

10. **Summary Budget**

Classrooms for the Future Grant Announcement and RFP Information can be found at: (Note that this information was updated for 2008–2009. http://www.edportal.ed.state.pa.us/portal/server.pt/community/grant_information/691)

district accomplish these goals? What *exactly* would your district accomplish? What are your *plans* for accomplishing these goals? How much money would you need to conduct this project? How can you assure the funder that the project will not die the moment the funds stop? An example of an outline for meeting the demands of an RFP is shown in Box 3.2. This outline was written by the Greenville Area (Pennsylvania) School District to fund a Pennsylvania Department of Education initiative known as Classrooms for the Future.

Summary

Apart from the myths, of which you are already aware, a major obstacle to novice grant writers is the vast array of acronyms and jargon. A list of common grant-writing terms is found in Figure 3.1. All experienced grant writers are encouraged to skip the glossary and continue on with the rest of the book. But if you are a stranger to the grant-writing world, your entry into this world will be made easier if you peruse this list and become familiar with some of the common terms.

Grant writing, like almost every new undertaking, will become easier and more fun with practice. The fun and ease of grant writing will increase rapidly once you establish a good place to write and fill it with the necessary tools. A personal grant-writing library and a streamlined process for using it are invaluable to those who are fortunate enough to have the space. But a special grant-writing room is not essential if you have a portable library, such as a briefcase with a three-ring binder.

Most grant proposal evaluators like numbers. This makes ready access to data critical to serious grant writers. A three-ring binder can house the necessary data, along with important quotable quotes.

Copies of your school district's mission statement and a rating form can be used to align your proposal with your district and with the funding agency's purposes.

RECAP OF MAJOR IDEAS

- A well-equipped personal library can add to the pleasure of grant writing.
- A personal library coupled with an efficient program for its use can enrich your grant-writing program and raise your success level.
- A well-equipped portable library is all that is required to support a successful grant-writing program.

- Most grant evaluators prefer numbers over words and data over verbal approximations; therefore, you need ready access to significant data, tables, charts, and graphs.
- Short, quotable quotes are more powerful than extensive dialog.
- Your school district's mission statement can be used to convince prospective donors that your district would be the ideal partner to help meet their mission.
- Rating forms can remind you to address every part of an RFP, and they can even tell you how much weight each part of the proposal carries.

LIST OF TIPS

1. If you have the means, designate a space in your home for a grant-writing office, and equip it with the essential tools.
2. Create a portable (briefcase) office.
3. Get a three-ring binder and a handheld hole punch so that you will be prepared at all times to gather important information.
4. Collect quotable quotes, data, tables, charts, and graphs, and put them in your binder.
5. Include your school district's mission statement in your binder.
6. When each journal arrives, immediately use sticky notes to tab those articles that focus on the concepts important to your goals.
7. Shelve your tabbed journals backward with the spines toward the back of the bookcase, leaving the sticky tabs visible. This gives you immediate access to articles on your favorite topics.
8. For each grant, request a copy of the rating form, and address all parts. If the criteria are weighted, focus more on those criteria carrying the most points.

Choosing Your Path

INTRODUCTION

Grant writing has two paths. To better understand these approaches, consider the strategies that the American and British bombers took in World War II. The British pilots bombed at night to reduce the chances of being hit by flack (ground fire). Willing to take that risk to get a better view of their targets and make a higher percentage of hits, the American pilots conducted their missions during the day. The two allies complemented each other, keeping the Nazis under attack around the clock. The choice is similar when writing grants; you can either select a request for proposals (RFP) and develop a proposal to meet its requirements (daytime bombing), or you can write your proposal and then attempt to locate a funding source (nighttime bombing). Obviously, each choice has its advantages, and depending on the variables, sometimes one strategy is better than others and vice versa.

Grant writing works the same way. Wanting to use their time wisely, novice grant writers often ask which path is best. "I know I could write my grant and then look for funding (sometimes called the *nighttime* or *shotgun* approach), or I could check out the funding first and then tailor my proposal to a specific grant. So, which should I do?"

If forced to choose, then the author would take the latter approach because it gives the writer more control. But, actually, there is a better alternative—do both! Start by *considering your reason* for writing grants. Will this be a teacher writing a small grant alone to garner materials for the classroom, or will it be a team of colleagues writing a large grant to meet a major need for the school or district? When writing a large team grant, remember that funders of big grants (both government and private) fund *ideas*, not things, wants, or needs. Then check the sources to locate agencies that share your interests. Choose an RFP, and carefully tailor a proposal to meet the funding agency's specifications. Because the funding source's needs trump the grant writer's needs, this rifle

| Audiences of this funder include school districts................**Yes/No** |
| This funder has previously funded grants on this topic......................**Yes/No** |
| The range of grants made by this organization is from......**\$__.__ to \$__.__** |
| Deadline ....**Day__ Month__ Year__** |

FIGURE 4.1   Source Map

approach is superior; therefore, you should tailor most of your proposals to meet the requirements stated in RFPs. But suppose you desperately want to write a grant for a special cause (e.g., your school or district wants to implement a new program needed to raise its test scores for English language learners), and you cannot locate any suitable RFPs? In such instances, I recommend you proceed using the shotgun approach; write your grant and then seek a funding source.

MAPPING YOUR SOURCE

When manuscripts are sent to editors, the sender often receives a generic rejection letter saying, in effect, the submission is "not right for our magazine or company." This may be a euphemism—the editors' kind way of telling you that they consider your work to be no better than junk. Or it can mean just the opposite, "We think your work is great and we surely would like to publish it, but we have recently accepted a very similar manuscript and, [in the case of a magazine or journal] we won't return to the topic for another year or two." So, the rejection letter can mean exactly what it says; it is not right for our journal—you have targeted the wrong source. The same can be true of grant proposals; therefore, you must learn to target the right sources. This also partially explains why so many excellent proposals are rejected.

A source map can save time by preventing you from applying for grants that are beyond your qualifications.

A good tool for making sure you are targeting the right source is a source map (Figure 4.1). Using a source map can save you some time. Far more important, it can expedite your grant-writing program by reminding you to make sure your district is eligible to apply for each particular grant.

TARGETED AUDIENCE/BLOCK GRANTS

Many federal grants are block grants. This means that a large amount of money is doled out in blocks to each state. The states have a lot of freedom in deciding how to use these funds, so they write their own guidelines for making awards to their various schools or school districts. For example, the grant may be targeted to higher education institutions, as opposed to PK–12 schools. PK–12 educators are wasting their time applying for these grants unless they plan to partner with a university. Or the opposite may be true; the grant may be directed to PK–12 schools. University personnel are wasting their time applying for these grants, unless they plan to partner with PK–12 schools.

RANGE

Once you have checked the audience and determined that you are indeed eligible to apply for one of these grants, you must check the deadline. If it's next Monday, then be careful to avoid the common pitfall of quickly throwing together a half-baked, poorly thought-out proposal. Perhaps the best choice is to take your time, go ahead and prepare your proposal draft as though you were going to submit it now, and then hold your draft and submit it during the agency's next funding cycle. This will give you plenty of time, perhaps a year, to collect additional data to enrich your proposal—time to make it *the best it can be.*

CHECK THE AMOUNT

Having learned you are eligible to apply for a grant and the deadline is reasonable, it is now time to check the amount of funds available. The specifications for most block grants include a range of money. The range statement usually includes a maximum. For federal grants, this is not a suggested, ballpark range. Serious grant writers take these maximums (and all other specifications) literally and seriously, being careful to avoid exceeding the stated amount. Foundations may be more flexible with the stated maximum, but unless you are told by a foundations officer that it is all right to exceed the stated maximum, you would be wise to stay within it. Put succinctly, don't do it. *Do not exceed a stated maximum, not even by one dollar.*

Sometimes the range statements for grants also have minimums, which should also be taken seriously. Funding agencies that are set up to give away millions, tens, or hundreds of thousands of dollars do not have the time or patience for dealing with a request for five or six hundred dollars.

RFP specifications are not mere suggestions and, therefore, must be strictly adhered to.

These ranges are usually stated in the RFPs. For grants whose RFPs do not provide a dollar range and for grant monies that do not have RFPs, a look at the history of the agency's funding will suffice. The *Federal Register* contains all grants made by every government agency during a given year. By reviewing a few months' history of this agency's grants, you can quickly see what amounts are reasonable for the agency. Stay within these amounts.

TABOO TOPICS

As in many endeavors, sometimes in grant writing, a little common sense goes a long way. You would never apply to a church, temple, or synagogue for a grant that runs contrary to the denomination's faith. You wouldn't apply to a green company for money to be used in ways that would pollute the environment. This is just plain common sense. But other necessary precautions are far less obvious. In recent years, so many companies have merged or taken over other companies that, without knowing it, a grant writer can easily violate one of the subsidiaries' interests. The message here is to *know your funding agencies.* Obviously, you can't know everything about all companies, but you can and should *gather data on those few agencies to which you want to target your proposals.*

MATCHING YOUR STRENGTHS WITH THE FUNDING AGENCY'S GOALS

Both the nighttime or shotgun approach to grant writing (writing the grant first and then seeking a funder) and the rifle approach (seeking a funder and designing your proposal to meet the specific demands of the RFP) require the proposal writer to understand the nature of the funding agency, the writer's own strengths, the strengths and needs of the writer's school district, and the strengths and needs of the writer's community.

Is it possible you might present such a strong need for money that the funding agency might take pity and fund your grant just because you need help so badly? Yes, this is a possibility, especially when applying to philanthropic foundations. However, for all other sources, it is much more likely that the funding agency will be motivated by your skills and strengths. People like to place their money on winners, not on losers. So, here are two **tips:** *Always put the desires of the funding agency above your own. Emphasize your unique strengths and those of your district and local community, using them to convince the funding agency you will do a better job than the other applicants will do in meeting the funding agency's goals.* Also, determine whether there are any major funding agencies in your area. **Tip:** *Remember the adage that most grants that are funded by corporations are funded in the shadow of the corporations' smokestacks.* This means that most corporations take care of their own neighbors before helping others. Remember in Box 3.1 that this strategy worked for Amy. It will also work for you.

People like to support winners, not losers.

Most corporate grants are funded in the shadows of their smokestacks.

THE TRIANGULAR MODEL

As indicated previously, successful grant writers work to gain control over their grant-writing program, but for most grant writers it happens gradually, spread over several months or even a few years. Nevertheless, grant writing is as much an art as it is a science; there is no perfect, fail-proof algorithm or prescription for writing grant proposals. Many novice grant writers are looking for a model. Figure 4.2 shows a model that has worked well, leading to the funding of over 30 proposals of all sizes. It is the triangular model for matching strengths with the funding agency's goals and practices, or, if you prefer, simply the *triangular model*.

Using this model, the writers keep one eye on the funding agency's goals and the other on their areas of expertise. The model includes the writers' personal strengths, the strengths of their institutions (school or school district), and the strengths of their community.

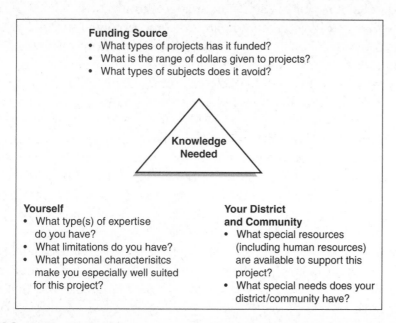

FIGURE 4.2 **Triangular Model for Matching Strengths with Funding Agency's Goals and Practices**

Also using the triangular model shown in Figure 4.2, select a topic of particular interest to you. For example, identify your district's or school's greatest need, and fill in the blanks in this box. Looking back at this model, notice that the potential funding source to which you are targeting your grant is at the top of the triangle. Think of this agency as a *senior* partner. This top location is important because it is a reminder that the funding agency is the partner who holds the purse strings. Too often, novice grant writers are either unaware or unwilling to do what it takes to get their proposals funded. They try to bend the funders' requirements (stated in the RFPs) to fit their preconceived ideas of how they would prefer to run the project. This is wrong headed. In fact, it is just the opposite of what successful grant writers do. They carefully shape their proposals until they perfectly match the funder's goals.

THE FUNDING AGENCY'S MISSION STATEMENT

If your proposal is funded, then you will be working for this agency; more specifically, you will be helping the agency meet its needs. So, your next step is to identify the agency's needs. This is easy. It can be done in multiple ways. First, you can discover the agency's needs by examining the RFP. Be careful to respond to *every* need mentioned throughout the RFP. Another common mistake made by a multitude of grant writers is their tendency to (1) get absorbed in responding to one part of the RFP, (2) go off on a tangent, (3) continue focusing and writing to this one concern, and (4) ignore other needs found buried throughout the RFP. This mistake is so common that I suggest you copy the RFP and highlight each part once it has been addressed. Although this advice may appear elementary, it can protect your proposal from a guaranteed rejection.

A second way to identify the agency's needs is by using your Google or Yahoo search engine. You are now searching online for this funding agency's mission (purpose and goals), the size grants it has funded, and the topics it funds—paying close attention to any topics it might consider taboo. If your Web searches fail, then refer to the *Federal Register*. This document gives the topic and dollar amount of each grant that gets funded.

Grant writing is a joint business of matching the funder's goals and the district's mission.

Now that you have gathered data on some potential funding agencies, it is time to look at yourself, your school, and your school district. Remember, grant writing is a joint business. Now it is time to determine with great clarity exactly what you and your school district bring to the table. Begin by looking at yourself. What strengths do you have to encourage grant evaluators to put their agency's money in your hands? This is not the time for modesty, but you must find a way to show your strengths without appearing immodest.

Start with your credentials, but don't overplay your hand. A college degree (including a master's or doctorate) is important only if it relates directly to your proposal; otherwise, it is pretty useless because it does not ensure that you are prepared to do the proposed job. Which of your experiences have prepared you for your role in this grant? You must look at your proposal more closely. For example, if you are looking for support for a proposed international student-exchange program or to develop or upgrade a program for students who do not speak English, then fluency in the appropriate language(s) is important.

For those of you who have had previous proposals funded, your track record as a grant manager and budget officer is extremely important. If your

a. **Unique experiences:**

b. **Academic expertise:**

c. **Unique strengths (suited to this project):**

d. **Awards:**

e. **Previous grants:**

FIGURE 4.3   List Your Important Strengths

grant requires you to speak in front of large audiences or to deliver special services, then a letter written on official letterhead thanking you for the moving speech you recently gave or for the *outstanding* services you provided is a great way to communicate your expertise, without showing off.

You can use Figure 4.3 to highlight your important strengths. An important yet often overlooked area of strength is enthusiasm. Superintendents and personnel officers will often tell you that when an applicant pulled out her portfolio and began showing pictures of her classroom activities, her face lit up, and she became so excited about her students that she forgot she was in an interview. That's when she got the job. This statement has two lessons. First, don't overlook the strength of portfolios because they include samples of your best work and samples of your students' best work. Second, if not by a portfolio, then find some other way to show your enthusiasm. Who in their right mind would invest their agency's money in a project in which the applicant seemed only mildly interested or only half-way committed to its course?

USING YOUR THREE-RING BINDER

Second, show your commitment. This can best be achieved through choosing topics you really care about. For example, if you are worried about child obesity and you want to do something about it at your school, then write a grant to curtail obesity. The next time you want to write a grant, write another grant on this topic. In Chapter 3, you were encouraged to get a three-ring binder and start collecting data and other information to use in your grant-writing *program.* Yes, we are *not* talking about a one-time, piecemeal writing of a grant, but a lifelong, personal, ongoing, grant-writing *program.* This ongoing practice of collecting articles on your chosen topic will do two things: It will add to your grant-writing resources, and, without your awareness, it will add to your grant-writing knowledge. As you use these examples and these data over and over, they will become second nature in your own thinking. This will automatically raise your level of enthusiasm and your skills for your grant topics.

Serious grant writers avoid piecemeal writing.

Finally, identify your limitations. If your writing skills are especially limited, then this is the perfect time to begin improving them. For example, if you want to tell the evaluators about your college degrees and you don't know whether you have a *masters degree,* a *Masters Degree,* a *Master's Degree,*

Your weaknesses can hurt your grant writing only if you choose to ignore them.

or a *master's degree,* then it's time to brush up on your grammar. The exercises in Appendices 7.1 and 7.2 can help. Furthermore, if, indeed, your grammar skills are limited, then you should get someone with far superior writing ability to read over your proposal and mark any grammatical errors. Even if you have good grammar, you will profit from having a colleague proof your proposal. If you are at a total loss with numbers, then seek the help of a more quantitative friend to review and correct your budget. Don't be embarrassed over any weaknesses; everybody has some. They can hurt your grant writing only if you choose to ignore them. Chapter 7 focuses on improving your grant-writing style.

YOUR SCHOOL AND SCHOOL DISTRICT'S MISSION STATEMENT

Now, using the form shown in Figure 4.4, examine your school and school district in a way you have never before seen them. Begin with their mission statements. A principal in Savannah, Georgia, has her school's mission statement posted on her office door. The sign reads, "Our business is learning, and we are getting better every day." This is a powerful statement because it is short and direct. The power of a short mission statement is illustrated by the mission statement of Southwest Airlines: "The low-fare airlines." That is about as concise as you can get, yet this mission has seen Southwest through both good and bad times for over 30 years. It is more than words; every decision to spend money is based on the simple question, "Will it help us remain the low-fare airlines?" If not, the proposed change is almost sure to be rejected. Once you find your mission statement for your unit, try to collapse it into one short, direct sentence. Then it will become a powerful grant-writing tool. If possible, build your proposals around this short mission statement; if not, at least align each proposal with your school's or school district's mission.

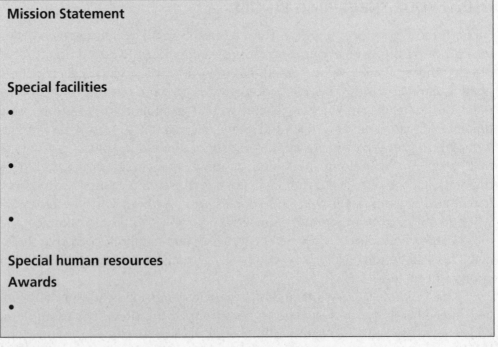

Mission Statement

Special facilities

-
-
-

Special human resources
Awards

-

FIGURE 4.4 Information About Your School or School District

SUSTAINABILITY

As addressed in Chapter 3, sustainability (measures taken to ensure that a grant continues after the funding stops) is important to funding agencies. Using your school's or school district's mission statement as a foundation for your grant proposals will capture the attention of funding agencies because they know it will enhance your grant's sustainability.

FACILITIES AND SPACE

Examine your school and school district's facilities. Make a list of those facilities that could be of use in grants. For example, suppose large conferences will be required to train teachers. The funding agency will want to know if you have the space and equipment necessary to hold those conferences. In downtown locations, parking space can be a critical asset to many proposals. Or, suppose your goal is to raise the number of National Board Certified Teachers (NBCTs). You may want to have your school serve as an NBCT testing site. Or suppose you want to start a driving school on your campus; then you must have the necessary space to build for a driving track.

HUMAN RESOURCES

An often overlooked strength of schools and school districts is their human resources. An important section to be added to your three-ring binder is the vitae of your teachers, counselors, administrators, and other school personnel. If your school and school district are large, then you must be selective; choose the vitae of those colleagues who have distinguished themselves at high levels and who are in your field of expertise. The Buffalo School District (Colorado) maintains a list of some of its faculty members' areas of expertise (Figure 4.5). The Buffalo grant director keeps this list at her fingertips and uses it when she leads a team of grant writers.

Some grant offices maintain a list of vitae of their grant writers and of other colleagues who have exceptional strengths.

AWARDS

Look again at your own field(s) of interest and expertise. If your department, school, or school district has distinguished itself by winning awards, then make a list of these awards, who issued them, and the date each was given. It's one thing to claim your school's industrial arts program is excellent; it's an entirely different thing to reveal that your school's industrial arts program has earned first place in the state's rankings. Claiming your school has a great cheerleading program is different from saying that your school's cheerleading team has made it to the national finals three times in the past decade. Including news clippings (saved in your three-ring binder) announcing these awards is an even better way to reveal your district's strengths. Although you might not always find it, you should search for this level of evidence to support every claim you make in your proposal. This is one of many ways you can make your proposal *the best it can be*.

Try to find evidence to support every claim you make.

Finally, you should also note your school's special needs. Although a school's ability to perform above the competition usually trumps the school's needs, needs still play an important role in funding. Therefore, you should know your school's needs. One grant writer, whose school district had the

QUALIFICATIONS

Areas of Expertise and Specialties

Message Development

Community Outreach and Capacity Building

Grassroots Engagement of Educational Community

Speech, Presentation, and Media Training

Facilitation and Mediation, Multistakeholder Public Processes

Situational Analysis/Issues Inventory

Graphic Design, Creative Direction

The Experienced Team*

Myra Adams, Principal

Myra Adams, owner of Adams Communications, specializes in strategic communications, collaborative problem solving, and public relations in the fields of energy, conservation, agriculture, and education. Adams's record of success is a direct reflection of her vast knowledge of Wyoming's unique grapevine and her extensive experience in message development, media relations, and grassroots coalition building.

From state and local initiatives to public involvement campaigns, Adams has combined her outreach and collaboration skills to develop innovative approaches to successful communication strategies. She has managed several statewide initiatives, including outreach and conference production for the Susan G. Komen Foundation, passage of the Wildlife Trust Fund, passage of the Wyoming Workforce Infrastructure initiative (supporting affordable housing for energy- and development-impacted communities), and several energy and open space–related projects on behalf of an institute at the University of Wyoming.

Active and well connected in state and local politics, Adams serves on many state and local boards, including the Environmental Quality Council, First Interstate Bank Advisory Board, CLIMB Wyoming, and the Community Foundation of Jackson Hole. She also served as Marketing Director for the Jackson Hole Visitors Council before starting Adams Communications. A Wyoming native from a fourth-generation Wyoming family, Adams earned her Bachelor of Arts in Organizational Communication from the University of Wyoming. She lives in Jackson with her husband, Bill Wotkyns, and their sons, Pete and Silas. Adams is a very bad fisherman.

Hanna Savage, Account Management

Hanna Savage has vast experience in community relations, strategic and crisis communications, and government affairs. Savage, a public relations consultant, focuses primarily on building community support—both grassroots and grasstops—for controversial energy and land use/development projects. Her ability to find creative ways to educate the public, build support among opponents, and encourage unprecedented partnerships has been met with great success in Teton County, Wyoming, where projects of this nature are normally met with strong resistance.

Before moving to Jackson, Wyoming, Savage worked for over 5 years in the White House. As Deputy Press Secretary to Vice President Cheney, she consolidated the administration's key policies into talking points and strategic message themes, and communicated them to national, regional, and local media. Savage also served as Special Assistant to the Chief of Staff to Vice President Cheney.

*The name of the district and personnel have been changed.

FIGURE 4.5 Buffalo School District Faculty Expertise (*continues*)

In this position, she drafted speeches, correspondence, and briefing papers on issues of domestic and foreign policy and prioritized information for the Chief of Staff's review.

Prior to her White House tenure, Savage was the Executive Assistant to the Vice President of Government Affairs at Halliburton Company. In this capacity, she was charged with congressional outreach and writing and editing the weekly company newsletter, which included all current legislative issues handled by the DC lobbying staff.

Savage received her bachelor's degree in Biological Sciences from North Carolina State University.

Dr. Barbara Wally, Education Consultant

Dr. Barbara Wally has been part of the Wyoming educational community for over 37 years. Wally received many of her degrees from the University of Wyoming (a BA in Elementary and Special Education, endorsements in Administration and Reading, and a PhD in Curriculum and Instruction); as a result, she has many educational connections around the state.

Wally has been deeply involved in the education of Buffalo County's children and teachers for the past 28 years. In 1996, she received the Presidential Award for Excellence in the teaching of science. This award is given annually to two teachers (one in science and the other in mathematics) at the elementary and secondary levels in each state.

Buffalo County has been a district known for its innovation in education and support of many of the smaller districts in the state of Wyoming. Wally has written, or been part of, many of the grants and opportunities offered throughout the state in the last 10 years. Examples of those are Title IIA and Title IIB grants (which have resulted in instructional coaching formats throughout the state and deep organizational change to the way Buffalo County teaches science and mathematics); a bridges grant, which set the foundation for summer school and beyond-the-school-day funding and organization throughout the state; a Reading First grant; and foundational organizational support to a book initiative called "Wyoming Reads," in which every first grade child receives a hardback book of their choice.

Wally has a tremendous ability to network throughout the Wyoming education community. The children of Wyoming are the key, and Wally can help make connections for those children.

Peggy Connors, Creative Director

Wyoming native Peggy Connors, an innovative graphic designer specializing in education and visual campaigns, has a successful record of capturing the essence of a client's message in a visual platform. Connors prides herself on closely studying the targeted audience and mastering a message that best presents the information and will resonate among the desired group.

Connors has served as creative director on numerous information campaigns, including a $30 million capital campaign for an art center; a statewide positioning for a national nonprofit; and a highly acclaimed domestic violence awareness campaign. She has also received national recognition for her creative work as the winner of Crane's Paper Identity.

Connors graduated summa cum laude as a Fine Arts and Graphic Design major from Illinois State University and was awarded the Outstanding Graphic Design Student of the Year. She was born in Jackson Hole, Wyoming, where she returned after completing her design education. And, yes, she can really ski.

FIGURE 4.5 Buffalo School District Faculty Expertise

highest dropout rate in the United States, turned this need into an advantage. She repeatedly made this case in all her proposals: "Let me show you that I can make my proposed program work here (where the dropout rate is the highest in the nation), and you will know that educators everywhere can make my model work."

Summary

Choose a grant topic for which you have a true passion, and the proposal readers will know that this passion will help sustain the program beyond the funded dates. Study the potential funding agency's mission statement, and carefully craft each proposal to deliver on that mission. This requires putting the funding agency's needs first. Study your own strengths and the strengths of your school and school district. Aim your proposal at convincing the proposal evaluators, not that you have the greatest needs, but that if your proposal is selected, you *can* and *will* do a better job than all the competition in meeting the funding agency's needs. The triangular model and a source map can be useful in designing your proposal.

- Appropriately used, your school's and/or school district's mission statement can strengthen each of your proposals.
- School districts benefit most when their educational leaders replace random, isolated grant proposals with a personalized, ongoing, grant-writing program.
- Educational leaders at all levels need ready access to data about their school and school district, including information about previous awards and grants, as well as the outcomes of those grants.
- Grant writers need to keep a list of their school's and school district's strengths, including the often-overlooked human resources.

RECAP OF MAJOR IDEAS

- In choosing topics, grant writers must search their own hearts and write about those causes for which they have a passion.
- Grant writers must decide whether to write grants and then look for funding, or they must review RFPs, select one, and carefully craft the proposal to meet the funding agency's goals. They can also use both paths.
- Many grant writers inadvertently fail to address some of the requirements stated in the RFP, and this mistake guarantees rejection.
- Grant writers need to align their personal strengths and their school's and school district's strengths with the needs of the potential funding agency.
- The first step in deciding to pursue a particular grant opportunity is to ensure a match between your grant and the funding agency—in terms of topic, dollar size, and deadline.

LIST OF TIPS

1. Choose topics for which you have a true passion.
2. Put the funding agency's needs above your own desires.
3. Emphasize your ability to outperform the competition rather than emphasizing your needs.
4. When listing your school district's strengths, don't overlook the strengths of your personnel.
5. Study each potential funding agency's mission statement.
6. Study your own school's and school district's mission statements, and shorten them to a few concise sentences.
7. Develop and use a source map.
8. Whenever possible, turn your weaknesses into strengths.
9. Use both the rifle approach and the shotgun approach.
10. Using the rifle approach, carefully craft *most* of your proposals to meet the funding agency's mission.

Including All the Right Parts

INTRODUCTION

Now that you can recognize and avoid the myths that discourage and trip unsuspecting grant writers, you have learned how to choose your approach by considering your circumstances, and you know how to select funding sources, it is time to decide what parts you will need to include in your proposals. Not knowing this can be one of the most confusing and discouraging parts of grant writing. Leaving out just one part can guarantee a rejection. But it doesn't have to be that way. This step will leave you knowing exactly what parts you will want to include in each of your proposals and will help you with the writing of each part.

When writing proposals for state, federal, and large foundations grants (i.e., grants that issue a request for proposals [RFP]), the first step is to check your RFP. Some RFPs tell you exactly what parts the readers of the proposals will expect to find in a proposal. For those grants that do specify certain parts, these specifications are not casual suggestions. On the contrary, they are mandates, and they must be adhered to rigorously. Each of this book's chapters contains some important guidelines, and by following each to a T you can increase the chances that each of your proposals will be funded. None of these tips or guidelines is more important than this. **Tip:** *Always address each and every part of the proposal as directly, clearly, and convincingly as you can*. In fact, as shown in Figure 3.2, each part will be counted when your proposal is evaluated. Missing parts will receive zeros. But this presents no problem to the alert writer. **Tip:** *Simply add a subheading for each designated part*.

Unfortunately, many RFPs do not specify the exact parts that their proposals should have, and what's even worse, the decision as to exactly which parts to include is somewhat subjective. For example, although one might argue that all proposals should require a budget or a table of contents, it is less certain that all proposals should contain an abstract or a title page. When

Correctly written, each proposal part becomes a tool for selling your dream.

written correctly, each of the proposal parts can become an opportunity to sell your proposal to the readers. **Tip:** *When you are in doubt as to whether to include one of the parts, err on the side of caution and include it.*

This chapter introduces those parts of a proposal that have proven successful in over 30 grants; therefore, although some of these parts are not offered as prescriptions, each is important and should be given close consideration. Think of each of the following parts not as a chore but as an opportunity or *tool* you can use to enhance the acceptance of your proposals. These parts include (1) a transmittal letter; (2) a title page; (3) an abstract; (4) a table of contents; (5) purposes, goals, and objectives; (6) timetables, timelines, and flowchart; (7) a sustainability statement; (8) an evaluation; (9) a budget; and (10) a checklist.

TRANSMITTAL LETTER

The transmittal letter is a short, one- or two-page letter written and signed by the senior officer in your school district. Its purposes are to introduce the proposal and to assure the potential funders that the district supports the proposal. By signing the transmittal letter, the senior officer agrees to stand behind the promises and commitments made by the investigators who wrote the proposal.

The importance of keeping the transmittal letter short can be appreciated by remembering the last time you saw a guest speaker or keynote speaker being introduced by a windy introduction that turned out to be as long as the anticipated speech. Perhaps you wanted one of the long hooks used in vaudeville acts to bring the introduction to an abrupt close. The evaluators have that power; if your proposal's transmittal letter is too long, then all they have to do is put it in the rejection file and move on to the next proposal. So, when you ask your senior officer for a transmittal letter, you might want to ask for a *short* transmittal letter. An even better approach is to *draft the letter yourself,* ask the senior officer to make the necessary adjustments, and then put it on the school district's letterhead. Like the rest of the proposal, the transmittal letter should be written in a clear, straightforward style.

Use common words, and don't try to impress others with your vocabulary. At a minimum, the transmittal letter should contain:

- The superintendent's phone number
- The superintendent's FAX number
- The superintendent's mailing address
- The superintendent's e-mail address
- A statement of purpose

A sample transmittal letter is shown in Figure 5.1.

This transmittal letter belongs in your three-ring binder.

Notice that the transmittal letter immediately defines the problem that the investigators plan to address. The letter also answers an important question, "Why us?" Why should we be the ones to study this problem? What special skills or resources do we have to suggest that we would do a better job than the others who are responding to this RFP? Notice too, that this letter uses recent data from a credible source to substantiate its claim that the problem *really is* significant.

Using the sample transmittal letter shown in Figure 5.1, you can develop your own generic transmittal letter template. Your template letter should include some of your special needs and some of your district's unique strengths. You can use this template each time you prepare a proposal.

Mr. Robert P. Anderson, Executive Director

Southwest Foundations, Inc.

108 Holly Hill Drive

P.O. Box 55

Lubbock, TX 79493

Dear Mr. Anderson,

A recent study released by the U.S. Department of Health has reported obesity as the number one health problem of America's youths.

The Nurse Practitioner Program in the School of Allied Health and Nursing at Southwest University seeks support for the enclosed proposal titled, "The Ashley Obesity Reduction Program for America's Youths." We have taken a holistic approach to this problem because we believe most of today's weight problems result from a consequence of changes in lifestyle. Our proposed program begins at the preelementary school level because this same report says that poor eating habits and sedentary lifestyle begin at this early age.

We chose to send this proposal to you because we know that your organization is committed to improving the health of individuals of all ages, especially teenagers and children.

Because our state has the highest rate of obesity in the nation, we believe the need to address this issue is acute. However, our decision to attack this problem is based on an even greater factor—our organization has studied health practices among youths and experimented with developing health foods for over 100 years. We have accumulated a knowledge base on which to build.

Please let us know if further information or explanation is needed. Thank you for considering this proposal.

Sincerely,

FIGURE 5.1 Sample Transmittal Letter

TITLE PAGE

A title page is a sparse page resembling the top page of a business report or the top sheet of a college research assignment. See Figure 5.2 for a sample title page. At a minimum, the title page should include:

- The project's title
- The name of the company or institution submitting the proposal
- The date

The title page may also include additional information such as the amount of money requested or the names, phone numbers, e-mail addresses, and FAX numbers of the investigators. Because the title page serves as a graphic organizer, enabling easy and quick identification of your proposal, and because yours is likely to be one of many proposals being evaluated, brevity is essential.

A Proposed Method for Enhancing the Purity of Steel

Submitted to: The Vulcan Foundation

by

The Rocky Mountain Bureau of Mines

July 21, (year)

FIGURE 5.2 Sample Title Page

ABSTRACT

An abstract is a short description of the proposal. Some grant writers make distinctions among the abstract, summary, program summary, project summary, program narrative, and executive summary; others do not. It is said that some nationalities do not care what you say or do as long as you say it correctly. Grant writing is concerned with both what you *say* and what you *do*. The important thing to remember is that it is the funder who calls the shots. You can also call a few shots as long as you respond to every one of the funder's calls. Some funders require an abstract, others do not. Check your RFP. If an abstract is required, (1) *use the term contained in the RFP,* and (2) *follow the specifications precisely.* Most RFPs requiring abstracts specify required lengths (e.g., *Include a 250-word abstract.*). This 250-word requirement is meant to be a maximum length. This common restriction reflects the purpose of abstracts, which is to enable evaluators to make a *quick* assessment of each proposal. They may begin the evaluation by conducting an initial screening and by reading *only* the abstracts. As mentioned in Chapter 3, many evaluators receive so many proposals that they must have a way to reduce the number they read to a small fraction of those received. In essence, *if you don't do an outstanding job crafting your abstract, then your proposal may never be read.* This makes the abstract extremely important. In addition to requiring the submission of abstracts, some RFPs specify the exact parts to be included in each proposal. Abstracts are easily written if you wait until the proposal is drafted. Once the content has "settled down," you can extract strong sentences from the full proposal. A sample proposal abstract is shown in Figure 5.3.

If poorly written, then your abstract may be the only part of your proposal that is read.

Responding to the critical shortage of high school physics teachers, the University of _____ proposes a 10-week summer institute designed to prepare secondary teachers who are now teaching physics, or who anticipate teaching physics next fall, but who lack certification in the area of physics. Each participant will be given a total of 266 contact hours of physics courses, laboratory experiences, tutorials, and seminars, providing students with the opportunity to earn 12 semester credit hours.

During the fall semester, each participant will be visited at his or her own school and provided with an opportunity to ask further questions and to share successes and criticisms of the materials developed in the institute.

FIGURE 5.3 Sample Proposal Abstract

TABLE OF CONTENTS

Some RFPs specify a table of contents as a requirement, but most RFPs leave the decision to include or omit it to their writers. Similar to the title page and abstract, the table of contents is a visual tool that can work for you, making it too important to omit. Furthermore, a table of contents can be constructed easily and quickly. For example, see the one shown in Figure 5.4.

Begin by titling your table of contents. Then, using Roman numerals, list the major parts of the proposal. On the right-hand side of the page, insert the

Table of Contents	
I. PROJECT SUMMARY	1
II. PROJECT DESCRIPTION	2
A. Objectives	2
B. Participant Selection	4
1. Number of participants	4
2. Policy for admission	4
3. Selection procedure	5
C. Program Content	6
1. Physics 110	6
2. Physics electives	7
3. Integrated laboratory	8
4. Seminar	9
D. Additional Components	9
1. Follow-up activities	9
2. Evaluation	9
III. STAFF	10
IV. FACILITIES	11
A. Instructional Facilities	11
B. Housing Facilities	12
V. INSTITUTIONAL SUPPORT	12
VI. BUDGET	14

FIGURE 5.4   Sample Table of Contents for Physics Teachers' Summer Institute Proposal

page numbers. When you have completed filling in all the parts, check your list to verify that you have not overlooked any parts. A simple omission can be interpreted as carelessness and can lose the confidence of funders, who may assume that you will be equally careless with the implementation of the proposal and when spending *their* money!

PURPOSES, GOALS, AND OBJECTIVES

Purposes are global statements used to explain the general expectations of the funder. For example, the purpose of a grant proposal might be to reduce the pollution in a particular part of the city. This is awfully vague. It doesn't tell what types of pollution, how great the need to reduce pollution, or how the forthcoming reduction of pollution is to be measured.

Goals are used to break the purposes down into parts. One goal might be to reduce the number of pollutants in the air, and another might concern the water. But neither goal answers the questions—What types of air pollutants or water pollutants? Or how much does the funder want these to be reduced? So, goals are broken down into objectives, which are much more specific. For example, one objective might be to reduce the amount of sulfur in the air to 1 part for every 10,000 parts. Each objective should be a short statement with an action verb written in the present or future tense. Get a copy of your school district's mission statement. Examine it for goals. Write one or two specific objectives indicating exactly how you and your unit can help reach each goal. Time spent improving your understanding of your district's mission is time well spent. A clearer understanding of this mission can bring clarity and power to your proposals.

TIMETABLES, TIMELINES, AND FLOWCHARTS

Funders always want to know the different stages in the project. When can you begin implementing the project? How long will each stage take? If the project has several steps or phases, it is the investigator's (grant writer's) responsibility to make a clear distinction between each phase and inform the funder as to when each phase will begin and end. Because funders often have many proposals to consider, failure to communicate the different phases and the time frame for each can be disastrous. Like incomplete proposals, unclear proposals usually get pushed aside and end up in the rejection pile.

Funders want to know when you will reach each stage of your proposal.

The *flowchart* is also an excellent tool to show the evaluators your sequence of events and when you expect to begin and end each event. As you assign the time for each phase, remember that funders give their support because they have a job they want to get done. If there is an urgency to get the program into operation, then the evaluators will be sensitive to the time frame and may be highly influenced by the ability of some investigators to complete the job sooner than others. This suggests that you should be ready to implement the first phase of your project as soon as you learn that it has been funded. But remember also that the funders demand quality work, so be sure allow as much time as you deem necessary to do a good job. The goal here is to present a timetable showing that you are ready to begin implementing your project, and once you begin, you will move the project forward from one phase to another, without unnecessary delays, until it becomes operational (Figure 5.5).

Include in your timetable and flowchart the date you plan to disperse your program to ensure that it benefits as many as possible.

Notice that the flowchart shown in Figure 5.5 shows the steps in chronological order and also includes specific beginning and ending dates for all project phases. In retrospect, however, it is easy to see that the timetable has

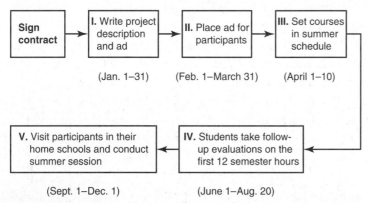

FIGURE 5.5 Project Timetable

a major omission. It fails to include plans to disseminate information. At the beginning of the first summer session (June 1), plans to have a news reporter on hand should have been included. Most funders like to have publicity on their programs, showing their generosity and commitment to the causes they support. You should also file copies of the publicity in your three-ring binder, so it is ready for use at any time to strengthen future proposals.

Make a list of at least three or four strategies you can always use to publicize your grants. Write these strategies down, including the addresses and phone numbers of consultants and news reporters. You might also want to include the names and addresses of the editors of journals to which you would like to target articles you write to help others use these new programs. *As you know, hindsight offers opportunities to discover omissions not previously observed. Examine the sample timetable shown in Figure 5.5 and determine whether there are other events and dates that can be added to the timetable to improve the project.*

SUSTAINABILITY

Grant funders know that when the funding period ends, most programs die.

Another factor to consider is extending the timetable to show your plans to continue the program *after* the funder's support is withdrawn. Obviously, not all grant proposals are written to establish programs, so providing information on how you plan to sustain your program once the funds dry up is not listed as a proposal part on the checklist provided later in this chapter. If, however, your proposal does involve establishing a program or an ongoing service, having a clear statement on how you propose to keep your program alive could be one of the most influential parts of your proposal. Grant funders know that for a very high percentage of programs, once the funding ends, the programs immediately die.

EVALUATION

Internal evaluations are always viewed with suspicion of bias.

Most RFPs require the investigators to arrange for external evaluators to make comprehensive assessments of their programs. Others, such as private donors and family-owned foundations, permit the investigators themselves to conduct the evaluations. When given the choice between conducting the evaluation yourself and hiring an external evaluator, seriously consider the latter choice. Regardless of how objective and accurate your own evaluation might be, it is always subject to suspicion; therefore, it is usually far better to commission a third party. Always select a company or evaluation consultant with no connections to your school district.

Pre- and posttests offer a simple and elegant approach to evaluating your program internally. In this context, *elegant* means the approach is both clear and convincing, two essential qualities of all effective proposals. The method is convincing because it establishes a baseline, letting the evaluators know where you were at the beginning of the program and where you expect to be after a given time. For example, when Paul Irish of the Integrated Arts Academy in Vermont, prepared a digital storytelling literacy grant, he included the one-paragraph evaluation statement shown in Figure 5.6. In the first sentence, he commits to having teachers "fill out evaluations before and after their training" to "determine their comfort level and understanding of digital

---

Evaluation

Teachers will fill out evaluations before and after training to determine their comfort level and understanding of digital storytelling concepts, vocabulary, and technology tools. To determine the efficacy of the program, teachers will collect benchmark writings completed before and after the project. These benchmark pieces will show growth in student understanding of writing organization. Students will use rubrics during and after the process to improve and evaluate work, complete pre- and postsurveys on technology skills and digital storytelling, and engage in reflection of their work through journaling. Fountas and Pinnell Benchmark Reading Assessments administered at the beginning of this school year will be compared with tests administered next September to assess how digital storytelling projects have affected student reading. Particular attention will be given to questions that assess comprehension and beyond-the-text knowledge and questions that ask students to elaborate on text construction and make inferences.

FIGURE 5.6   Paul Irish's Digital Storytelling Grant Evaluation

storytelling concepts, vocabulary, and technology tools." In the same paragraph, he also commits to using a nationally recognized assessment tool at the beginning of the school year. These test results "will be compared with tests administered next September to assess how digital storytelling projects have affected student reading."

If you decide to use an internal evaluator, then you should also consider collecting your own data. These data can be quickly and easily gathered. The grant whose timetable is shown in Figure 5.5 won over the competition for 5 years running. This continued success can be attributed to a very simple annual evaluation. Each year, *after the summer institute was over,* the investigator drove to visit the participants, asking them two simple, yet poignant questions: *"What did you learn in last summer's institute that you have been able to implement?"* and *"What might we have done in the institute that would have helped you even more?"* Having the proposal win over the competition for 5 consecutive years was a great payoff for asking two simple questions. (Of course, each year the investigators used the answers to these two questions to rewrite and improve the proposal. Year after year, this strategy kept the grant-writing team one step ahead of the competition.)

A carefully planned evaluation can provide improvements that ensure funding.

BUDGET

Because the budget plays such a major role in determining whether a proposal is funded, Chapter 6 discusses how to prepare a budget that will make your proposal irresistible.

CHECKLIST

To guard against omissions, some grant writers make a checklist of the major parts in their grants. This is an easy task if you list each part of the grant under

Your own credibility may be your greatest strength, and it can be enhanced by providing data to support every claim you make.

a subheading. It is further simplified by putting each subheading in italic or boldface letters. The checklist for this proposal is as follows:

- Transmittal letter
- Title page
- Abstract
- Table of contents
- Purposes, goals, and objectives
- Timetables, timelines, and flowcharts
- Sustainability
- Evaluation
- Budget
- Checklist

Summary

Grant writing can be made easier by knowing exactly what parts your proposal should include. Many RFPs list the parts that the evaluators will expect to see when they examine and evaluate the proposals. If your proposal is to have a chance to be funded, then you absolutely must include all of these parts. Some evaluations are given guides or rating sheets with instruction to give each proposal part a numerical rating. When the scoring is complete, these evaluators simply add the scores and award the grant to the proposal with the highest total score. Therefore, it will behoove you to (1) follow the directions and include every part listed in the RFP, and (2) ask whether a proposal evaluation score sheet is available for you to use in preparing your proposal.

For the many RFPs not specifying the exact parts they want to have in these proposals, remember that when used appropriately, each part can be a tool to sell your proposal to the evaluators. Therefore, you should seriously consider including all parts discussed in this chapter.

Because many evaluators receive an unmanageable number of long, poorly written proposals, brevity and clarity should be paramount when writing each part. Include just enough to do the job, which, of course, is to communicate clearly and persuasively. Putting quality above everything else is an equally important principle to use as a guideline when preparing proposals. Although it is to your advantage to be both economical and expedient, promising to deliver too much too soon can be disastrous. Caution and good judgment should temper your temptation to overcommit.

Credibility is an indispensable quality for all grant writers. Experienced grant writers who have successfully implemented previous grants have an advantage over novice grant writers *if they have collected data and maintained records to substantiate their success*. Novice grant writers can offset this advantage by keeping careful records and by using their first grant, and each succeeding grant, to establish their own credibility.

Although this may appear as a catch-22 situation for novice writers, it is possible to put credibility into that first proposal by citing the literature. Funders expect to see evidence of need for the proposed program or product, and they expect to see data to support the investigators' claims, including any claims of expertise or claims of other resources such as personnel or facilities needed to successfully implement their proposal. Locating and citing studies to support your generalizations can be tantamount to taking that extra step to ensure acceptance of your proposal. Chapter 3 suggests that all grant writers develop a system for collecting and storing data so it can be retrieved easily and quickly. This same chapter also presents an easy, yet highly functional system for doing so.

When your proposal is complete, check it against your parts checklist to verify that all parts have been included. As incredible as it may sound, sometimes investigators become so wrapped up in the writing of their proposals that they inadvertently leave out some of the most important parts, including the budget, when mailing their proposals. Therefore, you should use this checklist again when you are literally putting the proposal in the envelope.

A final check is also needed to remove any grammatical or mathematical errors. Simple errors give the impression that the investigator is careless, leaving the evaluators to suspect that similar carelessness will be exercised in overseeing the grant (if, by some miracle, the flawed proposal should eventually be funded).

RECAP OF MAJOR IDEAS

- Some RFPs specify the parts that the evaluators expect to see in all proposals. These evaluators frequently assign points to each part of the proposal and total the scores to determine which proposals will be funded.
- Clarity and brevity should be the goals for preparing each part of the proposal.
- Through careful construction, each part can be used as a tool to garner support for the proposal.
- Most funders value the ability to deliver a quality program or product over the investigators' needs.
- Investigators should be prudent but realistic when preparing their budgets.
- RFPs should always be followed meticulously.
- Investigators can strengthen their proposals by citing reports and articles.
- Each proposal should include a plan for publicizing the program.

- Each investigator should explain how the proposal will be continued after the financial support from the funder is discontinued.

LIST OF TIPS

1. Be sure to include every part stipulated in the RFP.
2. Make every part as concise and clear as possible.
3. Even when it is not requested in the RFP, always include a table of contents and a timetable.
4. If you are not the designated senior officer in your district, then present a preliminary transmittal letter to your senior officer, along with your request for the senior officer to write a transmittal letter using your draft as a guideline.
5. When an abstract is required, never exceed the stated maximum length.
6. Create a flowchart to be used as a timetable.
7. Make sure the budget mirrors the narrative, with the major expenditures being the most important parts.
8. To avoid overlooking an important part of the RFP, try to acquire a copy of each grant's rating form. If you succeed, then create a subheading for each part of this form.
9. Do not emphasize your needs over your ability to carry out the purpose of the grant.
10. Develop a clear statement explaining how this program will continue beyond the funding period.

Preparing the Budget

INTRODUCTION

As mentioned in Chapter 5, the budget is considered by many to be the heart of any grant proposal. It should drive the grant. If all other parts of a proposal are perfect but the budget is less than excellent, a mediocre budget can, and often does, lead to rejection. So, as you study this step, do so with the goal of learning how to develop a budget that will make your grant irresistible—a goal that is reached when your budget is clear, concise, reasonable, and convincing.

The budget is such a key part of any grant that it is virtually impossible to discuss grant writing without mentioning it. In this chapter, you will see, beyond a shadow of a doubt, that an otherwise near-perfect proposal can be rejected because of its budget. For this reason, the budget has been mentioned throughout this book. Its significance makes it the only grant part with its own chapter. But recognize, also, that budget writing can be a very positive experience (and once people have written a couple of them, some look forward to writing their next budget). To achieve this goal, you must make your budget irresistible. The purpose of the budget is to show exactly how much money you need and exactly how you plan to use it. This book describes *budget* as a blueprint for *planning* and *explaining* the costs of a grant. Unfortunately for them, but fortunately for you and your teachers, most grant writers focus only on getting the money. You can do better by beginning working on your budget at the outset; this causes you to think about how you are going to use each part of the budget. Of course, you must write a short sentence or two each time you add an item explaining *exactly* how this money will be spent.

Some people are threatened by the task of writing a budget. It may be because they have no idea how much things cost. If you feel unprepared to put together a good budget, don't worry. Instead, just start putting down

The budget is a blueprint for planning and explaining the costs in a grant.

some numbers (broad estimates). Then you can begin phoning and checking them out. This applies to both intangibles (e.g., labor costs) and concrete objects to be purchased. One grant writer describes budget drafts as "opportunities to think on paper."

Clarity

Above all, you must make your budget clear, not only to yourself but also to the evaluators. You can achieve clarity through brevity and structure.

The budget must be crystal clear not only to yourself but also to the evaluators.

Brevity

Chapter 3 indicated that most proposal evaluators are bean counters. They are left-brain, quantitative thinkers who live in a world of numbers. Like accountants, proposal evaluators have heads for numbers, and they have mind-sets that demand detailed accuracy. The beauty of numbers lies in two dimensions: their brevity and their exactness.

Most teachers are short on numbers and long on words. This is unfortunate because verbosity and rhetoric enable your teachers to discuss topics they don't fully understand. Rhetoric is a great tool for politicians, who often purposefully cloud their meanings, but both rhetoric and verbosity are defeating to grant writers.

The budget offers your teachers an opportunity to jump ahead of the competition. **Tip:** To develop an irresistible budget, begin by thinking like an evaluator; *think in numbers and dollars*, using your left-brain mentality.

But grant evaluators also demand details. This seemingly mutually exclusive pair of conflicting demands—details and brevity—may appear to be an oxymoron, but it is not, at least not for those who learn to think and speak with numbers. So the next question is, how do I include all the necessary details and still manage to keep my budget brief? The answer is by using a process known as *front-end loading*, which means starting your budget at the front end of your grant-writing process. By the end of the budget process, you should be able to describe each part, clearly and succinctly. A budget should have two parts: a one-page listing of all items showing exactly how each amount is derived and a short summary (or narrative) explaining anything needed to clarify the budget list. **Tip:** In your summary, *write no more than two or three short sentences about each major category on your budget list.*

Your narrative should have no more than two or three sentences about each budgeted item.

When correctly ordered, a one-page table can do the job. Note the budget summary for a Science, Technology, Engineering, and Mathematics (STEM) grant shown in Table 6.1. The first category listed in this table is Personnel (Salaries). This is typical of most grants, especially training grants, because salaries are usually a budget's most expensive cost. However, because this is not primarily a training grant, personnel is not the most expensive item in this budget.

The budget summary is followed by a budget narrative. Many requests for proposals (RFPs) include sample budget sheets. **Tip:** When responding to an RFP with a budget sheet, structure (or *order*) *your main topic categories according to the directions set forth in the RFP.* **Tip:** *If your RFP does not have a budget sheet, study the written information supplied by the funder.* Follow the sequence in which the funder introduces the items. This makes

Table 6.1 Budget Summary

Object Category	Instructional Series (100)	Support Services Total (200)	Total
Personnel (Salaries) (100)	$148,436	0	$148,436
Employee Benefits (200)	$38,532	0	$38,532
Purchased Services (300)	0	$13,032	$13,032
Supplies and Materials (400)	0	0	0
Capital Outlay (500)	0	0	0
Other (600)	0	0	0
Total	$186,968	$13,032	$200,000

Entries are based on Charleston County average salaries by position or actual salary of CATS employees.

Personnel	Salary	Health and Dental	Retirement	Social Security	Total
CATS Guidance Counselor	$44,600	$3,441	$5,749	$3,411	$57,201
CATS Teacher	$43,953	$3,441	$5,666	$3,362	$56,422
WRAP Teacher	$39,464	$5,001	$5,051	$3,410	$52,926
Afterschool Teachers @ $35 hr	$20,419	0	0	0	$20,419
				Total	$186,968
Transportation	$13,032	0	0	0	$13,032
				Total	$200,000

your proposal look familiar *to the evaluators*. For example, this book recommends that you begin your budget list by using a category titled Personnel, which the grant shown in Table 6.1 calls Personnel (Salaries). But suppose the funder begins with a category titled "Travel," then you should also put Travel at the top of your list. To achieve brevity, this book advises you to include only broad categories on your budget list. Suppose a particular RFP either tells you to include items within each category or shows a list that includes all items under the main categories. Then, you should do likewise in both your budget list and your budget summary. **Tip:** *Always let the RFP dictate the order*. If your proposal contains items not included in the RFP's example, you might want to phone the granter and ask about the proper location for these items.

PERSONNEL

Tip: Unless the RFP says otherwise, *keep your budget to one short page*. For each item, include any in-kind contributions and salaries. Add a total column (Table 6.1). As just noted, for most types of grants, Personnel is either *a* major expense category or *the* major expense category; therefore, it deserves to be listed at the top of your budget page. But in the absence of any type of ordering clue the most important *reason for putting Personnel at the top is because most* *evaluators will expect to find it there.* Here, you will list first those salaries or fees that will be paid in part or in full by the grant. For example, these might include a district-appointed grant director and a principal who will codirect the project. For the services of each salaried person, include a numerical explanation of how that dollar amount was reached. For example, a principal who is giving half her time to directing this project would be listed as: one principal @ $62,000 ÷ 2 = $31,000. Because the actual implementation of most projects requires either a little or a lot of secretarial help, this is usually expected to be included in the budget. If you do ask to be compensated for secretarial help, then you must show the derivation of the amount requested, basing it on the secretaries' salaries and the percent of time each secretary will be working on this project. You can either ask the funder to pay for these personnel services or list them as in-kind contributions. **Tip:** *Always check the RFP to determine whether a certain percent of the budget is required to be covered by in-kind contributions.* Exceeding this minimum limit by a wide margin will be viewed positively and can provide acceptance leverage, not only because it relieves the funder of some of the expenses but also because it gives grant writers vested interest, deepening their commitment to work harder to make the project succeed.

FRINGE BENEFITS

Tip: Check with your district office to determine whether it has an established rate (percent of salaries) allowed for fringe benefits. The benefits for each person who will work for this project should be itemized. The district may have a separate rate (percent expectation) for determining the fringe benefits for full- and part-time employees.

INDIRECT COSTS

Indirect costs are the overhead items required to keep your district operating. Check with your district to see how much to assess as indirect costs. Your district may stipulate a given percent of the overall budget costs. These can be surprisingly high. Next, check the RFP to determine whether a maximum percent of allowable indirect costs is stipulated. Sometimes the grantor's maximum allowable percent is less than the district's required percent. In other words, the grantor will not allow you to charge as much overhead as your institution requires you to charge. This presents a problem. **Tip:** With your RFP in hand,*inform your district budget office and see if it will make an exception to accommodate this proposal.* **Tip:** If not, once a funder begins negotiating a transaction, *suggest a meeting between your financial officer and the potential funder to attempt a negotiation.*

Fringe benefits and indirect costs maximums vary from district to district.

This is also the appropriate place to list the disposable item that you added to enrich your program but can eliminate without hurting the quality of the program, should you be forced to negotiate. When the funders indicate that they want to fund your proposal but are unable or unwilling to pay the full asking price, they might inquire as to whether you can complete the project for less money (they may do this as a standard practice as a guard against budget padding). In this case, you can tell them that there is one component that can be removed without affecting the program or the rest of the proposal.

The funders may agree to fund the program without this part; however, once they see that you have not exaggerated the rest of the budget, chances are they will tell you to retain the part, indicating that they will find a way to pay the full amount originally requested.

Since budgets have been mentioned repeatedly throughout the book, this chapter reviews important points that have been made. When programs are being evaluated, many evaluators immediately check out the budget. By doing so, they can obtain important insights into the grant writers' levels of competence. Former Foundations Director John Beineke offers grant writers a good tip: *Read widely and gain in-depth understanding* of each grant because knowing that the grant writers have a deep understanding of their grant can weigh heavily into the funding decision. This is another reason every grant writer should also prepare an accurate, well-thought-out budget. The budget is the first part many grant evaluators will see, and like the abstract, if they don't like what they see, then it may be the *only* part they will ever see.

Two common budget errors are asking for too much money and asking for too little money.

We also learned that two common errors in budget making are asking for far too much money (making the grant writers appear greedy) and asking for far too little money (appearing that the grant writers gave their proposed activities too little thought). To ensure your budget is the right size, always do the leg work needed to itemize everything (this will be especially important to foundations).

One may argue whether the budget is really the most important part of the grant, but one cannot argue against the premise that *integrity is the most important quality of a grant writer*. Grant writing is a business partnership process. No partnership is likely to survive, let alone happily prosper, without integrity. Because budgets use numbers, and numbers are exact, leaving little room for confusion (or camouflage), experienced proposal evaluators can spot dishonesty faster by examining a proposal's budget than by any other means.

A LOOK AT SAMPLE BUDGET PARTS

Most evaluators bring some definite expectations to the table. These include certain parts they expect to find in your budget, some of which are absolutely indispensable. **Tip:** *When the parts are spelled out in the RFP, include each and every one.* **Tip:** *Put these parts in the exact order in which they appear in the RFP.* Most education grants include sections commonly labeled as Personnel Expenses (including fringe benefits); Other Expenses, Indirect Costs, or Overhead (except for foundation grants); In-Kind Contributions; Other Contributions (for multifunder grants); Evaluation; and Sustainability.

PERSONNEL EXPENSES

If you want to have the director's responsibility shared among multiple coworkers, then the salaries of all codirectors must be included. If the codirectors spend only part of their time with this project and also have teaching, administrative, or other duties not directly related to this project, then the percent of each codirector's time given to this project must be shown in the budget and must be used to calculate the cost incurred by this project. For education grants targeted to nongovernment funding agencies, project directors' costs are very often given as in-kind (noncash) contributions, showing the grant writers' and their district's commitment to the project.

Referring to Table 6.1, we can see the budget used in a high school technology grant written to help at-risk students learn mathematics. Note that the bottom half of this table is used to break down the personnel costs shown in the upper half of the table. This is an effective way to make the main part of the budget concise and clear.

The Emergency Response and Crises Management Grant Budget shown in Figure 6.1 lists Personnel at the top, as do most program grants, followed by Fringe Benefits and Travel. These lines are followed by Equipment, the largest item in this budget.

Personnel Salaries are not used as an in-kind contribution. Before using salaries as an in-kind contribution, make sure your district policy allows you to claim them as such. Salaries are often considered as indirect costs, exemplifying the need to always work closely with your district office.

Be Reasonable

Virtually all RFPs require budgets to show how much money they will be asked to provide and how that money will be spent. Naturally, a major concern is always the need for the investigators to be good stewards of funds. Two principles should be remembered at the onset of constructing a budget. **Tip:** First, unless you are writing a grant whose main purpose is to garner technology, do not succumb to the common temptation to purchase an expensive piece of technology or other items not absolutely essential to perform the responsibilities of the grant. Even if a certain expensive piece of

U.S. DEPARTMENT OF EDUCATION	OMB Control Number: 1890-0004	
NON- CONSTRUCTION PROGRAMS	Expiration Date : 10/31/2003	

Name of Institution/Organization
Cullman County Schools

Applicants requesting finding for only one year should complete the column under "Project Year L" Applicants requesting funding for multi-year greants should complete all applicable columns. Please read all instructions before completing form.

SECTION A - BUDGET SUMMARY
U.S. DEPARTMENT OF EDUCATION FUNDS

Budget Categories	Project Year 1 (a)	Project Year 2 (b)	Project Year 3 (c)	Project Year 4 (d)	Project Year 5 (e)	Total (f)
1. Personnel	5,000.00					
2. Fringe Benefits	635.00					
3. Travel	12,000.00					
4. Equipment	106,400.00					
5. Supplies	22,400.00					
6. Contractual	5,000.00					
7. Constructions						
8. Other	5,000.00					
9. Total Direct Costs Oines 1-8)	$156,435.00					
10. Indirect Costs	3,896.00					
11. Training Stipends	30,000.00					
12. Total Costs (lines 9-11)	$190,331.00					

FIGURE 6.1 Total Project Budget

technology is essential, but only to get the program underway, to avoid making the evaluators suspicious, *consider renting the equipment instead of purchasing it*. **Tip:** Second, *treat the grant money as though you were spending your own money*. Always ask for enough money to do a good job, but don't be overly generous with someone else's money.

Grant writer and evaluator Wendy Wingard-Gay says, "As a judge, I turn to the budget page first because I want to know what the grantee really wants and whether the need justifies the wants and desires of the grant writer. Be careful not to ask for things the school or district should already be supplying, i.e., paper, pens, writing tablets, and computers. Basic supplies should not be included in a budget."

When the budget is written, it must reflect the mission of the proposal. This means that the items that cost the most should be funding the most essential parts. It also means that *all* items included in the budget must also be included in the proposal's narrative and vice versa (Figure 6.2). For example, when Paul Irish prepared his literacy grant on interactive storytelling, under

BUDGET PAGE

Item	Description	Total
Professional Development (25% Minimum)	Stipends for attending webinar/training sessions for four members of the team: three mathematics teachers and one Technology Integration Specialist. Each team member will spend 3 hours in training. Rate is 20/h per person for a total of $240.	$1,440.00
	Funds to purchase three one-hour webinar/training sessions for each member of the team. High quality webinar/training sessions will be conducted by the trainers from Turning Point Technology. Rate is $100/h per person for a total of $1,200.	
Evaluation (10%)	Evaluation will be performed by a third party.	$450.00
Hardware	Turning Point Technology (three sets)	$2,400.00
Software	Microsoft Office	$0.00
Business Office	Overhead for administrative expenses <5% of total	$210.00
Total Budget		**$4,500.00**

BUDGET NARRATIVE

The objective of writing this proposal is to incorporate twenty-first-century technology into our daily teaching to improve student learning and achievement by way of active engagement in our classrooms. The data collection aspect of Turning Point Technology helps readily determine who needs immediate intervention. Turning Point Technology helps to have all students participate and respond in class and compels otherwise nonparticipatory students to be actively involved in their learning. It also encourages healthy classroom discussions and makes learning fun for all students.

Currently, we have only one set of clickers in our department and that is woefully inadequate for the 11 mathematics teachers we have at BHS. The equipment needed to make this emerging technology work is already in place at BHS, so the bulk of the money from this proposal will be geared toward competently training teachers to become comfortable using this technology in class.

FIGURE 6.2 Paul Irish Budget Page and Narrative

the Evaluation section, he committed to administering a specific test to all participants. **Tip:** *Always give your completed proposal a mirror test*. A *mirror test* is a comparison of the budget and the proposal narrative. It is given to ensure that each item included in the budget is explained in the proposal's narrative.

Tip: *Begin by listing the most costly, tangible items. Then list the most costly intangibles*. Salaries are often among this latter group. Don't forget to include overhead expenses. If you work in a large school district and are not the director of the grants office, check with the Office of the Superintendent or with the district's grants office for the exact amount to ask for overhead. If your school district is small and does not have a grants office, your superintendent's office can provide this information.

Proposal evaluators run checks to ensure that each budgeted item is included in the narrative.

Make In-Kind Contributions

A part of the budget that has become increasingly important in recent years is in-kind contributions. *In-kind contributions* are noncash contributions that your school district makes to the project. In-kind contributions have become increasingly important because funders have expected investigators to make increasingly greater contributions. Indeed, in recent years, many grants require an even, dollar-for-dollar match.

In recent years, many grants require a dollar-for-dollar in-kind match.

But, again, the investigator can use in-kind contributions to make this match. These include items such as portions of salaries of employees who spend time working on the project. As mentioned previously, the investigators themselves may offer to spend a portion of their time codirecting the program and, therefore, should list the percentage of their salaries reflected in the percentage of their working time spent on the project. Don't forget to also count the time that secretaries and other clerical employees might spend on the project. The cost of building space required to house the project can be calculated and counted as an in-kind contribution. The space includes buildings and rooms rented especially for the project, including buildings and space your employer already owns. Don't forget to include the cost of utilities and photocopying.

Once your budget is drafted, review it for missing items and to verify that it mirrors the body of your proposal. For example, the most expensive items should *not* include expendable items.

Remember that once the program is in operation, you may not be able to adjust the budget for at least a year. Furthermore, the funder may want to negotiate for a smaller budget. Desperate to have their proposal funded, some grant writers accept cuts in their budgets so severe that they cannot conduct the project effectively. This is a common mistake.

Some grants do not permit budget adjustments during their first year in operation.

OTHER EXPENSES

This part of the budget lists all types of expenses (except salaries and benefits) required to make the project successful. Looking again at Table 6.2, we see that our at-risk technology grant lists Purchased Services, Supplies and Materials, and Capital Outlay. These are considered *Other Expenses*. As mentioned, some large schools and school districts have a standard amount set to cover all administrative expenses. The budget for Vermont's Burlington High School grant is shown in Figure 6.3. This school expresses its overhead costs (Business Office Administrative Expenses) as a percentage of the total grant expenses. Using a percentage of the budget's overall cost is the normal way of stating overhead.

Budget			
	Items	**Cost per Item**	**Total Cost**
Professional Development			
8 teacher workshop stipends for 4 half-day sessions	8	200	1,600
3 facilitator wokshop stipends for 4 half-day sessions	3	200	600
Book for workshop participants: *Digital Storytelling in the Classroom: New Media Pathways to Literacy, Learning, and Creativity*	11	22	242
Digital storytelling books for professional library	2	29 (approx)	58
Subtotal			*2,500*
Equipment			
Scanners	2	125	250
Flip video cameras	25	130	3,250
Flip video camera cases	25	11	275
Tripods	2	60	120
Microphones	5	10	50
MP3 players (SanDisk Sansa Fuze 4 GB)	25	60	1,500
MP3 chargers	5	11	55
MP3 skins	25	15	375
Splitters	25	6	150
Headphones	25	10	250
MP3 player screen protectors	25	3	75
Subtotal			6,350
Business Office Administrative Expenses	**1.5%**		**150**
Evaluation			1,000
Total			**10,000**

Thank you so much for considering our needs—we appreciate any and all contributions your organization can help us with. And, more important, thank you for stepping up to support our community—there are not many organizations who are as philanthropic!

FIGURE 6.3   Burlington High School (Vermont) Grant Budget

EVALUATION AND SUSTAINABILITY

Chapter 5 introduces two proposal parts titled "Evaluation" and "Sustainability." Because of their importance to most grants, when done right, both of these activities cost money and, therefore, should be addressed and given dollar amounts in the budget. The appropriate place for them is under the heading Other Expenses. For sizable grants, especially those written to federal agencies, an external evaluation conducted by experts outside your school district is usually required. Making a few phone calls to get a ballpark cost estimate for having an expert or team of experts evaluate your project is well worth the time. It tells the grant evaluators you are serious, thorough, and committed to the success of your project.

Adding a "Sustainability" section sends the same message. Suppose in your budget summary, you said you were committed to extending the life of this project beyond the duration of this grant. This statement is fine, but, by itself, just saying this isn't enough. What have you *done* to make this happen? Here's your opportunity to prove your commitment by asking other sources for funds to help make it happen. **Tip:** *Ask your community leaders to provide their time and energy to write other grants for submission to other funders to keep this project alive.* Then use these partners' salaries and the projected number of hours they commit to pursuing other funders to determine the cost of their time. List this item as an in-kind contribution.

Project Sustainability

All funders are keenly curious to learn how you plan to continue operating your program after the funding stops, and most funders insist on having this explained to them up front before they approve the proposal. You must think through this process and offer a convincing plan. Several steps can be taken to ensure that the life of your proposed project continues beyond the funding period. Here is a very easy and effective way to make this happen. **Tip:** *Involve a broad base of your community in preparing the proposal.* The more people who become vested in the program, the more support you will have in ensuring its continuation. The BP grant proposal shown in Figure 6.4 does just that; it expands its support base by involving the local college and by offering to cover teachers' travel expenses, or to pay them to take their grants to fruition and also help five of their fellow teachers do the same.

The more people who become vested in the program, the more support you will have for ensuring its continuation.

A second way to achieve sustainability is to gather evidence of the program's success. **Tip:** *Collect letters and newspaper clippings showing how people benefitted from the program.* Include these in your three-ring binder so you will have them on hand and readily accessible to share with new faculty members and new members of the community, both of whom you may want to encourage to join the project team.

Letters and newspaper clippings are great sources of evidence that your program is benefiting people.

From the beginning, solicit the involvement and endorsement of elected officers in your community. Mayors and other city officers who are involved with the grant may find ways to extend its life. Local legislators may be able to pass legislation to continue the funding of all or parts of the program. Such was the case with one American Heritage proposal; a legislator created a line in the state budget to finance doctoral students at the local university to research the community's history.

Chapter 3 suggests that you consider adding a part to your project that can be removed for the purpose of negotiation. This is a reminder to add that

BP must agree that districts can apply for this grant and that all teachers involved can be counted toward the 300 participant requirement (e.g., Rock River works with Elk Mountain to do a windmill project and every teacher in both schools is involved). Otherwise, this is doomed to failure from the start.

Let's hook into the January science conference at Casper College and the state presidential dinner for the Presidential Award winners in math and science. It needs some boosting activity to keep it viable, and this might just do it.

Many of these teachers would love to network, but their districts cannot pay their expenses so they have to take personal days and pay their own transportation, room and board, and sub. An idea is to individually contact each winner and offer to pay their way (up to $500), or pay them $500 for materials for their classrooms. We take the whole expense as a donation, so there is no tax on it for reporting purposes. If they agree to take the $500 check, then they agree to a 2- to 3-hour grant support symposium. They also agree to sponsor and support five other teachers in their bids for a grant and help them take their ideas to fruition. I would recommend that they come with the people that they hope to work with before we give them a check. Teachers are very busy; they don't mean to put stuff like this on the back burner, but they will. Any chance the governor would highlight some of the best projects publicly? We can call it kid-to-kid teaching about Wyoming energy. If we are lucky, then we could get 20 teachers × 5 sponsored grants = 100 grants. If each grant involves three teachers, then we have our 300 teachers.

During the symposium, they will be given ideas for the grants and introduction to the statewide web page. They will also be given the blog and podcast support that we will need. I recommend that there is a juried panel of experts who will determine what content gets posted. I am also suggesting a 50% up front award and a final 50% award of the grant on posting so BP gets what they are hoping for.

Some quick cost ideas:

20 teachers to the symposium	$500 × 20 = $10,000
Lunch	$400

A web page that could include blog and podcast capability and could hold video that is hosted on a page that will stay put (state website, BP website?)

I have no idea how much that would cost—can Bill do this?

Creation of a potential project idea page—digital would be best here for use at the syposium.

20 hours of work? × $100 an hour for a total of $20,000

Printing for some fliers and possible phone costs (this will be minimal because it is people-to-people that will work) $200

FIGURE 6.4 Cost Proposal for BP Grant

part to your budget. Remember, this is an extra that can be removed to reduce the overall grant cost without damaging the rest of the project.

Some proposal evaluators are very tough. Before writing your next grant, study the review scores one of the evaluators gave the West Ashley High School technology proposal, shown in Appendix 6.1. A breakdown of these scores is shown in. Notice that this evaluator gave this grant writer a perfect score on the budget and then slammed him on the evaluation part. The budget report, shown in Appendix 6.1, explains this great disparity, saying that "the budget report provides strong evidence of the specific use of the funds in detail," but there was "no evidence provided to continue (sustain the program once the grant funds were depleted)." This example gives indisputable evidence to the previous statement saying that a grant writer, or a grant-writing team, can prepare an impressive proposal and yet can be taken down by just one oversight. It also shows how important it is to use the budget to convince the evaluators that you will deliver on every promise.

The good news is that although a mistake can be a setback, it does not have to be fatal. Such a well-thought-out program as the one described in this proposal deserves to be funded. This particular team has experienced success with previous proposals, and it will make sure that each of its proposals receives the adjustments required to make it acceptable.

As stated previously, the best set of guidelines you will ever get for preparing a proposal—including the budget—is the RFP. Kathy Haven, a California parent, who is discussed further in Chapter 8, has an outstanding track record for writing one funded grant after another. Kathy follows the advice given throughout this book. She chooses topics for which she has great passion and determination. After all, she is writing grants to make her local school better for her own children. The budget for one of Kathy's grants in shown in Table 6.2. This bilingual grant can be seen in its entirety in Appendix 6.2. Notice that Kathy has followed a format set forth by the potential funder, responding to each question. Although she has placed Personnel Costs in a section other than at the top of the budget (she may be following the sequence set by the funder), she has produced a very unobstructed and clear list of expenses. Although this proposal is concise, her use of data shows an in-depth understanding of the challenges her school is facing (87.5% on free and reduced breakfast and lunch program) and that she has a grasp of exactly what is needed to help her school overcome its bilingual challenge. Kathy has a very well-thought-out plan to achieve this goal.

Notice, too, that Kathy has provided a Web site in the event that her targeted funder wants more information about the program this grant will support. She also gives an additional Web site address for the district's annual program and budget, providing convincing data on how important this proposed program is to the school and the school district. **Tip:** *Showing how a grant's benefits will spill over to other schools and into the community always strengthens a proposal.*

A Web site can be created to give funders evidence of how the program is meeting its goals.

GIVING THE MIRROR TEST

When responding to an RFP, don't begin writing a proposal until you first verify that your proposal is in the funding range stated in the RFP. Your budget should be large enough to do the job well, but no larger. Remember to include an expendable item to use in the event that the funding agent requires you to negotiate the funds.

Tip: *You can increase the chances of your proposals being funded by including large in-kind contributions.* Always remember to investigate the possibility of directing or codirecting your project and including part of your salary and the salaries of other personnel in your district as in-kind contributions. Always take a variety of measures to ensure your project's sustainability beyond the funding period.

Poorly written, vague proposals stand very little chance of being funded. Above all, make your proposal and your budget clear. Chapter 7 prepares you to develop a special writing style, which will make your proposals more attractive to funding agents.

Summary

Do not wait until you have written your grant narrative to prepare your budget. Draft your budget first and adjust it as your proposal progresses, keeping in mind that your budget must mirror your project narrative. Keep your narrative short, writing only two or three sentences about each budget item.

Always check the RFP to see if budget categories are provided. If so, use them and keep them in the same order as you find them in the RFP. Keep your budget short, no longer than one page. Include plenty of in-kind contributions, and don't ask for more, or less, than required to do a good job. For the purpose of negotiation, include a part that can be removed, reducing the overall cost without damaging the rest of the proposal.

Involve a broad community base on your grant-writing team, and solicit written promises from leaders throughout the community of their commitment to help sustain the program once the funding stops. Target your proposal to a funder who has funded similar projects in your project's cost range. Just before mailing it, give it a final read, making clarity to the readers a top priority and ensuring that it contains all parts listed in the RFP.

RECAP OF MAJOR IDEAS

- The budget is such a key factor that it can determine the fate of the proposal.
- Budget clarity, from the view of the evaluators, is absolutely essential. Proposal evaluators expect and demand clarity and justification.
- Integrity is essential, and it can be earned through the budget.
- Budgets that are too extravagant or too lean draw suspicion.
- The budget spreadsheet should mirror the narrative, allocating the most money to the items most critical to the program's success.
- In recent years, larger-than-ever amounts of in-kind contributions are being required; therefore, making a large in-kind contribution can tilt the scales in your favor.

- In the budget, exact numbers and percentages trump approximations.
- Evaluation and sustainability are important to large grants and, therefore, must be covered in the budget.
- By developing a strategy to overcome them, rejections can reduce failures to delays.

LIST OF TIPS

1. Ask only for the items and services required to carry out your program effectively.
2. Ask for enough to do a good job but never exceed the maximum stated in the RFP.
3. Exceed any specified required amount of in-kind contributions.
4. Never exceed the amounts your district allows for overhead and fringe benefits.
5. Consider donating time to manage your program as an in-kind contribution.
6. Include an expendable item that can be deleted without damaging the rest of the program.
7. Spend the time and effort needed to prepare a clear and accurate budget.
8. Include these parts in each budget: Personnel Costs; Fringe Benefits, Other Services, and Indirect Costs; Evaluation; and Sustainability.
9. Think of grant funders as partners and never misrepresent or withhold information.
10. When responding to an RFP, let the sequence of RFP parts shape your format.
11. Whenever possible, use exact costs instead of approximations.
12. Include internally conducted evaluations for small grants and external evaluations (or both) for large grants.
13. Determine the costs for sustaining your program beyond the funding date, and list these as requested costs or as in-kind contributions.
14. Develop a plan to respond to each rejection and reduce the would-be failure to only a delay.
15. Run a mirror test to ensure your budget mirrors the budget narrative.

Developing a Succinct Writing Style

INTRODUCTION

Most grant proposals are evaluated by a team of readers: men and women who have been assigned the task of spending hours, days, and often weeks reading and discussing dozens or even hundreds of proposals. The enormous number of proposals received for a single grant, coupled with the poor writing style employed by many of the writers, often renders the evaluation job almost impossible. But you can turn this negative situation into a positive situation for you. Put clearly, you can use this knowledge to increase the likelihood that your proposal will be among those few selected and approved for funding. Although you cannot change the number of proposals received, you can make your proposal stand out among its competitors by developing an effective writing style.*

A strange thing happens to people when they begin writing any type of scholarly works, including papers written in graduate classes, manuscripts to be submitted to editors of professional articles or books, or grant proposals intended for funding. Just knowing their work will be evaluated casts a mystical spell over writers, and, unaware of the spell, their behavior is dramatically affected. Unfortunately, the change in behavior is not for the better. On the contrary, it diminishes the quality of their work. For the few writers who are aware of this mysterious phenomenon, this is good news; they can use this knowledge to produce grade A papers, published books, and funded grant proposals.

In the event that you are skeptical about mysticism and spells, consider the work of muses. Many fiction writers say the characters in their stories or plays sometimes come to life and take over the plot. At first, this sounds crazy, until you consider that once characters are fully developed, they must behave accordingly. But that is fiction writing. So, now let's return to the business of grant writing. Knowing that the competition is keen, and assuming that to

Knowing that their proposals will be evaluated casts a mystical spell over most grant writers, destroying their ability to write clearly.

*This chapter is based on the author's book, *Writing for Professional Publication: Keys to Academic Success*, Needham Heights, MA: Allyn & Bacon, 1999.

make their proposals fundable they must make them appear scholarly, grant writers often make their works unnecessarily complex. Several strategies are employed to achieve this goal—unusually long sentences and paragraphs, unfamiliar words and sentence structures—leaving the reader wondering what the author really meant. Ironically, instead of impressing the evaluators and leaving them believing that the author is a real scholar, the evaluators are at best disappointed and at worst completely put out because they cannot understand the proposal. When this occurs, rejection is virtually guaranteed.

The good news is that an alert writer can reverse the results. All that is required to make your proposal more attractive than the competition is to unravel those strategies that made it obtuse, and use the opposite approach. In other words, *writers can make their proposals attractive by developing a simple, straightforward writing style*. There is further good news; this is easy to do, and the rest of this chapter is a simple recipe for developing a style that will gain the attention and respect of your proposal evaluators.

WRITE SIMPLY/AVOID UNNECESSARY JARGON

Have you ever noticed the change that comes over our vocabulary when we are introduced to strangers? This change also occurs when we speak publicly. We are like the medieval archers who were extremely valuable in wars. They served the same role cannons served during the Civil War and heavy artillery played in later wars. Like today's jet bombers, the arrows, cannons, and heavy artillery had the ability to reach out and strike over a distance. To appreciate the importance of these long-distance weapons, consider the alternative; without these long-distance warriors, all war becomes hand-to-hand combat, forcing each soldier to meet the opponent face to face.

Archers who used bows and arrows carried quivers over their backs, and each quiver contained a variety of arrows. Each type of arrow had a special purpose. We writers are like archers; we have quivers we carefully load with words used to achieve specific purposes, and we use these words accordingly. Knowing that our proposals will be evaluated, and assuming that the judges will be highly educated people, we choose words we believe will make us sound highly educated. To impress, we use a lot of long words because we believe long words are evidence of scholarship. For example, when we are talking to a friend about the type of instrument we use to write grants, we might be embarrassed to say that we use a pencil or ballpoint pen and tablet. It just sounds more impressive to say we use our keyboard, computer, or laptop. And if we want to further impress our audience, we can even crank it up a level and instead of saying we *use* our computer to write, we might say we *utilize* it. The word *utilize* has a scientific ring, implying a high level of precision. But, guess what? It doesn't have any other meaning other than that conveyed by the shorter, more familiar word *use*. The only differences in these two words is the one we choose when we write is about three times as long and has three times as many syllables. By using such words, we also ensure that our grant proposals will be three times as long and three times as difficult to understand.

So, the next time you read a book on grant writing and the author advises you to choose words that grant writers use, take this advice with caution and skepticism. Your attempt to spice up your proposal by using high-toned,

The only differences between the words use *and* utilize *are that one has three times as many letters and three times as many syllables as the other.*

sophisticated language to impress the readers can easily backfire and have the opposite effect.

Connie Phelps of Wichita, Kansas, says, "My first grant proved productive, painless, and pleasant! Writing a successful grant application requires a compelling rationale with accurate facts....I wrote succinctly and targeted the most essential information with three to five sentences for each short-answer question." For a look at this grant, see Figure 8.2. Even the humblest of us are guilty of switching arrows; we can't resist the temptation to select a word, now and then, that we know some of our readers won't recognize, thinking surely this will somehow leave the impression that we really know our stuff. (Several years ago, I read the word *defenestration*, and since then, I have been itching to use it in an article or book.) The only reason I want to use it is to let others know that I know a word they probably don't. If I thought about it at all, then I would realize how juvenile and ridiculous this is, for I'm sure all my readers know words I don't. For those who might argue that on rare occasions we may need to select a word unfamiliar to some of our colleagues, my response is these occasions should, indeed, be *rare*. Grant writer Wendy Wingard-Gay says, "Watch the educational lingo! Use common language. Grant readers do not always include educators on judging panels. Someone from the community or a business leader may judge your grant. Abbreviations like IEP, AAC, LD, and ABT have no meaning to these judges. *Have someone from the community read your grant before submitting it so your proposal is understood.* Be sure to check for spelling and grammar."

"My first grant proved productive, painless, and pleasant."
—Connie Phelps

A good precaution against using unnecessary jargon is to imagine you are meeting with one of the evaluators of your proposal. Pretend you are sitting down in front of this person, just talking as you would talk to a colleague. Simply put the words in your proposal that you would use if you were having an informal chat, explaining the proposal to a colleague. This does not suggest that you should appear folksy, or that you should ever use slang, but rather that you should avoid using unfamiliar, high-toned words.

Tip: My advice to you is simple; when writing grants, *never use a two-dollar word when a twenty-five cent word will work.* Following is a list of unnecessarily long words, along with a corresponding list of shorter words.

Never use a two-dollar word when a twenty-five cent word will work.

utilize	use
prioritize	rank
origination	origin
medication	medicine
establish	set
administer	run
irregardless	regardless

Of course the word *irregardless*, although a common expression among educators, isn't even a legitimate word, but that stops only a few writers. Take a moment to examine your own tendency to use unnecessary, high-toned words. Make a list of two or three pretentious words you frequently use, and for each word, list a shorter, more common word.

USE SIMPLE STRUCTURE

Imagine an evaluator who is exhausted from hours of reading over dozens of grant proposals, and you will appreciate the need for making your proposal quick and easy to read. Replacing unnecessary jargon with everyday words is just one of several techniques you can use to clarify your writing. You can also clarify your meaning by shortening your sentences and paragraphs. Strunk and White (1979, p. 23) said it clearly: "A sentence should contain no unnecessary words, a paragraph no unnecessary sentences, for the same reason that a drawing should not have extra lines and a machine unnecessary parts." Imagine the damage that could be done to a drawing by adding an unnecessary line or to a machine by adding just one extra part. One extra cog in your watch would render it completely dysfunctional. Just one unfamiliar word can draw the reader's attention away from the proposal. Consider the additional damage that could result from a few unnecessary sentences, paragraphs, or pages. The same is true with a paragraph. **Tip:** *Each paragraph should have only one idea.* Any additional sentences should be deleted. If your paragraph runs for longer than a quarter or third of a double-spaced page, it is probably too long and should be made into two paragraphs.

Just as one additional cog in your watch can render it dysfunctional, one unfamiliar word can render your sentence unintelligible.

REPLACE PHRASES WITH SINGLE WORDS

Having too many words often ruins sentences. Our language is filled with unnecessary phrases that can be replaced with a single word. Consider the list shown in Figure 7.1.

These lists include just a few of the many expressions that make our writing awkward and murky. When you are drafting your proposal, don't worry about them. Yes, you read this sentence correctly. As a writer, your main goal is to get your ideas down on paper. Once the first draft is complete, you will have time to return and tighten your sentences. Look for adverbs. Adverbs slow down the reader. Use them sparingly or not at all. After your draft is complete, delete most of the adverbs. **Tip:** *Replace long phrases with shorter ones or, when possible, with single words. Good writing is good self-editing.* Is it work? Yes. Does it require self-discipline? Yes. Is it difficult? No. Incidentally, did you notice that the same unnecessary word was used twice in this brief paragraph? Furthermore, this was the same part of speech the paragraph warned you not to overuse. I am referring to the adverb *down*. I chose to make an exception because the word is very short and because it feels good to me. Writing is like driving a car. You can't dodge every pebble on the highway. Use some judgment. Now, it is time to develop an awareness of some of your larger rocks and stones.

Adverbs rob sentences of their power.

Using the list of bulky terms in Figure 7.1, identify some that you frequently use. For each term, think of a single word that can replace the bulky term.

WRITE FORCEFULLY

Clarity is unarguably the most important quality in any serious, nonfiction writing, particularly in grant proposals. Put simply, as a grant writer you must write clearly. But grant writers must go beyond this goal. Because grant writing is a buyer's market (meaning the supply of proposals greatly exceeds the demand), and those who read and evaluate poorly written proposals are quickly lulled

Bulky Terms	Concise
until such time as	until
a high rate of speed	fast
on account of	because
in the event that	if
provides information	tells
in the majority of cases	usually
each and every one	all
has to do with	concerns
has the capability of	can
in spite of the fact that	although
cancel out	cancel
mandatory requirement	requirement
at that point in time	then
at this point in time	now
in attendance	there
improve the quality of	improve
a new innovation	an innovation
in short supply	scarce
in the final analysis	finally
in the foreseeable future	soon
she is a woman who	she
in view of the fact that	because
on a daily basis	daily
in a hasty manner	hastily
in close proximity	near
there is no doubt that	certainly
a large percentage of	most
once upon a time	once
during the past year	last year
can't help but think	think
almost everyone	most
need to be established	needed
filled to capacity	full
give consideration to	consider
rank order	rank
put in an appearance	attend
revert back to	revert to
with the exception of	except
have no other choice	must

FIGURE 7.1 Replacing Bulky Terms with Concise Terms

Clarity is the most important quality in grant writing.

into a stupor, you must develop a style that reaches out and grabs the reader. One of the best examples of grabbing the readers is found in the opening lines of Charles Dickens' *A Tale of Two Cities*.

> It was the best of times, it was the worst of times, it was the age of wisdom, it was the age of foolishness, it was the epoch of belief, it was the epoch of incredulity, it was the season of Light, it was the season of Darkness, it was the spring of hope, it was the winter of despair, we had everything before us, we had nothing before us, we were all going direct to Heaven, we were all going direct the other way.

In these few short lines, Dickens grabs the reader's attention and, like an assailant, with a firm grip on the neck, shakes the reader back and forth. Notice each short line is a paradox. Dickens uses contrast to hold attention. Notice, too, the length of the lines. Each line is short. Dickens is able to keep the readers totally involved and deliver tons of information without the use of complex paragraphs, unfamiliar words, or complicated sentences.

FORMULA FOR WRITING A POWERFUL SENTENCE

Grant writers must write powerfully and forcefully.

This is powerful and forceful writing. Because of the supply and demand mentioned previously, grant writers must write powerfully and forcefully. Following is a clear formula for achieving this goal.

Tip: Begin by *using a concrete noun for the subject of each sentence, and put this noun at the beginning of each sentence.* For example, suppose you are writing a grant to improve traffic safety on snowy, icy highways. Instead of saying, "There are many times in January when the weather makes driving on the highways dangerous," just chop off the front of the sentence. Note that this sentence begins with the word *there.* But *there* refers to location, and this sentence is not about location; it's about the effect January weather has on driving. So, why not begin with the subject, *January weather.*

Tip: *Follow the subject immediately with an action verb written in the present tense.* So, now you have "January weather makes driving dangerous." Does it say the same thing the longer sentence says? Yes. The big difference is it uses fewer and more exact words. Precision and economy are essential to powerful writing. Note, too, that the verb is written in the present tense. The past tense slows the reader because it requires reading additional words.

Powerful writing is achieved through using fewer and more common words.

Most people who have written dissertations or theses were taught to preface almost every meaningful statement with a conditioner, a qualifying statement intended to protect the writer and committee from being sued for saying something not absolutely true. A similar practice, on a smaller scale, was found in high school, where many of us were taught to avoid all-inclusive terms, such as *all* or *always*, and all-exclusive terms, such as *none* or *never*.

To be successful, you must keep the evaluators of your proposals engaged and interested, and you can do this by (1) using a concrete noun for the subject; (2) using an action verb, written in the present tense; (3) putting the subject at the beginning of the sentence; (4) following the subject immediately with the verb; and (5) deleting all unnecessary words. The result will be short, crisp, clear, and powerful sentences.

Here is a final suggestion to help you write forcefully. Note that this paragraph starts with the word *here*, and, yet, this sentence has nothing to do with location. Advice about starting each sentence with a concrete subject, and other advice in this book, should be a good guideline, but not a strict recipe. For example, a final suggestion to help you write forcefully is to *begin with a concrete subject*. I had two reasons for beginning this sentence with the word *here*. To be honest, it was the first word that popped into my head, which exemplifies the need to always edit our own writing. An experienced author said this about his own writing. "Often, I find myself saying, 'I didn't know I knew that.'" Editing and rewriting clarify the product. More amazing, they clarify our thinking. Occasionally breaking a few rules is all right and is actually recommended because it can keep your work from being stilted; yet, the closer you follow these guidelines, the more competitive your proposal will be.

The advice in this chapter is an intended guideline, not a recipe.

You can use the exercise shown in Figure 7.2 to improve your skills in using editing to shorten your sentences. The first goal is to get your ideas on

---

Delete the unnecessary words.

1. The truth of the matter is that the company was not successful.
2. The judge, who was a distant cousin, set him free.
3. She is a woman who does not usually stumble forward without giving considerable thought to the possible consequences.
4. His cousin, who is somewhat older than he, himself is, will stand a good chance to inherit the entire estate.
5. The fact is, he's finished.
6. His job is a highly demanding one.
7. There is no doubt but that he responded in a highly hasty manner.
8. The reason why is that the Hawthorne control group was shocked out of its complacency by the supervisor's presence.
9. There is no doubt that the jury was right in finding him guilty.
10. Were you aware of the fact that excessive salt produces hypertension?

Note the effect of close editing.

1. The company was not successful.
2. The judge, a distant cousin, set him free.
3. She does not usually proceed without considering the consequences.
4. His older cousin will stand a good chance to inherit the entire estate.
5. He's finished.
6. His job is highly demanding.
7. He undoubtedly responded hastily.
8. The supervisor's presence removed the complacency.
9. Undoubtedly, the jury was right in finding him guilty.
10. Were you aware that excessive salt produces hypertension?

FIGURE 7.2 Writing Concisely

paper. Then you can edit, edit, edit. Few people realize how many unnecessary words we use in our daily conversation. This spills over into our writing. But if there's one thing that the proposal readers don't want, it's more words.

Examine Figure 7.2 and, in the first list, *delete as many words as you can from each sentence without changing the author's meaning.* Sometimes this is difficult because you don't always know someone else's intended meaning. Fortunately, this is not a problem when you are editing your own writing. Once you have finished editing, check your revisions against the second list. Perhaps you have gone further and tightened your statements even more. That's good.

The first sentence begins with *the truth of the matter is.* Because this is nonfiction writing, we can assume it is true; therefore, this phrase can be eliminated. Next, notice the word *not.* Negative words usually slow the reader, so *unsuccessful* is preferred over *not successful.* The sentence can be further improved by simply saying, *The company failed.* Notice that even when editing such a simple sentence, the process occurred in steps. Good editing seldom occurs in a single step. It is like shining a piece of furniture; each treatment makes a slight improvement, and, if polished several times, it will take on an entirely new glow. And to illustrate the point that even the best writers must edit and rewrite their work again and again, consider this bit of data. Most people consider Ernest Hemmingway to be one of America's greatest writers. We tend to believe that the truly great writers are born with such a gift for writing that they don't have to work at their craft. Not so. Hemingway's book *Farewell to Arms* proves this; I once read that the archives hold 119 drafts of the final chapter of this book!

Writing concisely is not difficult, but it does take time. One of the world's great writers, Samuel Johnson, once began a letter to a friend by apologizing for writing such a long letter and saying that he would have written a much shorter letter had he had time. Clarity is achieved through editing, and it does take time. Figure 7.3 shows several sentences being rewritten to achieve clarity. You may want to cover all columns except the first to determine how much you can improve each sentence.

WRITE CORRECTLY

You can use the exercises in Appendices 7.1 and 7.2 to refresh your grammar skills.

WRITE POSITIVELY

Sometimes negative words have their purpose, but, like adverbs, they slow down the reader. Did you notice this sentence uses an unnecessary adverb? Instead of slowing the reader, it slows *down* the reader. Adverbs and negative words will sap your proposal of its energy and lose the evaluators' attention. Consider the following examples:

"Grant writers do not often need to use more negative words." You can use several easy strategies to improve this sentence. Did you notice that it breaks several rules previously discussed? The sentence begins with a noun, but this noun is not the subject of this sentence. The sentence begins by

Original Sentence	First Revision (to shorten)	Second Revision (to shorten more)	Third Revision (to make active)
It will help if teachers will identify routines that need to be established.	It will help if teachers will identify necessary routines.		Teachers should identify necessary routines.
Teacher preparation programs typically spend a great deal of time acquainting prospective teachers with how to teach information.	Teacher preparation programs typically spend considerable time acquainting prospective teachers with how to teach.	Teacher preparation programs typically spend considerable time on teaching about methodology.	Most teacher preparation programs emphasize methodology.
Such fear may well be a result of a lack of understanding of some ways of preventing problems and responding to them once they do occur.	Such fear may result from a lack of understanding of ways to prevent problems and respond to them.	Such fear may result from a lack of understanding of ways to prevent and respond to problems.	Not knowing how to prevent and respond to problems can frighten teachers.
However, repetition should not be overdone. If it is, boredom can set in.	Repetition should not be overdone. If it, is boredom can set in.	Excessive repetition can result in boredom.	Excessive repetition can cause boredom.
In general, people who are acknowledged to have a great deal of expertise in a given area exercise considerable influence over others.	In general, experts in a given area exercise considerable influence over others.	Experts in a given area exercise considerable influence over others.	Experts often influence their peers.
Efforts are being taken in nearly every industrialized nation to improve the quality of their schools.	Efforts are being made by most industrialized nations to improve their schools.		Most industrialized nations are working to improve their schools.

FIGURE 7.3 Good Editing Is a Step-by-Step Process

talking about grant writers; yet, the sentence is not so much about grant writers as it is about negative words and their effect on writing. Another warning to the experienced writer is that this sentence contains the negative word *not*. **Tip:** *Remove unnecessary negative words such as* not. Sometimes using this word is appropriate, but when you see it in your writing, consider it a warning.

Try to rewrite the sentence so the word *not* is unnecessary. For example, you might change *do not often* to *seldom.* "Grant writers seldom need...". But remember, the subject belongs at the beginning of the sentence and *grant writers* is not the subject; this sentence is about the use of negative words. Take a breath, step back, and think, why shouldn't grant writers use more negatives? Because negatives weaken the sentence. So why not say, "Too many negatives weaken a proposal." or "The overuse of negatives weakens the author's message." Either of these rewrites is a major improvement.

TREAT GENDERS FAIRLY

For centuries, the English language practically ignored females, but this ended in the 1970s with the advent of the twentieth-century women's liberation movement. Authors wanted to be fair to females, but they didn't know how to achieve gender equity without constructing awkward sentences. The results were sometimes so ridiculous that they were entertaining: "He or she wants to develop an effective grant writing style so that his or her proposals will be funded." A similar version of the same sentence often reads like this: "He/she wants to develop an effective grant writing style so that his/her proposals will be funded."

Tip: *The easiest way to remove gender bias is to pluralize,* replacing he/she with *they* and his/her or his *or* her with *their.* When pluralizing does not work, rewrite the sentence. In the original sentence, "He/she wants to write excellent grants so that most of his/her grants will be funded," pluralizing will improve the sentence, but not enough because the subject of this sentences needs to be moved to the beginning of the sentence. "Excellence in grant writing enhances funding." Perhaps you can improve this sentence even more.

Do not be discouraged if you have to rewrite a sentence or paragraph several times to make it clear and powerful. All good writers know that the best writing usually takes the form of editing.

Some of us have very weak backgrounds in grammar, but we have creative minds capable of forming good ideas. We should never let our writing limitations deter our desire to write grants. Chapter 4 contains grammar exercises that focus on the most common mistakes made by educators.

People with creative minds should never let a lack of writing skills deter their desire to write grants.

USE GRAPHICS

Apart from the actual writing, another thing affecting the clarity of writing is organization or structure. You can strengthen the clarity of your grant proposal by using a combination of devices that work to organize the major concepts in the readers' minds. Among others, these include using numbers, tables, graphs, and tables of specification. Following is a brief discussion on the use of each to enhance clarity.

NUMBERS.   Some grant writers are naturally quantitative; they think and express their ideas using numbers. Other grant writers are qualitative; they think and explain their ideas using prose. All grant writers can benefit by using numbers. Numbers draw the readers' attention and communicate expectations more accurately than verbal descriptions. Grant writers can use numbers to make commitments. This is important in garnering the evaluators' support for the proposal. It is also valuable when the writer conducts a self-evaluation. For example, a grant proposal author who is asking for money to improve dental health in a community assesses the existing condition before the improvement program begins. If that assessment is recorded in the number of cavities per hundred patients, then a reassessment of the condition can be made easily and accurately. Put simply, grant evaluators like numbers because they communicate expectations clearly and because they make evaluation accurate and easy.

Grant evaluators like numbers because they communicate clearly and accurately.

TABLES.   Tables enable us to view a wide rage of data at once, making comparisons easy, and should be used in lieu of pages and pages of words, which often bog down the reading of proposals.

GRAPHS.   Graphs are visual representations of variations. One of the most familiar graphs is the bell curve, which shows the varied distribution of all sorts of things in nature. Examples of things subject to this type of distribution are the weight and height of animals and plants, the margin of error of humans and machines, and, of course, the intelligence quotients of human. But not all items in the universe are distributed so evenly. For example, if high and low temperatures or the highs and lows on the stock market are plotted on a graph, you would not expect to see the bell (or normal) curve.

Some grant writers are reluctant to include projections in their grant proposals. They worry that if their prediction fails to come true this could be interpreted as false representation on their part. This concern is absolutely unfounded. Graphs showing projected trends should be used because they can be powerful communicators and convincing tools. Like all visuals, graphs facilitate our ability to grasp complex concepts that would be much more difficult to communicate in words alone.

Like all visuals, graphs facilitate our ability to grasp complex ideas.

Graphic Organizers.   A graphic organizer is a visual representation designed to show the relationships among several or many concepts. If a proposal is very long, then a written abstract is often required to help the evaluators gain an overall understanding of the entire operation. Even if the request for proposals (RFP) doesn't require an abstract, proposal writers always have the option to include one. The fact that many RFPs have a maximum word limit for abstracts testifies to their purpose, which is to facilitate a quick and easy understanding of the proposal. Although, to some writers, the absolute word limitation may seem unnecessarily restrictive, it should always be followed because some evaluators will refuse to read proposals if they do not adhere to all the guidelines. The main difference between the use of abstracts and graphic organizers is that the graphic organizer is visual and, therefore, can be interpreted at a glance. For example, Figure 7.4 shows a graphic organizer for a proposal.

Flowcharts.   Flowcharts are graphics designed to show the sequence of events. Each flowchart has boxes or circles separated by arrows. Programmed instructional materials make extensive use of flowcharts, replacing the need for a teacher to be present to tell students what to do next. Figure 7.5 shows a flowchart being used in programmed instructional materials.

TABLES OF SPECIFICATION.   A table of specifications is a particular type of chart that can be useful to grant writers. It is unique only in that it

FIGURE 7.4 Developing an
Appropriate Writing Style

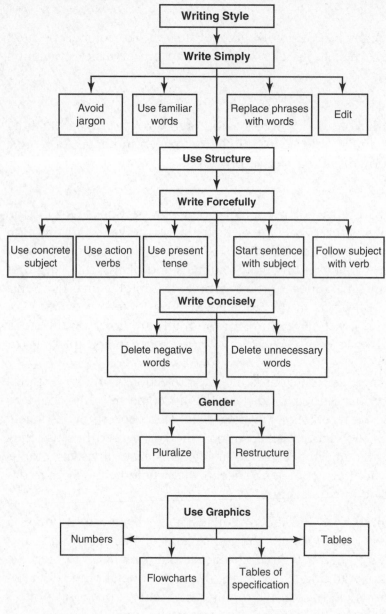

FIGURE 7.5 Sample
Flowchart

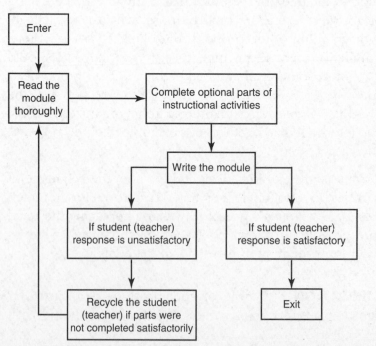

uses labeled rows and columns. Tables of specification can be used by grant writers who want to make certain they are covering all intended elements. Failure to do this could be catastrophic. For example, the grant writer could lose credibility quickly if an evaluator reads about part of the grant and learns it was overlooked in the table of contents, the proposal body, or the budget.

Each table of specifications uses a matrix with labeled columns and rows. For example, Table 7.1 was developed to be used in a municipal government grant written to curb red light violations. A quick glance at this table of specifications shows, in a convincing flash, the need for a solution to a rash of accidents resulting from red light violations in this particular town. Future grant writers could extend this investigation by developing and testing different devices to measure and compare their ability to deter red light violations.

Table 7.1 Table of Specifications for Traffic Light Violations Grant

Frequency of Violations per 10 Minutes Time Interval

Washington and	1	2	3	4	5	6	7	8	9	10	11	12	13	14	15	16	17	18	19	20
1st	X																			
2nd			X																	
3rd			X																	
4th									X											
5th												X								
6th																				
7th	X																			
8th								X												
9th													X							
10th			X																	

Rose Avenue and	1	2	3	4	5	6	7	8	9	10	11	12	13	14	15	16	17	18	19	20
1st							X													
2nd																				
3rd														X						
4th	X																			
5th	X																			
6th										X										
7th																				X
8th																				
9th														X						
10th															X					

Summary

Successful grant writing demands a special writing style that can be developed by anyone. The major goal is clarity. The best approach to achieving clarity is to ignore style and grammar until the first draft is complete. Then go back and edit your draft copy several times, removing unnecessary paragraphs, sentences, and words.

Powerful and clear sentences can be written by placing a concrete subject at the beginning of the sentence, followed immediately by a present tense action verb. Jargon and other unnecessary and unfamiliar words should be eliminated or replaced with shorter, more common words.

Such visuals as graphics, tables, graphic organizers, and tables of specifications can simplify and clarify your proposals. Do not be afraid to make projections part of your proposals.

- We tend to use fancy words that often confuse readers when we write.
- In grant writing, the use of qualifiers should be limited because they rob each sentence of its power to communicate clearly.
- Unnecessary jargon should be avoided because it is confusing.
- Many common phrases can be replaced with single words.
- Overuse of adverbs diminishes clarity.
- Negative words signal the need to rewrite or tighten up a sentence.
- Gender equity can be achieved in grants by pluralizing.
- Graphs, tables, graphic organizers, and tables of specification should be used to improve communications with evaluators.

RECAP OF MAJOR IDEAS

- Successful grant writing demands a special writing style that can be developed by anyone.
- The proposal writer must craft each proposal using a writing style that is clear to evaluators.
- Style should be of little or no concern until the writer completes the first draft.
- Self-editing and rewriting are essential steps in grant preparation.
- Brevity facilitates clarity.
- Beginning sentences with concrete subjects, followed by present tense action verbs, increases the power of writing.
- Whenever possible, avoid using the past tense because it slows the reading.

LIST OF TIPS

1. Put clarity above all else.
2. Avoid the use of unnecessary jargon.
3. Use everyday words that everyone can recognize.
4. Keep sentences and paragraphs short.
5. Use concrete nouns and active verbs written in the present tense.
6. Start sentences with their subjects, followed immediately by verbs.
7. Include only one idea per paragraph.
8. Replace bulky terms with single words.
9. Use graphic organizers, graphs, tables, and tables of specification to show relationships.

Reference

Strunk, W., Jr., & White, E. B. (1979). *The elements of style*. New York: Avon Books.

Finding Funding Sources

INTRODUCTION

In my grant-writing workshops, I find that many participants start their grant-writing activities by searching for funding sources. Ideally, what many of these teachers need and want most is a comprehensive list of grant funding sources. Let your teachers know that such a list does exist and direct them to the *Federal Register*. As Chapter 3 indicates the *Federal Register* is a government publication containing all requests for proposals (RFPs) issued in a calendar year. It tells who is funding what topics and for how much—two bits of information that your teachers must know to effectively target funding sources. Teachers who rarely or never use the Internet can probably find a hard copy of the *Federal Register* in the local library. Because it is updated daily, locating a funding source for a particular proposal topic may require several trips.

Those teachers who are Internet savvy can find a wealth of information about funding sources online at www.gpoaccess.gov. Here they can search for funding sources by selecting the current funding year and entering their proposal topic. An alternative source that many grant writers find easier to use than the *Federal Register* is the Grants.gov Web site (www.grants.gov). On this site, grant opportunities can be found by searching on keywords, categories, agencies, or other specific criteria. In addition, completed grant application packages can be submitted and tracked online via this site.

More recently, an increasing percent of federal funding is being shifted to the state level. Your teachers will want to check with their state department of education and with such warehouse sites as GrantsAlert.com, grantwrangler.com, and Oneida-Herkimer-Madison (OHM) BOCES Program and Professional Development (PPD) grants (www.ohmboces.org/ppd_grants.htm).

Maximum grant-writing success for school districts requires a core of skilled educators and parents who are dedicated grant writers.

Most school leaders who are responsible for helping their schools acquire money by writing grants realize the importance of having a team of experienced grant writers on whom they can depend. Although involving community members is important, ongoing success requires a core of skilled educators and parents who are dedicated to grant writing. Some school leaders are fortunate to have such a team, others are not; their units have not progressed this far in grant writing, and they simply do not have a functional team.

Regardless of which category better describes your school district, much value can be derived from encouraging and helping teachers write individual grants to improve their school, their classroom teaching, or both. Value can also be gained from encouraging teachers to collaborate with others to write school- and district-wide grants. This book begins by teaching you how to help your teachers write small, single-authored proposals, and later focuses on assisting teams in collaborating on large proposals. Following this sequence, this chapter begins by providing sources that you can use to help individual teachers write grants to improve their classrooms. The significance of local community sources must not be underrated. Grant writer Cindy Brown says, "I have written lots of grants to big companies, but have found our local service clubs to be the most supportive." The second part of this chapter identifies sources of larger funds for improving schools and school districts. Each of the chapter's two parts will identify some of the most fruitful sources and provide samples of grants funded by these sources.

But preparing successful proposals requires tailoring each to its targeted funding source; therefore, this chapter contains suggestions and stories from the authors of these grants. To be successful with their own proposals, your teachers must develop a "feel" for the types of grants each source funds. Ideally, the perfect approach would be to arrange a meeting between each teacher or team who is writing a grant and a teacher who has written a successful grant on that topic. If such a meeting is not possible, then the next best service you can provide would be to ask someone who has written a successful proposal similar to the once you have underway to answer a few key questions:

- "May I see a copy of your proposal?"
- "Why did you write this grant?"
- "Why do you believe that the evaluators funded your proposal?"
- "What did you learn from this experience?"

Fortunately, at each level (classroom, school, and district), two or more successful grant writers have been asked these questions. Reviewing these sample grants and the authors' comments will enable your teachers get a "feel" for the types of proposals that succeed with these funding agencies.

PART I: FUNDING SOURCES TO IMPROVE CLASSROOMS

The Preface to this book alludes to a new grant writer who finds grant writing incredibly easy and fun. Now listen while Christine File, an elementary school teacher at E. A. Burns Elementary School in Charleston,

South Carolina, tells, in her own words, about her first grant-writing experience.

FUNDING SOURCE: DONORSCHOOSE
WWW.DONORSCHOOSE.ORG

I want to tell you about my favorite funding source for teacher grants. DonorsChoose is an online charity that makes it easy for teachers or administrators to help students in need. It is one of the most user-friendly grant sources for busy teachers to use. I heard about DonorsChoose from an e-mail on grant opportunities sent by my school's media specialist. After reading the e-mail message and talking with other teachers who had used the charity, I decided to write my first grant. Let me say it again: the DonorsChoose Web site is very user friendly and easy to navigate, even for the most inexperienced grant writers.

DonorsChoose.org was developed in a Bronx high school where teachers experienced, first-hand, the scarcity of learning materials in the public schools. Charles Best, a social studies teacher, sensed that many people wanted to help distressed public schools but were frustrated by a lack of influence over their donations. He created DonorsChoose.org so that individuals could connect directly with classrooms in need. Since its launch in 2000, DonorsChoose.org has helped more than 200,000 teachers and citizen philanthropists connect and make a difference.

Here's how it works: Public school teachers from every city and state in America can post classroom project requests on DonorsChoose.org. Requests range from pencils for a narrative writing unit, speakers for a computer class, to drums for a music class. Potential donors can browse project requests and give any amount of money to the grant(s) that inspires them most. Once a project reaches its funding goal, DonorsChoose delivers the materials to the school. The donor will get photos of the project, a thank-you note from the teachers, and a cost report showing how each dollar was spent.

I teach first grade, and my students enjoy reading Eric Carle books. As a young teacher starting out, I didn't own any Eric Carle books. Writing a grant to get these books for my students was a natural step. These books are very popular and quite expensive. As a teacher, I wanted to write a grant requesting money to buy these books for my students to help them read and to foster the joy of reading. It is extremely important for students to learn to enjoy reading if they are to succeed in the majority of their classes. Kids who enjoy reading will read more often and will be more inclined to do the schoolwork that requires reading. Once they enjoy reading, a whole new world will open to them.

It's This Simple

Let me take you through the DonorsChoose writing process, using DonorsChoose.org. *The first step: Create your own account.* The profile requires you to enter personal information such as your name, phone number, address, and e-mail. School information is also needed, such as district, school, phone, address, and teacher affiliations (Figure 8.1a). Also, a photo section is available to upload pictures of your school or classroom. Please remember to be careful when uploading pictures—don't show recognizable faces.

The next step: Create your project (Figure 8.1b). After you have made a profile, select *"create a project."*

1. ***Name your project:*** Think of a title that will catch the eye of potential donors.
2. ***List the resources:*** List the resources you need to complete your project (Figure 8.1c).
3. ***Summarize your resource request:*** Keep your summary short.

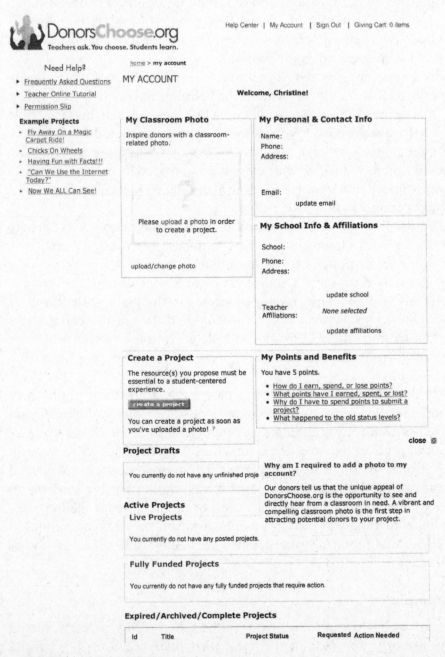

FIGURE 8.1a Create Your Own Account

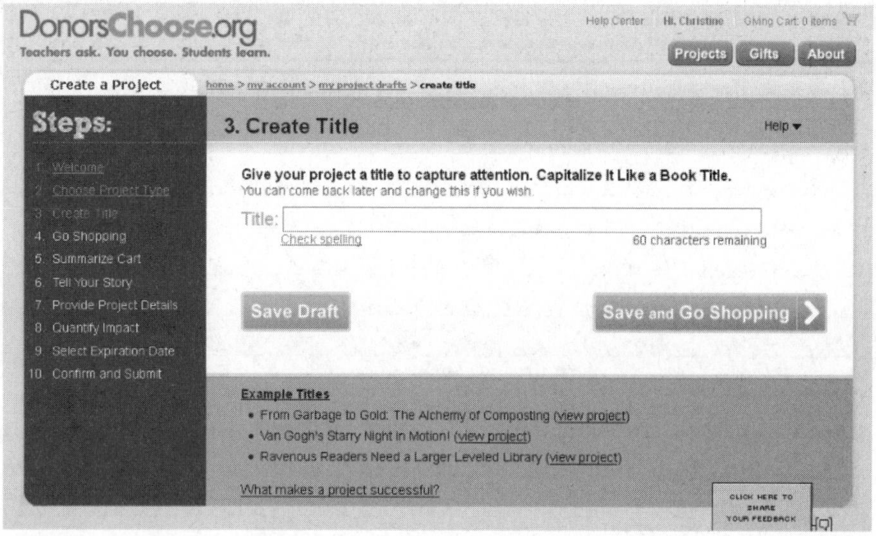

FIGURE 8.1b   Name Your Project

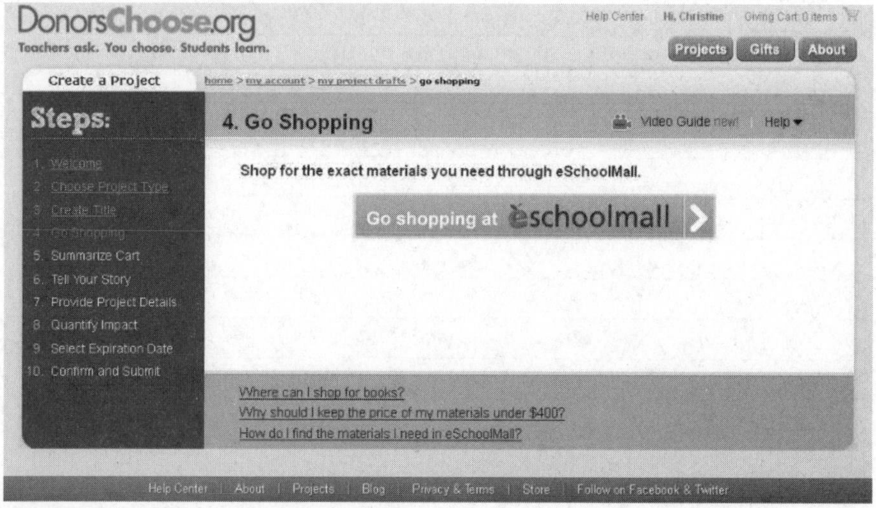

FIGURE 8.1c   List the Resources Needed

4. ***Write an essay:*** This is the section where you describe your students and their challenges. Be sure to explain what your students will be able to learn and do if your project is funded.
5. ***Save and submit:*** Once you have submitted your grant proposal, the DonorsChoose team will review and finalize it, completing your grant-writing experience.

I wrote my Eric Carle grant in March 2008, and it was fully funded within 1 month. All 20 Eric Carle books were delivered to my school by May 2008. I spent 30 minutes writing and submitting a fully funded grant worth $225.00. I now have the materials to help my students become better readers. DonorsChoose is truly one of the easiest ways to get much-needed materials for your classroom.

"DonorsChoose is one of the easiest ways to get materials for your classroom."
—Christine File

> **REMINDER: Please refrain from the use of your name, your school's name, or any other identifying words/marks in the body of the application. Thank You.**

Grant Application

Project Title _School Newspaper_

Number of students reached by the project _~~Near~~ 1200_   Age/Grade level to which project is directed _6-8^th_

Brief Description of Project _The gifted class (25 students) in our middle school has designed the school newspaper for the past 4 years for each grade level. This year, due to funding, we are doing one newspaper for all three grades, but can do only one for the first quarter. We need funds for a 4-page paper for three more quarters._

How is the project innovative or why is this an area of special need in your building or classroom? _Students design, write, compile and deliver the newspaper to all students and staff in the building. They learn organization, language arts skills, technology, social and business skills, and higher level thinking and problem-solving skills._

What is the projected long-term effect of this project on your students, school, district? What are the project objectives and how will they be measured? _Quarterly newspapers document and chronicle school life. As a student-initiated endeavor, our newspaper (~~This~~ ~~School News~~) have provided a proud tradition. Additionally, students may claim publication credits. They feel this is their own project._

Time line of project implementation/completion _Jan - 2nd Quarter; March - 3rd Quarter; May - 1st Quarter 2004   2004   2004_

Currently or previously, have there been similar projects underway in your district? ☐ Yes ☒ No _I don't think so. This is not a journalism or writing class._

If yes, were the past projects successful? Why or Why not? _Schools w/ journalism or writing classes - yes. Our grade level newspapers the past 4 years were very successful. Students always want to begin on the next one right away. Parents asked about it at conferences - where is it?_

Project Budget: (materials and itemized costs) _Printing of 1200 copies at School Service Center ($60.00 for each run) Ink Cartridges ($50.00) $60 × 3 = $180 + $50.00 = $230.00 + $20.00 for possible cost increases and miscellaneous costs._

Additional Comments _Without funding, the paper cannot continue as the school budget and personnel is no longer available to cover cost and labor. Thank you for your consideration._

AMOUNT OF FUNDS REQUESTED $ _250.00_   (Minimum $25.00 – Maximum $250.00)

www.cuofamerica.com ▲ 316-265-3272 or 1-800-256-8049 in Kansas

FIGURE 8.2   School Newspaper Grant

Funding Source: Credit Union of America

Another excellent source for classroom improvement grants is the Credit Union of America (www.cuofamerica.com). Like Christine, Wichita, Kansas, journalism teacher Connie Phelps had a similar experience with her first grant. According to Connie, it was easy because she followed a sequence of simple grant-writing steps. See if you can identify the steps in Figure 8.2 as she tells you in her own words why she wrote the grant and why she believes that her application was funded.

Now let's break down Connie's steps. *First*, she had a real need, not a contrived need made up to get a grant. **Tip:** *Remember that funders fund dreams and plans, not just requests. They give opportunities, not just money.*

Second, because one of her colleagues had received a similar grant, she believed she could, too. *Third*, she did the necessary research. She was fortunate to have worked in an office that gave her access to convincing data, including receipts. *Fourth*, she wrote short, data-based answers. Finally, her handwritten application, with some marked-out words, was finished. Once you get your ideas on paper, you can clean up your proposal by writing multiple drafts. Connie's grant source was TGIF (Teacher Grants . . . Ideas Financed!). The URL is CUofAmerica.com/tools-and-resources/tgif.aspx.

As you continue examining Connie's proposal, look beyond the fact that this proposal draft is handwritten. Beyond the crossed-out words, you will see that she has a real need. For the past year, her students have designed, written, compiled, and delivered a school newspaper. Through this work, they have improved their organizational, language arts, technology, higher-level thinking, and problem-solving skills. But due to the economy, they are being forced to give up this project, of which they hold proud ownership. *Sharing your passion increases your chances of getting your proposal accepted.*

Sharing your passion increases your chances of getting your proposal accepted.

Connie has also done the legwork required to produce specific costs, showing exactly how much money is needed and exactly how it will be used. Remember, *grant proposal readers want evidence, demand exactness, and love numbers*—without which this proposal probably would not have been funded.

WHAT HAPPENS WHEN SOMEONE'S FIRST PROPOSAL IS FUNDED? (BRENDA MESCHNER'S STORY)

A trend repeated when teachers begin writing classroom improvement grants on almost any topic is they become hooked on grant writing. The beginning of this book recognized the fact that no one is a born grant writer. We are born with neither the appetite nor the necessary skills for grant writing. Nevertheless, most of those who accept the challenge, and succeed, experience an emotional high, leaving them hooked on grant writing. In effect, they quickly become more than people who write grants; grant writing becomes part of their personalities, and they change from being people with the ability to write grants to being grant writers. Michigan middle school teacher Brenda Mescher is a good example. Over the past 4 years, Brenda has written a dozen grants. Thus far, seven of these grants have been funded. Following is a list of these grants accompanied by a short explanation of why Brenda believes that each proposal was funded.

No one is born with an appetite or the skills for grant writing, but one funded grant is all it takes to hook most grant writers for life.

Grants I have received within the past 4 years:

Spring 2007, Kappa Delta Pi, "Integrating Children's Literature in Middle School Math," $150. This money was used to purchase around 10–15 kids books with math topics in them—for example *Sir Circumference and the First Round Table, One Grain of Rice, Bats in Parade,* etc. I have used these books with my eighth-grade classes to explore the math concepts in these simple kids stories. My eighth-grade students, however, have to explain the math concepts their books represent.

Spring 2008, Kappa Delta Pi, "Capturing Math in the Real World," $150. This money was used to purchase one digital camera. The teacher and students use the camera to capture images in our everyday environment, showing various math concepts. The pictures are used in conjunction with the Ti-Navigator system as background images for graphing. Students take pictures of buildings to find geometry concepts in the architecture and pictures of lines and slopes to categorize them as positive, negative, slope of 0, parallel lines, and perpendicular lines.

Spring 2009, Target Field Trip Grant, "Canoe Trip," $800. This money financed an eighth-grade field trip, canoeing on a local river. This coincided with a unit on water quality in the science class (I am not the science teacher, but wrote the grant collaboratively).

Grants received through the local educational credit union:

- ***Fall 2007, Ti-73 Calculators, $1,500.*** This grant bought a set of Ti-73 calculators which are used on a daily basis in conjunction with the Ti-Navigator system to create a wireless network between the teacher's computer and students' calculators, enabling assessment tools, interactive activities, etc.
- ***Spring 2007, Laptop, $600.*** This grant was used to purchase a Windows laptop to be used with the Ti-Navigator system. My school is a Mac school, and a Windows laptop was not in the budget.
- ***Summer 2009, Math Whizz Summer Program, $800.*** This money was used to help implement and maintain an online summer math program for my middle school students, offered through Math Whizz Education.

Spring 2010, Kids in Need Grant, "Capturing Math in the Real World," $450. This money was used to purchase five additional cameras to expand on the project mentioned previously.

Grants I am waiting to hear about:

Elizabeth Ann Setan Professional Development Award for the Diocese of Kalamazoo—I am awaiting information on this grant. If awarded, it will be used to further my master's degree in the Catholic Educational leadership program at the University of Dayton, specifically to pay tuition costs for "Leadership in Diverse Communities."

Meemic Insurance Grant—I am awaiting information on this grant. If awarded, it will be used to attend the National Council of Teachers of Mathematics (NCTM) annual conference in Denver.

Tips from Brenda:

- Collaboration with other subject areas such as technology, science, and language arts is beneficial to your project.
- To purchase supplies for the classroom (e.g., calculators), you really need to tie it into a project. It is vital to inform the reader how valuable these supplies are to everyday student learning.
- Use technology to connect your grant to the real world.
- Describe your proposed project's impact on student learning and future students.
- Indicate how many students your grant will help.
- Seek LOCAL grant providers! The grant impacts the community directly.

JUST TRY IT!!! You would be surprised at what you can get! It does take time and effort, but it can be rewarding for the teacher and definitely for student learning.

As you read about each proposal, didn't it become obvious that to Brenda Mescher grant writing is more than writing grants? Couldn't you feel the difference it makes in her daily teaching? If I were a middle-level student, then I would really enjoy taking a camera and searching for examples of numbers in my world. If I were a middle-level math teacher (and I was), then I would love to have a wireless navigation system in my classes. I hope her Ti-73 calculators grant gets funded!

PARENTS: AN IMPORTANT SOURCE

Researching the background needed to write this book involved literally hundreds of computer searches, as well as e-mails and phone calls to funding agencies, grant writers, and school- and district-wide grant directors. Confirming some of the generalizations that I had already made from my own grant-writing experiences made it all worthwhile. But I would also get a surge of excitement when an unexpected insight would seem to fall from the sky, leaving me thinking: "Why have I never thought of this idea?" Such a moment occurred when I phoned California parent, Kathy Haven. Although I have encouraged grant writers to reach out and get community members and parents involved in grant writing, my intention was to solicit letters of support from businesses and agencies and also use these members and parents on grant-writing teams. I had never fully realized the power that a single parent can have in writing individual grants to support a school. Kathy tells her own story:

Over the past 3 years, I have turned myself into the volunteer grant writer of our school, Bijou Community School, in South Lake Tahoe, CA. I was a math and science teacher for nearly a decade, and then I started a family. I have had NO training as a grant writer; yet, this year, I might actually clear $50,000 for our school by writing little grants from local foundations and community organizations. I have had about 20 small grants funded in the past 3 years, and I chose to write grants to make a difference at my children's school. We, the community, started a Two-Way Immersion (TWI) program at a local elementary school, and whereas the district was happy to start the program, we realized the TWI classes would cost more than your average classes. So, I took it upon myself to try to help out financially by taking a shot at these grants. And, now, I am pretty successful at getting most of the grants I apply for.

For this article, I have chosen one of the most recent grants I received because it is representative of my work and the types of grants that I choose. This particular grant application came from a foundation (Echo) within a large business (Heavenly Ski Resort) in our community. I was writing the grant to receive funds for reading books for the TWI program at our school. With the grant money we received ($1,000), we will buy more leveled books in Spanish for our students. Because our program requires our students to have all books in English and Spanish, the Spanish books are obviously an additional cost. So, I believe that this grant helped our school and district by keeping costs down for buying supplies for this new TWI class. Also, I am always careful to *hopefully really "help." I don't assume, but always ask to make sure I write for "things" that the teachers, staff, and administration at our school really want. They have actually given me a "box" at school where teachers leave me requests or grant applications they find. It has become my "job" at school.*

I have learned that in my grant applications, I am as descriptive as possible about the program I am trying to get funds for (e.g., the TWI program); I am clear about why these funds are necessary from outside sources, rather than the district itself; and I usually provide the organization that is sending out the grants with a detailed list of how their money would be spent. This detailed list also allows the organization to partially fund my grant (as in this Echo grant application). Most of the grantors have awarded me the total I have requested, and I believe that this is because I give them this detailed list, but I have also learned that some foundations have a particular amount to donate each year, and they like to donate to many groups. So, if my applications have three different options for money that would be helpful to our program, I give them flexibility and ease in accommodating everyone applying. I have also found that local foundations like supporting local programs, especially if the programs are well organized and specific. I believe that the last piece of my success has been in the acknowledgment of the grant sources. As I am now in the third year of doing this, I am often getting grants from foundations or organizations that supported our program and school the previous year. After our school receives a grant, I am quick to write a letter of appreciation to the organization, and I always submit a "kudos" in our local paper. Also, I try to keep a running list of the groups that have helped us out and make an effort to "toot their horn" when it's appropriate.

Last, I found grant writing to be very fulfilling work. As I am a stay-at-home mom of three, the grant writing (which I usually do at 1 a.m. when everyone's finally asleep) gives me a tangible accomplishment. Also, through this process, I have met many interesting and influential people who have helped broaden my contacts with other organizations and foundations. It has been personally gratifying to contribute to my children's education by doing more than helping them with their homework or volunteering in their classroom. I also strongly believe that each of us has an obligation to make the world a better place for our children, and this is one of the small ways I hope I am making a difference both for my children and all the children at our school.

Kathy Haven
Parent Volunteer
Bijou Community School
Lake Tahoe Unified School District
South Lake Tahoe, CA

ANOTHER EXCELLENT SOURCE: PROFESSIONAL ASSOCIATION GRANTS

Many professional associations support their members by funding their grant proposals.

Teachers who are looking for funding sources to improve their lessons should know their professional associations exist to serve them and one of the services they provide their members is supporting grants. **Tip:** *As a leader, you can advise your teachers to first check their content specialty associations to determine whether they provide grant opportunities.*

Associations that cover all content disciplines fund grants written by their teacher members who need supplies or services to improve their lessons, or who want to improve their schools.

Funding Source: Kappa Delta Pi

Several of Brenda's grants were funded by the educational society, Kappa Delta Pi (http://kdp.org/). Kappa Delta Pi offers up to 50 Classroom Teacher Grants to pre-K–12 private, public, parochial, and home-school teachers. These grants provide members who are practicing teachers with the funds to support specific programs or activities. Designed to engage students in the learning process through interactive activities, they allow teachers to purchase supplies or fund field trips for which school funds aren't available.

Interested teacher-members must submit a brief proposal outlining why the funds are needed and how the grant will be used. Proposals are reviewed by a team of esteemed practicing educators, and up to *25 grants of $125–$150 each are awarded*. For a list of other grants funded by Kappa Delta Pi, see Appendix 8.1. Your teachers should notice that this list sometimes includes the number of students each grant will fund.

Also remember that one of Brenda's *tips* was to always *tell in your grant how many students will be affected by the grant*. Kappa Delta Pi asks all recipients to write a letter outlining the differences the grant made in their classrooms. By doing so, your teachers are positioning themselves for submitting their next proposal to that funder.

Funding Source: Phi Delta Kappa International

Another professional society that gives grants to teachers is Phi Delta Kappa International (intltravel@pdkintl.org). If you have teachers who want travel to other countries to enrich their teaching or to help foreign schools and students, a program is available to help you do just that. Christie McWilliams, President of the Texas Lone Star Chapter of Phi Delta Kappa, explains how she got a Phi Delta Kappa grant enabling her to provide help for a school in Tanzania (Figure 8.3). As you share Christie's letter with your teachers, call their attention to the tips Christie offers to preparing future proposals.

A Phi Delta Kappa International Regional Project Application form is shown in Appendix 8.2. Rating forms are such a valuable tool that a section was devoted to this topic in Chapter 3. Notice the rating form (Evaluation Criteria Regional Project Application) on the last page of this appendix. The very first item is an explanation of the significance of your proposed activity to Phi Delta Kappa and the second item is clarity. **Tip:** *Make sure your teachers state clearly how their proposed projects will benefit Phi Delta Kappa*. A copy of Christie's grant is shown in Appendix 8.3.

Small/Individual Grant Summary

The first half of this chapter introduced a few of the many sources that fund individual teachers' applications for money to be used to enrich their personal teaching skills and their classrooms. Each source has been shared using a success story that provides a step-by-step guide for novice grant

Background Information

In August 2008, I accompanied seven other educators from the United States and Canada to Tanzania, where we learned about their school system. This trip was organized by Phi Delta Kappa International (PDK), an organization promoting service, research, and leadership in education and of which I served as a member and chapter president at the time. On this trip, Tanzanian government education officials escorted us to city, rural, and bush elementary and secondary schools, as well as teachers' colleges. Because we knew school resources are scarce in Tanzania, we delivered boxes of books and school supplies to the elementary and secondary campuses. Although the city and rural schools were equipped with at least some books and supplies, the bush schools had none whatsoever. In fact, when we distributed pencils, some of these students did not know what they were for and licked them!

On returning home, I began making presentations about the Tanzanian school system and my experience to my school faculty, my students, PDK chapters, and other organizations. At the end of each presentation, audience members showed interest in continuing to send books and supplies to these schools. However, shipping expenses are high, as it costs $120–$200 to mail one box from the United States to Tanzania. Although I could easily organize a book and supply drive for Tanzania's neediest schools, I could not fathom where I would get the money for such exorbitant shipping costs.

Idea for the Grant

I expressed my idea of a book and supply drive as well as my concern about shipping costs with a friend. As the PDK region C representative, she reminded me that PDK awards regional project grants for up to $1,000 annually, and, as a PDK member and chapter president, I might consider submitting a grant proposal to help offset shipping costs. However, part of the grant evaluation criteria states the project must have significance to PDK. She explained that this criterion means the activity must produce new PDK members.

As I reflected on the presentations I had already given, I realized not only had I been spreading awareness about the Tanzanian school system, I had also been promoting PDK in the process—some audience members even joined PDK as a result of my presentation. I could therefore easily request up to $1,000 for shipping assistance by creating a grant proposal with two objectives: (1) increase awareness of PDK and generate new members, and (2) provide a service project for educators and students.

Grant Application Process

I downloaded and completed the regional project grant application from the PDK Web site. Consisting of only four pages, it was much shorter than I expected and included the following components: cover, project information, narrative, and budget. I also added one page of additional notes to provide adequate background information. I titled the grant, "Teacher to Teacher: Supplying Tanzania's Schools with Essential Resources." Before I submitted my final proposal, I revised it multiple times after seeking feedback from my peers and the PDK region C representative. I then sent the application to the region C representative, who distributed it to a three-member committee for review. The committee responded favorably overall to my grant application. One member, however, requested more specific information on how I would evaluate the project. I revised the assessment information, resubmitted the enclosed application, and the grant was approved.

FIGURE 8.3   Christie McWilliams' Story (*continues*)

Project in Action

After receiving approval of the grant, I gave eight presentations to a total of 123 participants. I gathered and shipped six large boxes, approximately 166 pounds, of the following materials:

- School supplies distributed among two bush elementary schools and one orphanage
- Solar-powered flashlights distributed among both rural and bush secondary schools to allow students without electricity to study at night
- Scholarly education journals sent to a teachers' college
- Books and journals on leadership to be distributed among district administrators

Furthermore, 55 audience members requested further information about PDK, five joined PDK, and one participant expressed interest in an institutional membership for the 2009–2010 academic year. All objectives for the activity were met, and I submitted a final report to PDK. From this experience, I learned that applying for a grant is not as scary or time consuming as I initially thought, and the benefits of owning and following through with a significant project are well worth the effort.

Tips for Writing Grant Proposals

- Most important, read the evaluation criteria beforehand. Be sure your application addresses all criteria.
- Request to review past successful grant proposals to use as models.
- Create a catchy and appropriate title for your project.
- Include specific and manageable project objectives and a plan to assess each objective.
- Prepare your proposal early to allow for revision.
- Ask someone involved in the grant-giving organization to offer feedback on your proposal.
- Remember all the rules of good writing. Write concisely and specifically—less is more. Have no errors. Proofread the application multiple times and have your peers review it before submitting.

I learned that applying for a grant was not as scary or time consuming as I initially thought.

FIGURE 8.3   Christie McWilliams' Story

writers. Because these stories are told in the first person by those who succeeded, their passions for their experiences shine through. Their passions will continue long after the grant money is spent, helping them become better teachers.

Sharing these novice grant writers' passions and the steps they used should enable department leaders to assist other teachers in taking the plunge into grant writing. But superintendents, principals, and designated grant directors want more. In addition to helping individual teachers find resources for their classrooms, these education leaders want to use grant writing to bring major improvement to their schools. School and district-wide improvements require much larger grants, which are usually written collaboratively. The second half of this chapter examines some larger, collaboratively written grants, with an eye on their funding sources. The chapter also shares ways of involving other community leaders and institutions in the preparation of major grant proposals.

PART II: FUNDING SOURCES TO IMPROVE SCHOOLS AND SCHOOL DISTRICTS

This part of the book is written to help leaders guide the preparation of larger proposals designed to improve schools and school districts. It stresses team writing and collaboration with peers, community members, universities, and other school districts, giving examples of each. **Tip:** *The goal here is to have a grant-writing team that writes a continuous flow of grants connected to the district's mission.* This team must also be able to write huge grants, some requiring the ability to form partnerships with other school districts and other institutions. Those districts that already have such programs in operation will want to improve their productivity. As you read the remainder of this chapter, consider how you can lead your schools in the development and/or improvement of a well-oiled, grant-writing machine.

Systematic improvement requires a well-oiled grant writing machine.

A Principal's Proven Strategy for Identifying Grant Sources

Some building-level leaders are charged with the challenge of bringing in money to support their schools. (We saw an example of this in Connie Phelps' newspaper grant.) Inside grants are to be encouraged, but the current national economic disaster has intensified the need for many school administrators to seek funding outside the district. Because leadership demands so much of principals, sometimes it is easy to forget you don't have to put all the responsibility for generating funds on your own shoulders or on the shoulders of your teachers. Any project that benefits the schools also benefits the community. Most businesses and foundations understand that their own survival depends on the well-being of their community. Former Kansas Principal Karen Hayes shares her effective strategies for involving the community:

Any grant that improves a school improves its community, and most businesses and foundations understand that their own survival depends on the well-being of their community.

"One of the first things I did when I was named principal of a blue-collar urban elementary school was to introduce myself to all of the local businesses within my school community. Many of the parents worked two jobs or double shifts; after school, students returned to empty homes, or they went to the local community center, which had an afterschool program. The community center's mission was to empower children and parents to reach their potential and enable older adults to maintain their independence. My school's mission was to serve as a team of staff, students, parents, and community working together to teach students to become high achievers, lifelong learners, and responsible citizens.

Because I was able to see a natural relationship between our school's mission and the community center's mission, and because so many of my students attended the community center's afterschool program, I saw it as a natural opportunity for my school and the community center to form a partnership. I immediately began volunteering as a member of the community center's board. Within a few months, I was asked to chair the Program Committee. I had a plan; I would creatively use the community center to support my school's and the community center's goals.

Because I was able to see a connection between our school's mission and the community center's mission, I saw an opportunity to form a partnership.

Many of my students needed help with their homework, or just needed an adult to read to them or to listen to them read. I wanted funds to create and support an intergenerational tutorial program for the center.

Intergenerational programs can provide a venue for children and senior citizens to come together to share talents, resources, and support. I found a funding source through the Omaha community United Way of the Midlands. I wrote an Intergenerational Tutorial Grant that would bring in grandparents to help students with their homework. I designed a program in which people of all ages could come together, interact, explore, and build meaningful relationships.

I found it inspiring to observe my students curled up reading a book with a "surrogate" grandparent, watching other seniors overseeing homework, helping students with their letters or numbers, or just listening to children sharing their day.

I received more interest from other local businesses who wanted to support our school through Adopt-a-School partnerships. One agency painted our second-floor landing, adding bean bags and bookshelves, which we turned into a reading nook. Another local partnership was an outdoor advertising/billboard agency. Our school became one of the first schools to be highlighted on billboards throughout our community. We eventually began showing student artwork through this venue. Talk about ego booster . . . our students and staff became quite proud of the school noted for such significant advertising. Students whose artwork was shown blossomed in their efforts to strive for excellence in all aspects of school.

"We partnered with a local advertising agency to show our students' artwork. Talk about an ego booster!"

Families became increasingly interested and wanted to be involved . . . enthusiasm is contagious! My PTA membership increased over 100%, and my school received the State PTA "Mighty Oak" award because of the significant increase in our membership.

I would encourage any school principal to get involved with your school community. Agencies such as Lowe's, Home Depot, the State Department of Education, and, of course, your local United Way will support the promotion of proactive, creative thinking. It doesn't take a paid grant writer to write your grant, but it does take committed adults who are willing to give their time to think creatively and to take the time to find the funding source. I find that grant writing means turning your ideas into a theory of action.

Writing your plan, answering the "who, what, where, and how," and then deciding on the budget you will need to accomplish your plan are the intentions of a grant. Local, state, and federal agencies may be able to support your ideas. Search their Web sites, call, or just stop by your local agencies. "It takes a village to raise a child" . . . and our children deserve nothing less.

United Way can help you get support from multiple funders, and this increases your proposal's chances of being funded.

One of Karen's major sources was her local United Way (www.uway. org). **Tip:** *Encourage your teachers to contact their local United Way office when their proposals directly enhance the community.* United Way can help you get the support of multiple funders, and this increases your proposal's chances of being funded. She also used Lowe's (Lowe's Toolbox for Education will donate $5 million to public schools and public school parent-teacher groups at more than 1,000 different public schools per year, www. toolboxforeducation.com) and Home Depot (Home Depot provides grants for facilities improvements, www.homedepot.com). By searching *Lowe's Grants for Schools,* you will find *Lowe's Toolbox for Educators/Lowe's Grants*

Recipients. Here you can click on the current or past year and find a list showing that a sample grant was awarded in every state. You can refine your search by clicking on *Community Service Grants* or *Campus Improvements.*

Several lessons can be learned from Karen Hayes. **Tip:** Perhaps the most important of these lessons is to *involve several local agencies in the same grant-writing goal.* Funders love it when they see other agencies are chipping in to help make an important dream become a reality. School leaders should treat grant writing the way a music maestro treats an orchestra. This requires getting out into your community, meeting the CEOs of local businesses and other community organizations, selling your faculty's dream, and making these community leaders full partners in this dream.

Two examples of United Way Grants are seen in an Atlanta-based grant titled *Beating to a Different Drum* in Appendix 8.3 and a grant titled *Reach for the Stars* in Appendix 8.4. The latter grant involves multiple funding agencies and is designed to benefit disadvantaged children over a wide geographic area.

ADDITIONAL EXCELLENT FUNDING SOURCES FOR SCHOOL DISTRICTS

In my two-year investigation of grant-writing programs in school districts located throughout the United States, I found the Burlington (Vermont) School District to be a shining example of the power a well-orchestrated grant-writing program can bring to making continuous improvements to its schools. Some of this district's grants are found throughout this book.

Funding Source: New England Dairy & Food Council

The New England Dairy & Food Council (www.newenglanddairycouncil. org/) funds grants to help schools provide healthy menus for their students. To qualify, your school must submit a letter of application. Vermont's Burlington High School received one of these grants (Figure 8.4).

The National Dairy Council and the National Football League in collaboration with the U.S. Department of Agriculture, have teamed up to bring you Fuel Up to Play 60—a nutrition and fitness program designed to help bring your school's wellness policy to life. Fuel Up to Play 60 encourages students to be active for at least 60 minutes every day and to fuel their bodies with nutrient-rich foods like low-fat and fat-free dairy foods, fruits, vegetables, and whole grains. Students need a healthy diet and regular physical activity to perform their best in and out of the classroom. You can find applications and procedures for applying for a Fuel Up to Play 60 grant at www. FuelUptoPlay60.com.

Funding Source: Ronald McDonald House Charities (RMHC)

The RMHC (www.rmhc.org) works to improve the health and well-being of children directly through its programs. It also works with nonprofit organizations around the world that are making an immediate, positive impact on children who need it most. Grants to these organizations extend the reach and impact of RMHC and quickly move donation dollars quickly to areas in their time of need. To see a sample RHMC grant application, see Appendix 8.5.

Fuel Up to Play Wellness Activation Grant Program Letter of Intent

This letter should be used by schools to communicate interest in participating in the 2009/10 Fuel Up to Play Wellness Activation Grant Programs with New England Dairy & Food Council. Participating schools will be chosen from those which apply based on the selection criteria and their desire to empower students around improving the school wellness environment. Completed letters along with a copy of your school district's wellness policy should be sent to Jill Goodroe at 802-865-9372 (fax) by 4:00 PM on Friday, May 30, 2009. Chosen schools will be notified of their acceptance on or before June 15, 2009.

Selection Criteria:

- Part of a progressive school district with an interest in wellness (please include a copy of your school district's wellness policy with the letter of intent)
- Supportive school district administration
- Progressive school serving grades 6–8 that is interested in empowering youth to make a difference
- Supportive Principal
- Engaged adult program advisor with a willingness to assist youth to carry out the program
- Ability to participate in all aspects of the program planning, implementation and evaluation

District:	Burlington
School:	Hunt Middle
Enrollment:	410
Grades:	6–8
School Contact:	Deb Anger
Contact Phone Number:	864-8469
Contact E-mail:	danger@bsdvt.org

In 100 words or less, describe why your school would like to be considered for the 2009–2010 Fuel Up to Play Enhanced Wellness Activation Grant Program.

Hunt Middle School is one of the most diverse schools in Vermont. We hive more than 70 ELL students, representing dozens of countries, and our total school free and reduced lunch rate is over 50%. We feel that we can use the Fuel Up to Play Program to make a positive change for our students' nutritional choices and activity levels. We have a wonderful food service staff, and would like to work with them to enhance our current breakfast program. We would also like to offer after-school options for our students, particularly those who do not participate in traditional sports teams.

Potential adult program advisor:	Deb Anger

FIGURE 8.4 Fuel Up Grant (*continues*)

In 100 words or less describe why you feel the above named advisor would be an asset to this program.

Ms. Anger teaches Family and Consumer Science at Hunt. Her curriculum includes units on nutrition and basic understanding of the food pyramid, BMI, and relationships between nutrition, fitness, and overall health. Deb has previously taught physical education and continues to be an active and fit adult. She understands the struggles of our students and has an established rapport with them. This background will make her a tremendous asset for this program.

Linda Carroll	Deborah Anger	Linda Carroll
Signature of Applicant	Signature of Potential Program Advisor (if different from applicant)	Signature of School Principal

FIGURE 8.4 Fuel Up Grant

Funding Source: Your Local College

Schools in a college town have excellent opportunities to get partnership grants.

Schools located in a college town have excellent opportunities to get partnership grants through their state Department of Education or through their colleges and universities. This is particularly true with universities that have Colleges or Departments of Education and Departments of Health, Business Administration, and Law Enforcement. Actually, you need not be located in a college town. **Tip:** *Just locate the teacher education college that serves your region of the state.* Dr. Bill Phillips, Dean of the College of Education at Eastern Kentucky University, explains by describing his college's grant program:

> The College of Education has made available, on a competitive basis, funds to support expenses associated with scholarly activities. Funds can be used to support P–12 collaboration, research efforts, or the work of writing a book, a chapter for a book, an article, or for the preparation of an external grant proposal.
>
> Awards may include
> - Graduate research assistantships
> - Faculty release time
> - Supplies, expenses, equipment, and travel
> - Summer salary
>
> Proposals are due biannually
> - December 1 for summer and fall start dates
> - July 1 for spring and summer start dates
>
> Contact: College of Education, Office of Grants and Research
>
> Contact Person: Beth Brickley, 622-2962

If your state does not have a college with a grant program serving your area, don't give up. Dr. Phillips offers this suggestion:

> Contact the Office of the Dean of Education at your local university to find out what grants are available for collaborative research projects with

teachers in the public schools. If none is available, make a proposal anyway and ask for special funding. The College of Education at Eastern Kentucky University provides up to $3,000 for any action research project a professor and a public school teacher work on collaboratively. There is a simple one-page application that asks you to describe the project, identify who will participate, and list possible learning outcomes for students. Ninety percent of the applications are funded for the 22 school districts in our region of Eastern Kentucky. The review is performed by a team of faculty and staff at the College of Education and takes only a few weeks. Grant proposals are accepted only twice a year, so be sure to ask about the deadline. The money can be used to pay for materials, travel, and/or a stipend for the extra time you will spend implementing the grant. A simple, one-page report is required at the end of the grant to provide a rationalization for the money spent and to give an accounting of student learning outcomes. It is important to file the report so you will be eligible for future grants.

Collaborating with Other School Districts

Increased power lies in the hands of those districts willing to collaborate with other districts. Often, such collaborative efforts result in larger grants than can be secured by districts who insist on writing every proposal without working with other districts. Mr. Steve Zadravec, Assistant Superintendent of Portsmouth School District in New Hampshire, says, *Collaborating with other districts provides opportunities to implement and sustain innovative programs otherwise impossible to afford.* For example, interdistrict collaboration can lead to school-to-career partnership programs.

Increased power lies in the hands of those districts that are willing to collaborate with other districts.

FOUNDATIONS GRANTS. Large government and industrial foundations are funding sources far too important for any educational leader to ignore. Dr. John A. Beineke, a professor at Arkansas State University and a former grant director at the W.K. Kellogg Foundation in Battle Creek, Michigan, explains the uniqueness of preparing grants for philanthropic and government foundations (Box 8.1). He provides an in-house view of foundations and concludes by offering some general advice for serious grant writers.

NATIONAL ASSOCIATIONS. Both of the nation's largest educational organizations issue grants.

Funding Source: National Education Association (NEA)

The NEA offers two types of grants. The first type of grant is a $5,000 Student Achievement Grant. This grant can apply to any subject or grade level. The goal of the grant is to promote critical thinking and problem solving and to develop a knowledge base. The other NEA grants focus on learning and leadership: $2,000 grants are available to individual teachers, and $5,000 grants are available to support group-written proposals.

Funding Source: American Federation of Teachers (AFT)

The AFT has an Innovation Fund to support risk takers. Proposals may be written by teachers or unions and may include school-community partners.

BOX 8.1   The World of Foundations: A View from the Inside

Giving money away is easy. Giving money away well is difficult.

Waldemeir Nielsen, author and observer of foundations, has written that when one joins a foundation staff, "you have had your last bad meal and your last honest compliment." The part about good meals held true, the disingenuous remarks not so much. I had the privilege of being a foundation program director for five years at the W.K. Kellogg Foundation in Battle Creek, Michigan. I worked in the areas of leadership, youth, and higher education.

Giving away money sounds like a terrific job—and it was. But Gerald Freund, another follower of the foundation world, has written that "giving away money is simple; nothing is easier. Giving money away well is very hard; nothing is more difficult." Freund has also said that philanthropy is different from charity because it has a creative edge. Its purpose is to produce something that does not already exist or to enhance and change something that does.

Each foundation must by law distribute a portion of its corpus each year. So there are assets for educators to tap into, but the requests need to match the mission of the foundation. Very few foundations provide unrestricted funds for grantees to spend as they choose. Most foundations have their particular areas of interest. Some, like Kresge, Mabee, or Reynolds, focus on academic or research buildings while others like the Robert Wood Johnson Foundation are committed to health initiatives. The Kellogg Foundation centered its priorities on agriculture, education, health, and leadership.

So what is it like to work inside a philanthropic institution? Having been a public school teacher and university professor and administrator, for me the occupation was definitely different. The environment was a mix of the private business sector and a think tank. The CEO of a foundation behaves much like the CEO of a business enterprise. The vice presidents operate much like deans in colleges. And the program directors, my role, are the worker bees that function much like research faculty. The corporate element of the atmosphere manifests itself with gray suits, white shirts, drab ties, and numerous meetings. The day-to-day work is formal with a definite hierarchy and teams that function around the foundation's themes. Foundation staff travel nationally and internationally making field visits to promising grantees and their projects.

One of the first things I learned and one of the first things a grant writer needs to keep in mind is that foundation funding is competitive. Stagnant or decreasing funding from government means that more individuals and organizations are often chasing the same dollars from foundations. University fundraising, with staff dedicated to solely writing grants, is making it more difficult for K–12 schools with one grant writer at most to compete successfully. Compounding the competitiveness is the limited number of successful applicants. With requests outnumbering available resources even billion dollar foundations like Gates, Rockefeller, or Kellogg are unable to meet all the needs of our society. Large national foundations usually fund only about 5% of the appeals they receive.

The Web provides a relatively easy method to research foundations' guidelines.

So what kind of proposals are foundations looking for? As a program director, I had to follow the guidelines of the foundation. The web provides a relatively easy method to research these foundations' guidelines. Most foundations produce annual reports and list who their grantees were the previous year and the size of the grants. This will give the grant writer a good idea as to what is being funded by the foundation, and at what level of support. When writing a grant, grant one does not want to overshoot or underestimate the amount being requested. Using online search engines such as the Foundation Directory can assist in targeting those foundations with interests that coincide with the needs of schools in the K–12 arena.

At the Kellogg Foundation all letters were acknowledged, even if the appeal fell outside our mission or our interest. If the idea was especially strong, but could not be funded, we would if at all possible, write a personalized letter that attempted to explain why the request was not competitive. I always tried to be encouraging in my letters, even making phone calls on occasion. I knew that when I had been on the "outside" I had never appreciated being dismissed after investing my time in writing the grant proposal. One response I received denying my application for funding was especially inconsiderate. "If your project idea is so good and such an important idea then your own school should fund it," the foundation official wrote to me. I made sure I never sent an aspiring grant seeker such a letter.

In addition to having knowledge of the mission of the particular foundation you are writing to, it is important to be aware of the common purposes they wish to achieve with their grant making. These may include: (a) providing needed services that cannot be met through usual financial means, (b) experimenting to find new solutions to societal and community problems, (c) educating the public on current and emerging issues, (d) convening stakeholders on common issues for discussions and action, and (e) developing workable public policy options for government and nongovernmental institutions.

So how do teachers successfully secure grant dollars? As a program director, I looked for several elements in a potential grant. These included creativity— was the proposal something that had not been done before or done in the way the proposal suggested? Did the idea seem workable? Did the individual or the organization have the capacity to carry out the idea? Was there a track record of success and did their commitment seem sufficient? I also looked for a well-prepared, well-written proposal. Was the proposal realistic in terms of budget? Was it sufficient to successfully complete the project or was the request beyond the amount the foundation could afford and the potential grantee could spend wisely?

Grant writing is a creative process and the most critical component is the idea.

The most critical component of the grant-seeking process is the "idea." Did the idea appear to me, as a program director, creative, original, and worthwhile? Did it demonstrate an understanding of the area being addressed? Was it an area that needed support? To be able to respond to these questions, grant seekers need to discover ideas. And where do these ideas come from. From my experience, there are several avenues that those seeking grants should pursue. These include:

1. ***Read, Read, Read***—Grant seekers need to be voracious readers. Their reading regimen should include journals of opinion such as *The New Republic, The National Review, The Atlantic, The Nation,* and *The Weekly Standard* to name but a few that cut across the political and social spectrum. These journals follow political, social, cultural, and economic trends. They have essays, book reviews, and analysis of the news. Grant seekers are unable to read all the books we would wish, so these sources give us overviews of important new works and ideas. We should also read news magazines such as *Time* and national newspapers like the *Washington Post* and the *New York Times.* And in education it is imperative to be knowledgeable of the field for which funds are being sought. National professional organizations such as the National Council of Teachers of Mathematics, the International Reading Association, or the Council

Grant writers need to be voracious readers.

(continues)

for Exceptional Children all have strong websites and excellent publications that keep teachers abreast of new trends in their disciplines and age appropriate groups. *Education Week* is essential reading. CSPAN's *Book TV* covers a variety of new books each weekend. I have also found that even the popular presses, such as *USA Today*, can be a valuable source for tracking new trends and ideas. And don't forget to read books like the one you are holding right now.

2. *Attend Conferences*—New ideas for potential grants can often be generated by attending educational conferences. These can be national conferences sponsored by some of the organizations named above or they can be stand-alone meetings tracking a single topic such as the achievement gap, leadership, teaching, or assessment. Listening to those women and men whom I termed the "smart people" when I was with a foundation proved to be immensely helpful in identifying the new ideas in the world of educational practice.

Foundations like collaboratively written interdisciplinary grants.

3. *Listen to Your Community*—Foundations like to view themselves as "close to the ground" and community-based in the work they do. They believe that problems can be solved by looking to community assets, not community deficits. The deficits will be the challenges that are the focus of a grant. Being aware of local needs that the schools can address along with the learning, curricular, or systemic issues K–12 teachers wish to address is pivotal in securing a grant.

4. *Be a Synthesizer*—An often forgotten arena that grant seekers should pursue is to take two or three ideas and integrate them into a new configuration of looking at an issue, topic, or problem. The taking of several independent ideas and reformulating them in a new fashion can be appealing to a foundation. Cross-disciplinary approaches are popular because they call for collaboration. Foundations find attractive those prospective grants that bring, for example, health providers or the business sector as partners into an education grant.

5. *Take Time to Think*—A veteran program director at a foundation can readily discern a proposal that has been given substantial thought and research. The proposal is well-documented, thoroughly investigated, and thoughtfully written. Craig Dykstra of the Lilly Endowment has used the phrase "a hospitable space for disciplined reflection" to describe the environment needed to make quality contributions to any field of endeavor. The five "P's"—Proper Preparation Prevents Poor Performance—are necessary in the writing of grants just as they are in most endeavors in life.

We at the foundation also looked for particular words in grant applications. These include collaboration, community partnerships, sustainability, replication, impact, diversity, and public policy. A few final words about three of these words—impact, sustainability, and replication. A *New Yorker* magazine cartoon shows a dozen wolves baying at the moon from a mountain top. One wolf at the back of the pack turns to another wolf and asks: "Do you think we are having an impact?" Foundations are like that inquisitive wolf—how will you know your grant has had an impact? Make sure you build an evaluation component into your grant proposal and make it a budget line in the funding request. As for sustainability, be sure you tell the foundation how you intend to carry on the work of the grant when the funding ends. And finally, can your project be replicated in another classroom, school, or district? Does it have "legs" to make a difference?

Foundations look for certain works such as collaboration, community partnerships, sustainability, and replication.

I have been fortunate to use my knowledge of life inside a foundation since returning to my work in public education and universities. With the collaboration of others we have written successful grants that have funded a variety of projects and initiatives. These have included professional development activities for faculty, creating a self-sustaining Advanced Placement Institute, leveraging a grant to increase student and faculty participation in international activities, helping to create a public school foundation for a local school district, and strengthening and creating school/university partnerships to enhance simultaneous renewal of schools and a college of education.

The air within a foundation can be rarified and the operations of these institutions are indeed often mysterious. But those on the "inside" have the same motivations that those of us on the outside have. How do we take resources that would not normally be available and use them to make a difference in the lives of those in this country and around the world? If we keep that idea in sharp focus as we write our grants, the chances of successful funding will increase significantly.

John A. Beineke
Arkansas State University
(formerly of the W. K. Kellogg Foundation)

SPECIALTY PROFESSIONAL ASSOCIATIONS. Many of the once-called *learned societies*, now referred to as specialty professional associations (SPAs), support grants. These organizations are excellent for department and grade-level chairs because each is aimed at a particular discipline. A list of these organizations is shown in Figure 8.5.

These grants are open to both middle-level and high school science teachers who teach a minimum of two science classes per day and who have at least 2 years' experience in a K–12 school prior to the year of application.

American Alliance for Health, Physical Education, Recreation Dance (AAHPERD): www.aahperd.org/whatwedo/grants/

Bill & Melinda Gates Foundation: www.gatesfoundation.org

U.S. Environmental Protection Agency, Catalog of Federal Domestic Assistance: www.epa.gov/ogd/grants/cfda.htm

Cisco's Product Grant Program (PGP): www.cisco.com/web/about/ac48/pgp_home.html

The Mr. Holland's Opus Foundation: www.mhopus.org/teachers.asp

W. K. Kellogg Foundation: www.wkkf.org/

USA Grant Applications: www.USAgrantapplications.org

National Council for the Social Studies (NCSS): www.socialstudies.org/

National Council of Teachers of English (NCTE): www.ncte.org/grants

National Council of Teachers of Mathematics (NCTM): www.nctm.org/

National Science Teachers Association (NSTA) Toyota Motor Sales, USA, Inc., Toyota Tapestry Grants for Science Teachers: www.nsta.org/pd/tapestry

International Reading Association (IRA): www.reading.org/Resources/AwardsandGrants.aspx

SMARTer Kids Foundation: www.teachlearning.com/

Foundation Center: www.foundationcenter.org

Walmart Grants for Schools grantsuforeducation.co.cc/bsrwp

Walmart Grants for Teachers grantsuforeducation.co.cc/bsrwp

FIGURE 8.5 List of Specialty Professional Associations and Other Grant Sources

Because the purpose of an award is to provide startup funds, rather than to sustain ongoing research, an award carries the responsibility to disseminate the results of any funded proposal either through publication in refereed outlets or a one-page report pertaining to student learning outcomes.

1. **Proposal Submission.**   Applicants may submit only one proposal per cycle (i.e., one proposal in December and one in July). A successful applicant may accept only one award per year.

    Recipients of a previous award must have completed all requirements associated with that award prior to applying for new funding. These requirements will be negotiated at the time of the award and will likely include final reports, result dissemination, and proposal submission to external agencies.

2. **Project Narrative** (maximum of one page double spaced)
    * *Statement of the activity*—A rationale for the project defining its scope.
    * *Specific goals and objectives*—An expansion of the discussion of the scope of the project, focusing on the goals and/or objectives of the research.
    * *Significance of the problem or impact of the goal addressed*— A discussion of the impact of the project on the following: the discipline, other disciplines, faculty, students, the university, and the world.
    * *Budget*—How much do you need, and what will you purchase?

SPECIAL EDUCATION

Special educator Wendy Wingard-Gay, who was quoted in Chapters 6 and 7, prepared Box 8.2 for special educators. Much of her advice is crucial to grant writers in all disciplines.

BOX 8.2   Getting Your Wishes "Granted": Persistence Pays

Eager to begin my first job in 1985, I contracted with the local speech and hearing center to provide speech therapy services for Head Start students in three counties in the Piedmont of South Carolina. Since Head Start was a federally funded program, I had ample tests, materials, and supplies. A year later, I wanted a public school job so I worked for a large school district, Cherokee County in Gaffney, SC, where materials and resources were also abundant. After traveling two hours per day to Gaffney, I made the decision to go to a smaller rural school district in York, SC, as it was closer to my home in Rock Hill, SC (located 20 miles south of Charlotte, NC). I literally went from working out of a broom closet at Head Start locations in the schools, to a library conference room at Draytonville Elementary, Gaffney, SC, then to sharing a mobile unit and finally into a large classroom at Jefferson Primary School in York, SC. Transitioning to the new setting of a large classroom with lots of space was ideal, but also had its drawbacks. Since my position was a new one for the district, there was no special education teacher budget. There were no tests, test protocols, materials, or supplies—not even one articulation picture card. I found myself between a building principal and special education supervisor, neither willing to relinquish funds for basic tests, resources, and materials, which would be found in most schools for a beginning Speech Language Pathologist (SLP). I quickly learned to be a creative and resourceful beggar. I would gather up pens and paper pads at the conclusion of every speech conference, obtain tongue depressors, penlights, and gloves and drug company-sponsored sticky note pads from doctor's offices and borrow tests from a neighboring school district. You learn to be very creative and resourceful when you are poor! (There were no dollar stores or computers at that time.) After-school hours were spent tracing pictures to make masters for the purple ditto machines as there were no copy machines in those days! Magazine pictures were cut and glued onto index cards and games were made weekly for speech-disabled students. As this was a very conservative district, there were no spare classroom textbooks or teacher guides. I even solicited a donation from the local hardware store owners for paint to cover the walls in my classroom. Preparation activities became time consuming, so grant writing became a necessity. Writing grant proposals became the easiest way for me to obtain basic materials for a speech therapy room and also funded special projects, specialized materials, and resources for students and teachers at my school.

Twenty-five years later and $100,000 dollars richer in supplies and materials due to grant awards (with no space in the purple painted speech therapy room to spare), students and teachers at Jefferson Elementary have been profoundly impacted and have reaped all the benefits from special projects.

In twenty-five years, policies have changed. Now, the district gives each special education teacher a budget of $500 yearly (this has diminished somewhat due to budget cuts). A beginning special education teacher receives a slightly higher budget than veteran teachers. The SC legislature gives each teacher $275 yearly, including SLPs. With deep legislative cuts, this may be eliminated next year. Due to school involvement with the Parent Teacher Organization (PTO), the SLP receives $25 to $50 annually pending income from special school-wide projects. The South Carolina Department of Education once offered Educational Improvement Act (EIA) grants yearly (up to $6,000 for unit grants), which have been eliminated due to state budget shortfalls. York School District One once offered an in-house grant for $1,000, which has been eliminated due to budget constraints. The district's special education department funded in-state professional development for SLPs but that budget has been eliminated. The district hired a grant coordinator for the district who not only writes grants but also communicates teacher grant offerings from around the state and country to district personnel. York School District One remains a small school district having four full-time American Speech-Language Hearing Association (ASHA) certified Speech/Language Pathologists and two full-time Speech/Language Therapists [having an MS or BA with no ASHA Certificates of Clinical Competence] and continues to grow as it is considered a bedroom community of Charlotte, NC. Like many other SLPs around the country, we are all scrambling for outside funding sources to supplement or fund the needs of our students.

Currently, Jefferson Elementary is a Title One school, which serves students ages pre-kindergarten to grade 5. It has a current enrollment of 651, with 502 white, 106 black, 23 Hispanic, 10 American Indian, 7 White/African American, 2 Asian, and 1 Pacific Islander/Hawaiian. It has 47% of students on free and reduced lunch. There are 20% of students in special education. The school has a preschool disabilities program (ages 3–6), an Applied Behavior Therapy program for autism (ages 3–6), two self-contained classes for mild and moderately disabled

(continues)

students, one resource program, and one full time SLP and a half time SLT who serve 66 speech-disabled students total.

Here are some of the project titles and focus that have been funded by grants, businesses, and foundations for Jefferson Elementary School over the twenty-five years:

Grant Title	Focus	Source	Award
Celebrate Communicate!	Pre-K to Grade 2: Articulation/ language materials and resources	EIA Grant	$6,000
Here They Come-Chit Chat Chums!	Kindergarten, First, Second Grade: Enlisting community speech partners and materials/ resources to support vocabulary	EIA Grant Family Trust Bank	$2,000 $ 250
Tales for Articulation	Pre-K to 2: Targeted articulation via puppet shows	EIA Grant	$2,000
The ABC's of Speech Pathology	Parents and Teachers: Materials/resources to support afterschool parent/teacher meetings on speech disorders	EIA Grant	$6,000
PLAY: Preliteracy Language and Young Children	Kindergarten: Dress-up kits with puppets and coordinated books; created a weekly puppet show targeting basic concept vocabulary	EIA Grant	$6,000
The Big Mac Attack!	AAC and AT devices for students with autism Pre-K to Grade 5	EIA Grant	$6,000
SPEAK: Special Products Educating Autistic Children	Provided reinforcers, materials, and resources for ABT assistants and the SLP for autistic students	EIA Grant	$6,000
Abound with Sounds!	Preschool: Resources used to provide weekly language lessons by the SLP for preschool and preschool disability classrooms Kindergarten: Provided kindergarten curricula which involves music, motor, listening, and speaking activities for letter and sound awareness	EIA Grant Family Trust Bank	$6,000 $ 250
Quick Artic!	Kindergarten centers for EIS services; provided resources for the SLP to teach a lesson once per week for 30 minutes in each kindergarten class targeting sounds and language	EIA Grant	$6,000
Sounds Good To Me	First Grade: Sound field equalization systems	EIA Grant	$6,000

Grant Title	Focus	Source	Award
Sound Investment	K to Grade 5: Sound field equalization systems	EIA Grant	$ 6,000
LIPS: Language Intervention Partner Support	Resources and materials for speech volunteers targeting speech, language, and fluency	EIA Grant	$ 2,000
Sounds Like Fun	Sound Field Equalization System: Speech therapy room	York School District One Grant	$ 500
START-IN: Students Are Responding To Intervention	Pre-K to Grade 5: Language EIS implemented	York School District One Grant	$ 1,000
E-I-E-I-O! Oh the Places We Will Go!	Preschool to Kindergarten: Field trip Grant to Charlotte, NC which targeted the topic of transportation for 180 students and their teachers	Target Field Trip Grant Family Trust Grant	$ 800 $ 250
Sounds Good To Us	Sound Field Equalization System for Pre-K to Grade 5: upgrades	York School District One Grant EIA Grant	$ 1,000 $ 6,000
Sounds Like Fun	Sound Field Equalization System: upgrade	BellSouth Teacher Mini-Grant	$ 250
TALK: Teaching Articulation/Language to Kids	Pre-K to Grade 5: Speech software and professional development	EIA Grant	$ 2,000
LIPS: Language Intervention with Preschool Disabled	Preschool: Oral motor tools	EIA Grant	$ 2,000
Can Hardly Wait to Communicate!	Pre-K to Grade 2: Puppet shows; technology	EIA Grant	$ 2,000
SPARK: School Puppetry And Remediating Kids	Pre-K to Grade 2: Puppet theatre and props	EIA Grant	$ 2,000
Whoo! Enraptured with Raptors!	Pre-K: Targets books with birds and live raptor presentation	Family Trust Grant	$ 250
Technology Speaks	Pre-K to Grade 5: Equipment and technology	Best Buy Community Grant	$20,000

There have been several different sources for grants over the twenty-five years. As you will discover in your grant-writing exploration, there are available sites for grants. Federal grants can be found in the *Federal Register*, a government resource book that is published daily. Copies can be found in your local library but it can be accessed cost free on the Internet. Federal grants are very complicated and lengthy but they offer large funding awards. State grants can be obtained by phoning relevant divisions with the state government telephone directory or using an Internet search engine and typing in your state agency. Generally, state agencies list grant applications on their web sites. State grants are less complicated to write than federal grants and have smaller monetary awards.

Your local government may have community block grants available through city or county planning commissions or departments. Local, state, and national

Generally, state grants are less complicated than federal grants, but they generate less money.

(continues)

foundations offer grants that can be found using an Internet search engine. Local, state, and national corporations offer grants and can be accessed through the chamber of commerce. Many large corporations and businesses offer teacher or education grants that can be found on websites. Many professional grant-writing courses offer the most current government agency grant sites, business, or foundation grants for a fee.

Having written a multitude of grants over the years, I became a grant reader for the SC Educational Improvement Act (EIA) grants. Grant judging gave me an opportunity to watch trends and learn about new and exciting products and ideas that teachers had across South Carolina. It also gave me a strong opportunity to collaborate with teachers and staff within my school. We have a genuine, mutual respect of each other's disciplines and methods. Many of the grants have allowed me to go into regular classrooms to work with students on articulation and language. Several have addressed early intervening services targeting students having difficulties with listening skills, preliteracy, and phonological awareness skills. Teachers and students have received high-quality programming, resources, materials, and supplies. Students, their parents, and teachers have learned what an SLP has to offer to enhance learning.

Here are some special tips on grant writing that are my personal preferences:

Take care that you do not waste time on grants for which your schools do not qualify.

First, there are several key steps in the general grant-writing process. Download a copy of the grant application with guidelines and read it. Check for your school or district's eligibility. Do not waste time on a grant application when your school is ineligible. Follow all instructions and pay attention to the "fine" print as there may be taxes that your school or district may incur if the grant is awarded. Fill out all necessary forms and obtain the proper signatures. Use blue ink for signatures, as copy machines so closely match originals.

Next, watch for deadlines. A late grant is never accepted. Stay within the page limits. If the grant requires you to write with 200 words or less in a section, do not exceed the limit or it is disregarded. You will need to have your district's federal tax identification number handy. Give yourself enough time to complete the grant application.

Stick to the requirements on margins, font size and spacing. Use a size type that is legible. If a grant reader is judging 200 grants or more, the eyes get very weary. Use bold letters to make sections of the grant stand out. It is helpful to use headers within the document as it makes it easier for the judge to see that all the sections of the grant are present. Complete each section of the grant completely.

The grant application usually comes with judging rubrics or guidelines. Once the grant is written, review the grant to see if you have all requirements and components of the guidelines or rubric. Review and revise the grant as needed. Make the appropriate number of copies and submit the proposal.

After you submit the proposal, there are follow-up procedures. If you do not receive funding, make a request for the judging notes so that you can improve the proposal for the next time the funding is offered. If you receive grant funding, complete the final evaluation or documentation required by the agency, business or foundation. Failure to complete a final evaluation can be devastating. Your school or district may have to return funding or you may forfeit your opportunity to write a future grant. Final evaluations may include expenditure sections so be sure to maintain receipts from budget items. Some evaluations include having the grantee document activities in pictures.

Finally, be sure to thank the grant agency, business or foundation for the opportunity. You never know when a thank you note might make the difference in whether a business offers a future grant.

The key components of a grant application include a title, needs section, program activities with measureable goals and objectives, a management plan, evaluation section, budget, and appendices. A focus of an educational grant should be the students and their learning. The goal is to make a situation in your school better for the student. A successful grant writer is able to convey and justify this in a grant application.

First comes the title. Make your grant stand out by using a short, creative title. Many grant proposals are written online; therefore, you have to have some way to make yours stand out among all the thousands of others.

The needs section should include school data, which is relevant. It can include, but is not limited to, state testing data, local evaluations, socioeconomics, gender, and ethnicity. The needs section should describe programming currently being used and why it has or has not been successful. It should have a statement about what funding is currently available. For example, if your school budget has been eliminated, then state this in the needs section. It is helpful to conduct a needs assessment or use surveys of students, teachers or parents to support a new idea or that changes are needed. The grant agency, business or foundation may have a purpose or mission statement. Match your grant's purpose and school's mission statement to the mission of the grant provider. Successful grants include a total team approach, which includes principals, staff, district personnel, students, and parents.

A needs assessment to determine your district's exact needs is helpful.

The goals and objectives section should clearly convey the direction for school improvement. Tie the goals with the needs of the students. Use words such as "increase" and "decrease" in your grant. The goal should directly link to student learning and should link the school's weaknesses or identified weaknesses of a targeted population within your school. It should also be linked to the mission statement of the school and grant provider. Finally, link the goal of the grant to the educational performance standards of the school. After reading the goals, the grant reader should have a picture of what the school or situation will be when the goals are completed.

Objectives within the grant must include a time component, be measurable, realistic, specific, and relevant to the goal. Use an evaluation instrument for each objective and to determine the overall success of the project. Evaluation instruments include, but are not limited to, observation, rubrics, surveys, questionnaires, published assessments, teacher-made tests, statewide or district testing and/ or criterion-reference assessments. There should be a comparison of pre- and posttesting to determine if objectives were met for the overall goal.

SLPs are some of the finest goal and objective writers in the country. We write goals and objectives every time we write Individualized Educational Plans for students. This is where we have an advantage over our fellow educators who often do not know how to write measurable goals/objectives.

The management section of the grant usually includes a timeline, which must make sense. This section should include dates, detailed activities, and periodic assessments within the timeline to ensure success of the grant. The overall vision of the grant should be conveyed in this section for the first year and subsequent years. It is helpful to put the management section in chart form with headers for the following: the date with month and year, activity, connection to the school educational standards, person(s) responsible, and assessment. Grants written with a collaborative effort are the most effective. Be sure to explain the role of each collaborator within the management section of the grant. For example, let the reader know what the teachers will do, what the SLP will do, and what activities they will do together in the grant.

On collaborative grants, be sure to describe each member's exact role.

(continues)

Make sure that you include a dissemination component in the activities section. Businesses and foundations will want to know how you are going to share your grant results. For example, you can consider sharing grant results through newspaper, list serve, district or statewide meetings or workshops. Dissemination is very important to businesses, particularly if you give them local, state or national publicity.

Allow enough time to develop a detailed budget. Obtain the most current quotes or prices from vendors. You will want to have the budget section of the grant reviewed by your district's budget director to determine your district or state's guidelines for budget policies and expenses.

Be sure not to ask for things your school or district should already be supplying

As a grant judge, I turn to the budget page first because I want to know what it is the grantee really wants and whether the need justifies the wants and desires of the grant writer. Be careful to not ask for things that the school or district should already be supplying, i.e. paper, pens, writing tablets, and computers. Basic supplies should not be included in a budget.

It is helpful to secure outside funding sources for your grant proposal, like funding from your Parent/Teacher Organization. If outside funding sources are mentioned in the budget, it tells the grant reader that you are determined to meet your grant proposal and that you have gone to the trouble to find other funding to support the idea. The budget should be set up with the item to be purchased, description of the item, quantity to be purchased, vendor who sells it and the amount it costs. It is helpful to see the budget in table format, if possible. Including the vendor demonstrates to the grant reader that you have searched for specifics. It is also helpful when you secure grant funding to know your vendors when writing your purchase requisitions.

Watch the educational lingo! Use common language. Grant readers do not always include SLPs or educators on judging panels. Someone from the community or a business leader may judge your grant. Abbreviations like IEP, AAC, LD, and ABT have no meaning to these judges. Have someone from the community read your grant before submitting it so that your proposal is understood. Be sure to check for spelling and grammar.

If you want a specific kind of equipment or software, be prepared to fully explain it in the grant need, activities, and in the budget. A grant judge may not be familiar with names of specific products.

A grant reader often looks at the impact of the grant. Power comes in numbers! A grant that will involve 500 students for $2,000 has more of an impact than a grant written for 50 students for $2,000; therefore, the one with greater impact may be funded. Also, a grant with resources that can be used from year to year has advantages over a grant with consumables or a grant that will only last one school year.

Attend workshops or your state or national conference for SLPS. My best ideas have sprung from presentations or discussions among my colleagues at the annual Speech Language and Hearing Conference (SCSHA), the ASHA public school conference or national ASHA conference. If you come back to school enthusiastic from a conference and write a grant based on what was heard, the more likely it is that your principal or coordinator will support your attendance at other conferences—especially if you get a grant proposal funded. Share your grant ideas with others—as I just did! I wish you success on your grant endeavors. Remember—persistence pays! Happy Writing!

Wendy Wingard-Gay
MS CCC/SLP

The final suggestion in Box 8.2 is a good answer to a commonly asked question, "Where do you find good grant proposal topics?" Her advice should be taken seriously by all grant writers. It just makes sense that educators, whose job is about helping students, would want to share their insights and sources with their colleagues everywhere.

Summary

Many novice grant writers tend to begin their grant-writing activities by reaching for a comprehensive list of funding sources. Such a list does exist because all funding agencies are required to report each funded grant. These grants are reported in a document called the *Federal Register*. Hard copies of this document can be found in local libraries, and it is also accessible online. Online access is preferred by most grant writers because new grants are added to this document each week. The *Federal Register* is also helpful because it is a doorway to learning the types of grants and the dollar range of grants made by each grantor, both of which are essential to a successful grant writer. As mentioned in the beginning of this chapter, a user-friendly alternative to the *Federal Register* is www.grants.gov.

But successful grant writing requires more than the names of grant funders. Each funding agency has its own unique purpose for giving money away. Successful grant writing requires the proposal writer to get a "feel" for the funder's reason for funding each grant. Only then can writers locate a funder that matches a particular proposal and tailor each proposal to the funder's mission.

Educational leaders should encourage both small, classroom-improvement grants and larger grants aimed at improving schools and school districts. Grade-level leaders and department chairs should remind their teachers of the need to preface each search for funding sources by alerting their district office, which may know of potential funding sources or other teachers in the district who are pursuing similar grants. **Tip:** To receive maximum benefits, principals, superintendents, and appointed grant directors should *encourage collaboration. Each proposal's potential for getting funded is enhanced when other members of the community are also involved and when multiple agencies are invited to share in the giving of the desired support.* Encourage your teachers to look for support within the local community and at the state and national levels. Another Web site worth checking is www. schoolgrants.org.

RECAP OF MAJOR IDEAS

- Words matter, especially to foundations' evaluators.
- Most foundations have specific areas of interest and are unlikely to fund proposals outside those areas.
- An increasing amount of funded grant money is being channeled into state departments of education.
- Involving multiple funding agencies enhances a grant's potential for being funded.
- Many colleges have partnership grant programs to support local school districts.
- Many schools have parents who are excellent grant writers.

LIST OF TIPS

- Be sure to alert the superintendent's office before writing any grants.
- When writing to foundations, include such words as *collaboration, community, partnerships, impact, replication,* and *sustainability.*
- Study each potential funder's mission, and target your search to funders whose missions reflect your proposal's goals.
- Maintain a current list of potential funders in your community (keep this in your three-ring binder) and get to know their managers.
- Involve parents and other community members in your search and in your grant writing.
- Tap local businesses for support, and solicit their partnerships.

- Contact local colleges and universities to determine whether they have school/university partnership grant programs.
- Involve your local United Way office in your grant search.
- Check your state department of education for any qualifying grants.

- Involve multiple funding agencies in the funding of your grants.
- Make a list of individuals who can be asked to join grant-writing teams (keep in your three-ring binder).

Forming Partnerships

INTRODUCTION

The No Child Left Behind (NCLB) law requires schools to increase their levels of involvement with their communities. Parents must be involved in their children's lessons, and schools must form partnerships with businesses and increase their involvement with other community agencies. The responsibility for initiating and overseeing these alliances belongs to the schools. Tens of millions of dollars have been sent to the states in the form of block grants, allowing the states wide latitude for designing their own request for proposals (RFPs) so that each state's particular needs can be met. Writing for this money offers a special incentive for those familiar with the specific needs most critical to their schools. The sources funding multimillion-dollar grants are favorably disposed toward partnership grants. All this spells out unprecedented opportunities for writing partnership grants.

Sources that fund multimillion-dollar grants favor partnership proposals.

This chapter gives you an inside look at five very different partnership grants. The school districts initiating these grants are located in urban, suburban, and rural areas in different parts of the United States. As you examine each grant, pay particular attention to the needs each proposal purports to meet, the evidence the writers offer to support their claims of the needs, and their strategies for meeting them. Note the proposal writers' strategies for showing how the goals set forward in their proposals will be met and for sustaining the programs once the grant monies are depleted. Look for each proposal's unique features. In other words, put yourself in the position of those who have evaluated these grants. See what they saw and liked enough to put each of these grants above other proposals competing for this money.

As you read this chapter, remember that many of your teachers have never attempted to write a grant. To the beginner, grant writing can be a slippery business. The nature of grant writing is such that you can write or talk about it at great lengths without enabling others to do it successfully.

Sometimes what is needed is a good example, a proposal written for major funding, one carefully crafted and submitted for evaluation, and chosen over its competitors for funding. Each of the following five sections focuses on a separate grant proposal that has met these conditions. Each section points to the strengths of these proposals—the unique features responsible for them being selected over their competition. These unique strengths are qualities that you and *your grant-writing team can include in future proposals.*

As stated previously, grant writing is an unnatural act, and if we are not careful, it can leave novice and would-be grant writers confused. That's why the first grant alluded to early in this book (Chapter 1) was a simple and easy one tailor-made for beginners. But those who are responsible for leading teams of teachers must wade deeper into the lake and discover the awesome power of collaboration and partnerships. To familiarize your teachers with this new experience, you will want to share the five partnership grants that follow. Sage grant writers with dozens of funded grants under their belts will admit that every proposal they write leads to new discoveries about the art of grant writing. Grant writing is an illuminating activity. Throughout this chapter, as each grant is shared, make certain everyone, including your beginning teachers, sees the insights that each author gained from being involved in the grant-writing process.

PROPOSAL 1: EMERGENCY RESPONSE AND CRISIS MANAGEMENT

Cullman County (Alabama) was first inhabited by the Cherokees. The county seat, with the same name, is a pretty little German settlement. Apart from its hospitality, Cullman is known for its Victorian architecture; its Garden River Walk with its bird watching and nature trails; and its Ave Maria Grotto, which sits on a three-acre site with a Benedictine Abbey and 125 miniature reproductions of famous churches, shrines, and other buildings. Cullman County Schools is a rural school district with 28 campuses. The rural nature of these schools has made them vulnerable to unwanted visitors and to the perils of severe weather. In addition to ice storms making the transporting of students hazardous, Cullman County is located in one of the country's major tornado belts, a huge belt reaching from Texas to New York. Due to this combination of threatening conditions, Cullman County School District needed help in its efforts to make its students safe. Understanding the gravity of this need, Cullman County Schools Superintendent Dr. Nancy Horton supported the decision by Heidi Walker, the district grant writer, to apply for a block Emergency Response and Crisis Management grant. The $200,000 request was approved. Following are this grant's Application Checklist, Table of Contents, Program (Proposal) Abstract, Budget Narrative, and Executive Summary Performance Report. A copy of the complete grant is found in Appendix 9.1.

Application Checklist

The application checklist shown in Figure 9.1a is a simple reminder to help applicants guard against accidentally overlooking parts of the proposal. The parts on this checklist are typical of those required for most grants.

Use This Checklist in Preparing the Application Package: (Please Submit This Completed Checklist with Your Application).

✓ Signatures AND details of involvement from law enforcement, public safety, health, mental health, and the chief executive officer (we recommend you use the Partner Certification Requirement provided for the signatures).

✓ An original and three copies of the application are enclosed. Each page of the application is numbered consecutively.

✓ All forms in the original application that require a signature in **black** ink.

✓ Application for Federal Education Assistance (ED Form 424) has been completed according to the instructions and includes the nine-digit DUNS Number and Tax Identification Number.

✓ A one-page project abstract.

✓ A narrative description of the project.

✓ A budget summary page and supporting budget narrative.

✓ All applications must include the required forms, assurances, and certifications. Required forms listed below:

   (1) ED 424—Application for Federal Assistance and Instructions

   (2) ED 524—Budget Information, Non-Construction Programs and Instructions

   (3) SF 424B—Assurances, Non-Construction Programs

   (4) ED80-0013—Certifications Regarding Lobbying; Debarment, Suspension & Other Responsibility Matters; and Drug-Free Workplace Requirements

   (5) ED80-0014—Certification Regarding Debarment, Suspension, Ineligibility & Voluntary Exclusion—Lower Tier Covered Transactions

   (6) SF LLL—Disclosure of Lobbying Activities and Instructions

✓ GEPA Section 427 Requirement.

✓ A copy of the letter to the State Single Point of Contact (see page 28).

FIGURE 9.1a Application Checklist

Table of Contents

This particular grant required a *Table of Contents* specifying the parts shown in Figure 9.1b. As Chapter 5 recommends, even when RFPs do not require the use of a tables of contents, including one is good practice because it helps make the proposal clearer.

Proposal Abstract

As explained in Chapter 5, one of the most important parts of any proposal is the *Program (Proposal) Abstract*. Proposal abstracts should be thought of as the grant writer's best tool for selling each proposal to the evaluators. The Proposal Abstract for the Cullman Community Awareness/Emergency Response Partnership grant is shown in Figure 9.1c. Perhaps you will remember that of all parts in a proposal, the Program Abstract may be your only chance to convince the reviewers that your proposal is worthy of funding because *it may be the only part that gets read*. This makes the contents of this short document extremely important. Notice that this particular Program Abstract begins with a purpose statement that tells what the proposed program purports to achieve. It

I. Title Page—ED form 424

II. Table of Contents

III. Program Abstract

IV. Program Narrative

V. Budget Information—ED 524

VI. Budget Narrative

VII. Appendices

    1. SF 424B—Assurances, Non-Construction Programs

    2. ED80-0013—Certifications Regarding Lobbying; Debarment, Suspension & Other Responsibility Matters; and Drug-Free Workplace Requirements

    3. ED80-0014—Certification Regarding Debarment, Suspension, Ineligibility & Voluntary Exclusion

    4. SF LLL—Disclosure of Lobbying Activities and Instructions

    5. GEPA Section 427 Requirement

    6. State Single Point of Contact Letter

    7. Partnering Agencies

FIGURE 9.1b Table of Contents

Responding to the critical shortage of high school physics teachers, the University of _____ proposes a 10-week summer institute that will better prepare secondary teachers who are now teaching physics, or who anticipate teaching physics this fall, but who lack certification in the area of physics. Each participant will be given a total of 266 contact hours of physics courses, laboratory experiences, tutorials, and seminars, providing students the opportunity to earn 12 semester credit hours.

    During the fall semester, each participant will be visited at his or her own school and provided with an opportunity to ask further questions and to share successes and criticisms of the materials developed in the institute.

FIGURE 9.1c Program (Proposal) Abstract

then tells who will be helped and exactly how they will be helped. The abstract also uses an important buzzword [*rigor*] to talk the talk, and it backs up this promise with exact numbers (12 semester credit hours). This short abstract achieves still another purpose: It tells how the program director plans to evaluate the success of this program.

Budget Narrative

One remaining proposal part was singled out in Chapter 5 as being of paramount importance to all grant proposals—the *Budget Narrative*. Because grant writing is all about money, the proposal evaluators are going to want to see exactly how you plan to spend their money. Making this crystal clear to the reviewers is your responsibility. Your tool for accomplishing this is the Budget Narrative, shown in Figure 9.1d. Most program grants are primarily training grants, and normally, the largest expenditures in training grants are salaries. But this is primarily an equipment grant; therefore, the major expenditure is

Personnel $5,000

These funds will be used to provide an interpreter at school functions and to hire a person to translate all safety documents into the native language of non-English-speaking students.

Fringe Benefits $635

These funds will be used to pay retirement (5.02%), FICA (6.2%), Medicare (1.45%), and unemployment compensation (0.02%) for personnel.

Travel $12,000

These funds will be used to pay travel expenses of the Superintendent and her designee to attend all meetings required through this grant. These funds will also be used for teacher participation in workshops and conferences dealing with school safety, emergency response, and crisis management.

Equipment $106,400

These funds will be used to pay for the following equipment to be used in improving safety on all Cullman County School campuses:

- Communication radios—Radios will be placed at 12 campuses at the cost of $1,500 per site.
- Surveillance equipment—Surveillance systems that will be linked with the Central Office and the Sheriff's Department will be placed at the seven high schools and will also serve related middle and elementary schools at the rate of $4,200 per site. Five cameras will be placed at each site at the rate of $200 per camera for a total of $7,000.
- An identification system to create badges for all employees of the Cullman County School System will be purchased for $10,000.
- Laptop computers for housing student records will be purchased for each of the 28 Cullman County School campuses at the rate of $1,500 per computer.

Supplies $22,400

These funds will be used to purchase supplies needed to provide each teacher with an emergency action kit. These funds will also be used to provide medical kits at each school. Furthermore, these funds will be used to develop printed materials used to inform parents about safety procedures at each school.

Contractual $5,000

These funds will be used to pay for consultants who are specialists in the field of school safety and emergency response/crisis management to conduct workshops for Cullman County School personnel.

Other $5,000

These funds will be used for public relations and to cover expenses incurred during team meetings.

Indirect Costs $3,896

Indirect costs for the system are calculated at the current rate of 2.09%.

Training Stipends $30,000

Training stipends will be used for teacher stipends for summer workshops dealing with school safety and emergency response/crisis management.

*We considered the 18-month grant to be one grant cycle. Please notify us if the budget needs to be broken down further.

FIGURE 9.1d Budget Narrative

equipment. Nevertheless, personnel training is important for using this equipment, so this budget includes a substantial stipulation of money for training.

It is worth noting that this grant requires periodic progress reports. Had the amount of dollars requested been half-a-million dollars or more, the district would have been visited each year by a team of auditors. Seeing this part of the proposal is a reminder that the work isn't over with the announcement of the award—in fact, it just shifts gears. For multiyear grants, the steps you choose to take in this higher gear will determine whether you will receive funds from this grant in future years. But this is no cause for alarm. Experienced grant writers view this as an opportunity to prove to the evaluators that their initial investment in this proposal was a wise decision, and nobody understands how this program works better than you do. This is, indeed, an exciting step in the grant-writing process because what you do now will determine how successful your program will be in reaching your initial goals.

When a proposal is funded, the work isn't over. In fact, it shifts gears.

You may be asking questions such as: What if I discover a more effective way to execute part of the proposal? Or what if we experience personnel changes requiring additional funds to hire the services of new people? Will I be able to shift part of the budget to adjust for these changes? Most grants do provide some flexibility. But you will never have total flexibility, and just how much you do have will be determined by the guidelines set for your particular block of grants.

Executive Summary Performance Report

By now, hopefully, you are curious to learn just how successful this grant has become. An *Executive Summary Performance Report* for this grant is shown in Figure 9.1e. By perusing this report, you will see that continuous tweaking has taken place as additional ways to increase the program's effectiveness have been discovered. This is a very natural development as the implementation proceeds. **Tip:** *The best grant writers usually discover ways to make the process more effective.* The grant has provided Palm Pilots for the principals, and surveillance cameras and visitor badges for the campuses. The grant also led to a well-planned and articulated system of procedures to be followed in the event of different types of emergencies. Of particular importance is the fact that this proposal began with a survey. A simple questionnaire is a powerful tool for gathering quantitative data. In this case, these data produced convincing evidence of the need the district had for the requested support. Steps for designing and using questionnaires are shared in Chapter 10.

A simple one-page questionnaire is a powerful tool for gathering quantitative data.

Lessons Learned from the Emergency Response and Crisis Management Grant

• Staying alert to major national legislation and national concerns pays off to grant writers who build these factors into their grants.

• A checklist is helpful to prevent accidental omission of proposal parts.

• Surveys are excellent tools for gathering quantitative data to convince evaluators of your district's needs and that your proposed program will be effective.

• A notice of grant approval signals that it is time to begin making your grant reach its goals. It is also time to take steps to ensure reapproval of your grant.

• All block grants offer some flexibility, the amount of which will vary with each block of grants.

U. S. Department of Education
Grant Performance Report (ED 524B)
Figure 9.1e Executive Summary

OMB No. 1890-0004
Exp. 10-31-2007

PR/ Number # (11 characters) Q184L040175

(See Instructions)

This is a performance report for grant award #Q184E030309. This 18-month grant focuses on Emergency Response and Crisis Management. This submission is for reporting period 9-30-03–3-31-05.

The Cullman County School System is a rural Alabama school system that services 28 schools, almost 10,000 students grades K–12, and spans a large geographic area. One of the primary goals of the management plan is to increase effective communication among the campuses, between the Central Office and the campuses, and between the school campuses and the over 100 buses that transport students. Each of the 28 campuses now has a base station that provides for continual and reliable communication with the Central Office and with the buses that service those schools. In the past, in the event of inclement weather or other emergencies, it has been very difficult to reach schools by telephone in order to inform them of emergencies and emergency measures to be taken. The base stations and two-way radios on school buses have eliminated that problem.

Another primary goal of the plan is to provide an effective and portable way to track students in the event of an emergency when students must leave the regular assigned classroom and move to a secure location, whether in terms of inclement weather, bomb threat, or other emergency. Palm Pilots and the accompanying STI (attendance software) have been purchased for each principal. Student schedules, emergency phone numbers, limitations on who may have access to the child, and other pertinent data will now be in the custody of the principal at the secure location providing for reliable tracking of the students.

In response to another need for Cullman County Schools, an identification badge system has been purchased and every employee of Cullman County Schools has been entered into the computer system, along with his or her picture, the school or department location, and the assignment. Those badges will be distributed to the employees at the beginning of the next school year with the requirement that they be worn at all times when on a school campus or at the Central Office. In addition, official visitors badges will be required of any and all visitors to the campuses or the Central Office.

Cullman County is fortunate to have available a resource officer for each school site. Workshops are planned for the summer months for resource officers, principals, and Central Office staff to completely review and update emergency procedures for each campus. A standardized, color-coded flip chart will be printed during the summer to make available to each teacher and all support staff.

Cullman County is situated in rural Alabama and many parents and guardians work in areas that are a great distance from the schools their children attend. In the event of an emergency closing, it is very difficult to contact all parents or guardians to inform them of the closing. After careful research, the school district purchased a 3-year contract with School Reach, a parent notification system. We chose this system because there were no requirements for computer support or software support since the system is housed at School Reach's offices. This is a user-friendly, very effective method of reaching parents for a variety of reasons. Alabama has

FIGURE 9.1e   Executive Summary Performance Report (*continues*)

implemented a new truancy notification policy, and this system has afforded us the ability to make multiple calls and to track those calls, without using valuable personnel time. The system did experience difficulty in fully implementing the program the first year because of a state-mandated attendance software change. This change created massive problems in our schools, and our principals and attendance officers were overwhelmed by the software errors in the new system. For that reason, some of our emergency data was corrupted and we experienced a number of problems in getting the correct data in the correct format to School Reach. We were able to overcome those issues, and schools are now using the call system. Actually, a positive came from the experience in that schools were forced to update emergency information on all students, so we are now more confident in that data.

After surveying teachers, we discovered that 193 classrooms in Cullman County Schools had no way of contacting the office in the event of an emergency or a safety incident. We were able to address that issue through use of the grant funds, and now 100% of our classrooms and outlying buildings are able to contact the office immediately.

Cullman County is fortunate to have seven school resource officers who are assigned to the major school sites. The presence of those officers and their contributions to the students and faculty is important and has been instrumental in preventing problems before they occur. The district has partnered with the sheriff's department and has hired a supervisor for those officers. The sheriff provides a car and equipment to the officer, and the school district provides the salary. The grant funds defrayed a portion of that cost. Deputy Cook has provided safety training and is available to be of service to the school safety coordinator. In addition, the superintendent and the sheriff are scheduled to attend safety training in September 2005. The district will then send a team of individuals to do follow-up training on the incident command system. It has been determined that further work needs to be done on our crisis response plan, and that team will be instrumental in helping to improve that plan.

In association with the resource officers, Cullman County has implemented a school safety hotline. This hotline is available to callers who wish to remain anonymous, but who have information that they believe to be important to the safety and well-being our students. Plans are underway to create a series of videos, featuring students, that will encourage students to inform law enforcement officials or school officials if they are aware of any student who poses a threat or who is a potential threat to himself or to others. The videos will be shown to all students and all students will be encouraged to help maintain a safe environment.

After attending the conferences provided in Washington D.C. and in Denver, Colorado, the superintendent recognized the need to provide a comprehensive plan of each school site to law enforcement and to emergency personnel. Aerial photographs of each school site, scanned and saved to scale were taken of each school site. Those photographs, along with the Incident Command System Plan and other pertinent information, are being saved to computer disks that will be housed at the school, at the sheriff's department, at the emergency management agency, and at the central office. In the event of an emergency, the school safety coordinator will have immediate access to the CD and will be able to make sound decisions based on information at the tip of his fingers. A laptop computer was purchased that is dedicated to that one purpose, so the safety coordinator will be prepared in the case of any emergency at any site. The fourteen major sites encompass all schools.

FIGURE 9.1e Executive Summary Performance Report (*continues*)

Another area that we were able to address because of funds from this grant, was providing defibrillators to all campuses and two at large sites where the field house or the band room was at a great distance from where the defibrillators that already were in place were housed. This need took a personal note to our system when the husband of one of our principals was saved because of quick response to his massive heart attack. The health teachers at each high school site are trained to be CPR trainers and they are undergoing training to be defibrillator trainers as well. Our goal is that every Cullman County employee be trained in CPR and in the use of the defibrillators.

Because of the training we received in Denver, and because the grant afforded us opportunities to pursue avenues we never would have been able to afford, we have learned a great deal about prevention, mitigation, response, and recovery. Cullman County Schools greatly appreciates the effort on the part of those people who guided us through this process and who gave us permission to make changes when we recognized that the funds could be spent in ways other than what we had originally intended. We are still in the planning and learning stages, but we are far past what we were in terms of effective communication in the event of an emergency. We quickly realized that communication and ground work plans were where we needed to focus our efforts and that is what we attempted to do.

FIGURE 9.1e Executive Summary Performance Report

PROPOSAL 2: CLASSROOMS FOR THE FUTURE

When Greenville High School's Principal John Ziegler learned from the Pennsylvania State Department of Education Web site that Governor Rendell had proposed as part of his Budget Address on February 8, 2006, a 3-year initiative called *Classrooms for the Future*, John knew he wanted to give his students a state-of-the-art, technology-based program that would change their lives. The program would couple interactive and wireless technologies with training that would transform teaching-and-learning-across-the-school-curriculum that would enhance teaching methods and student motivation to raise academic learning at his school to an unprecedented level. But suspecting that in addition to learning about the specifics of this proposal, you would also want to learn about the qualities causing the evaluators to choose his proposal, I asked John why he believed that his proposal was funded. In Figure 9.2, he tells his success story in his own words.

The proposal can be seen in its entirety in Appendix 9.2. As you read John's story, look for the following **tips:**

• You can and should learn from both your successes and your failures.

• You must make your proposal clear, not only to yourself but also to the reviewers.

You must make your proposal clear, not only to yourself but also to the reviewers.

• Don't stir in your responses to the RFP throughout the proposal as if you were mixing *ragu* into a pot of spaghetti; put your answers in bite-sized pieces, and put these pieces in the order in which the RFP asks for them.

• When you learn your proposal is accepted, immediately begin the research required to make the format simple and the information powerful.

> *"I witnessed the power of collective energies that flow from a diverse team of people with the common goal of serving others."*
> *—John Ziegler*

I am John Ziegler, and I have written a number of grants over my 36 years in public education. Something I had to learn to fully understand is that grants or *requests for funding need to be written so that the reader, in contrast to the author, can quickly understand what the author is proposing and can easily score the proposal against predetermined selection criteria.* I recall once having written a compliance report and a grant for the Pennsylvania Department of Education. The reviewers from the state department were in the area and were kind enough to stop by and explain why both the report and the grant were turned down. After an hour of trying to justify and tell them that the information they requested was in both documents, I finally said, "It's like Ragu, it's in there!" The sauce and my analogy they understood, but they still wanted me to *break down the information into bite-size pieces and answer their questions in the order they were asked, providing the exact level of specificity requested.* By the end of the conversation, the reviewers agreed to give me an extension for submitting the compliance report, but the grant remained unfunded. The moral of this vignette for prospective grant writers is to make the format simple and the information powerful.

As a result of this experience, I made it a point that when applying for grants to provide the information in an easy to-read numbered format that addressed the particular questions asked and listed the exact information requested. My stepped preparation was to research the topic, collectively generate a vision for the future, and align the school's academic and technology standards to the goals, objectives, activities, and evaluative criteria used throughout the project. An action-packed timeline and a budget sensitive to realistic needs rounded out the format.

After getting all the groundwork done, I met with many people to discuss the action plan and seek their support. Each draft of the grant proposal appeared like a persuasive essay in itself and involved a great deal of thinking and writing. I finalized my draft proposals by reading them several times to correct vague areas, typographical errors, and grammatical errors, and by asking colleagues to review the proposal. Understandably, this was not my project alone; it was a collaborative act. I took responsibility for authoring the grant and, for that reason, collected information from students, parents, faculty, technology technicians, librarians, and fellow administrators. However, in so doing, I witnessed again the power of collaborative energies that flow from a diverse team of people with a common goal and willingness to serve others.

From these sharing activities, I collected and listed the details to each section that demonstrated a well-thought-out project, eventually weaving the wishes of the CFF (Classrooms for the Future) Leadership Team into the final proposal. For example, many funding entities expect your proposals to clearly state your plans to evaluate the results of the project before you make a decision; several entities expect you to state that a formal outcome-based evaluation will be conducted and forwarded to the entity at the end of the project. Conversations about the evaluative nature of the project drew much discussion and helped bring clarity to the outcomes we expected to serve as milestones and indicators of success.

Author's note: John's proposal was accepted and approved for $439,000 (2006–2009).

FIGURE 9.2   It's Like Ragu

Here are three additional **tips** provided by John's grant:

• Take responsibility for writing your proposal draft.

• Share your draft with all stockholders, and carefully weave their input and their desires into each future rewrite.

• Engulf yourself and your partners so thoroughly into your dream that no evaluation team member could resist the opportunity to become part of it.

PROPOSAL 3: PROJECT ELEMENTARY AND SECONDARY COMPETENCY APPROACH TO PERFORMANCE EDUCATION (ESCAPE)

It was early December and Sandy Brooks was barely out of her doctoral program. She had moved 500 miles to take her first higher education teaching position at a Midwestern university, choosing this position over several others because it provided ready access to a mainframe computer, a half-time editor for the faculty's use (just wishful thinking at most universities), and the opportunity to work with a nationally known professor in the department, a prolific writer who enjoyed sharing his expertise by teaching a course to the faculty titled, *Writing for Professional Publication.*

Having received a doctoral degree in curriculum and research, and having the level of optimism characterizing most recent graduates, Sandy was determined to create a better teacher education program than anyone had ever seen. She wanted a very different program, and if her wants were granted, this program would be totally field based; all the pedagogy would occur, not on the university campus, but in elementary and secondary classrooms. A second major condition for this new program was that it would be totally performance based.

So, Sandy checked with the university's office of grants and contracts to locate a potential funder for a performance-based, school-based, teacher education program. The news was disappointing; no known source was funding experimental performance-based higher education programs. She then talked to her new colleagues, who found her idea interesting but knew of no possible funding sources for such a program.

Sandy's school had a nice teachers' lounge where professors often retreated between classes for a quick cup of coffee to prime themselves for their next class. As she sat quietly, enjoying a moment of silence and a good cup of hot coffee, two colleagues entered the room, barely acknowledging Sandy's presence because they were engrossed in their own conversation. One was telling the other about a new teacher burnout program he had heard was coming to the local schools through block grants. That last word was enough to get Sandy's full attention. As these colleagues talked, Sandy quietly sipped her coffee and listened. The purpose of the forthcoming grant money was to design programs to rejuvenate teachers who were experiencing emotional burnout.

As the discussion continued, Sandy thought about her desire to create a performance-based, school-based teacher education program, wondering whether the new teacher burnout program and her personal dream for a model teacher education program might, in some way, be connected. Being an early riser, Sandy was fortunate to have her teaching load in the mornings, freeing her afternoons for conducting research, preparing lessons, and taking care of other professional responsibilities, including grant writing. The next morning Sandy taught her classes, went directly to her car, and drove to the state capitol, where she began asking about the proposed teacher burnout program. Sandy wasn't professionally mature enough to solicit the help of her legislators, but she had one powerful force on her side, persistence. Sandy was determined to have her model teacher education program.

The state department of education office had both good news and bad news. The good news was the rumor was true—money had been appropriated to support teacher burnout research. However, the bad news was that the money was earmarked, not for universities, but for elementary and secondary schools. She could handle this; she would write the grant for the local school district and submit it through the district. The further less-than-good news was that the request for proposals (RFP) had already been issued, and it had a short deadline. The job was too big for an individual to do alone in the time available. In retrospect, for an inexperienced individual or even an inexperienced group of writers, it wasn't very realistic. Fortunately, Sandy was too inexperienced to realize the odds she was facing. Even if she had known the slim chances for success, she was probably too determined and self-assured to be deterred by these odds. All she knew for sure was that if she didn't try, she was certain not to have her dreams become a reality. Even with an outside chance, the only way to meet this challenge was to locate some interested partners willing to work on a grant proposal through part of their Christmas break. Still determined, Sandy located three equally inexperienced colleagues who agreed to spend part of their holidays preparing a grant proposal.

Suggestion: If your school does not have its own organized grant-writing team, examine your workplace. Determine whether your teachers have a coffee room or a lunch group; a golf, racquet ball, or other exercise group; or a civic club where they can gather ideas for research project topics, or, as in this case, a place where they might learn of funding opportunities. If so, select one of these group gatherings to routinely discuss your creative ideas, and keep an ongoing record of the positive or negative reactions of your colleagues. Should you choose to lead your teachers to collaborate on a proposal, this record will help you identify colleagues who share your commitments. Advise your teachers to spend more time gathering data and writing grants than talking about their grants.

Provide your teachers a place to discuss their ideas, but advise them to spend more time collecting data and writing grants than talking about their grants.

Purpose of the Proposal

The proposed program was not created to replace the existing, traditional teacher education program; rather, it was aimed at a small cohort of exceptionally bright students who sought to escape the traditional route to teacher education, and students who would prefer to develop their pedagogical skills in elementary and secondary classrooms. As with all successful grant-proposal writing, this team's own professional and personal goals had to become secondary to the potential funders' goals. According to this RFP, the Department of Education's goal was to reduce the level of teacher burnout in elementary and secondary schools throughout the state. So, to be competitive, a proposal had to proclaim reduction of teacher burnout as its *paramount goal*, and this team of writers would have to devise a method to convince the evaluators that the proposed program would meet this goal.

The program would not purport to erase all teacher burnout in the state; instead, it would identify a manageable number of highly competent teachers who just happened to be experiencing burnout. Deciding that a manageable number of participants would be 50 teachers, the team settled on 25 elementary school teachers and 25 secondary school teachers.

These novice grant writers had heard that sometimes the best proposals are not always the ones selected for funding, but they did not know if this was true. The rumor is 100% true; sometimes some of the best proposals are over-looked. The most important thing this team knew was that *each proposal accepted for funding is selected because it is different* from the others; it has one or more qualities to make it stand out above the many other competing proposals. Because this was about all the inexperienced writers had working for them, they knew that to give their proposal any chance at all they had better use this knowledge well. Somehow, they had to make certain their proposed program had some unique features that the evaluators would view as strengths.

Each funded proposal has one or more unique qualities that make it stand out from the competition.

In a sense, this program would be unique because it was performance based. Sandy knew the evaluators would probably consider this to be desirable because performance-based programs were becoming popular and performance-based assessment was being proposed for all schools. But she also knew this uniqueness might not be enough; after all, some of the other proposals might also be performance based. This experience illustrates the need all grant writers have to read the journals and *stay apprised of the many trends in education.*

A REJUVENATION PROGRAM.   When choosing unique qualities for your own proposals, it is important that you *keep your attention on the purpose of the program, not your desires but the funder's purpose as stated in the RFP.* Sandy's own personal purpose for this proposal was to develop a superior, performance-based model for a teacher education program, one her college and other colleges could use to prepare future teachers. But, to Sandy's knowledge, the evaluators for this program weren't at all interested in *her* goal; they wanted a program that would eliminate some of the teacher burnout, which was pervasive in elementary and secondary schools throughout the state. These writers would find a way to jump-start those teachers who had emotionally burned out. [Author's note: Teacher burnout is still a major problem. Half of all teachers in the United States leave the profession within their first 5 years.]

Keep your attention not on your desires but on the desires of the funder.

The team researched the literature related to the funder's goal—teacher burnout—and discovered that there was agreement in the literature (which means they found at least two articles that agreed) that the point at which most teachers experience the most burnout is during their sixth or seventh year. So, they said so, citing these articles. **Tip:** *Citing current journal articles, books, and research has value in itself; it earns the evaluators' confidence,* reassuring them they are entrusting their money to individuals who are knowledgeable and current in their fields, and who are willing to put forth the energy required to substantiate their work. Citing references also suggests that the proposal writers are thorough, reassuring the evaluators that if this proposal is chosen for funding, these writers will make the extra effort needed to ensure their project succeeds.

SETTING GROUND RULES.   Keeping the potential funders' central purpose in mind, the writers decided to design a program to rejuvenate teachers who were experiencing high levels of burnout. They were careful to specify that the teachers chosen would be exceptionally talented. This served their grant proposal well because many of their competitors were building a case only on the basis of their *needs* (a common mistake among grant writers). Sandy and her team were basing their program, not on their *needs*, but on their *strengths.* Remember that some investigators (grant writers) believe the prize goes to the school district with the greatest needs. But people like to identify with winners, and people like to invest in winners, so this proposal would have the markings of a winner throughout.

So far, it sounds as though the collaborators were in perfect agreement on all issues. Actually, nothing could be further from the truth. They were the clumsiest collection of individual thinkers imaginable, and this will be revealed later; however, they were congenial, and they used their different points of view to strengthen their program.

No member of a grant-writing team should be allowed to disrupt the team's progress. The best interest of the team must prevail.

Too often, teams fall apart when they learn they cannot agree on all issues. Actually, differences can be helpful if managed appropriately. Once a decision to collaborate has been reached, the leader should immediately call a meeting to plan and organize the strategy for this group. During this first meeting, all members should agree to express their feelings and beliefs *and then go with the majority*; unanimity is not necessary. If the group has a member who is known for being argumentative, or a member who has a record of writing minority reports, then you must persuade that member to either be more cooperative or leave the group. Perhaps you can offer to give the teacher individual help on personal grants. No matter how excited that member may be over the proposed grant topic, *the best interest of the team must prevail.* From the onset, the group agreed to let all members express their preferences on every issue, but the majority also agreed to let no member impede the progress of the proposal. The majority would always rule!

Through surveying the literature, they learned that other performance-based programs used modules to develop the desired skills. Knowing that modules were an effective way to develop teaching skills, they chose to use modules in their program. Modules provide a way to ensure that the program has clear objectives and activities to cover all objectives. To teach their teachers and students about modules, they even wrote a module on modules. See Appendix 9.3. Sandy's team also knew the value in shared ownership; people work harder when they perceive the project as theirs, not a job to be done for somebody else. Because they had chosen to use the best teachers, it seemed to make sense to give them a lot of leeway. These were the brightest of the bright and the best of the best, so Sally wanted to use their talents and, at the same time, give them ownership in the program. People will work hard to succeed in a program they perceive to be their own.

Unlike other performance-based programs, which were written by professors and research and development (R&D) experts, these writers decided to trust their teachers to write the modules. They went a step further. Unlike other performance-based programs they found in their review of the literature, whose objectives and topics were chosen by professors and R&D teams, they decided to let their teachers choose the topics for their modules. This was a good decision because it increased member ownership; however, the decision to put the teachers in charge of the writing was flawed because most of the teachers had far worse writing skills than the team had envisioned. The team simply began by telling the teachers they had been chosen for this program because their respective principals had identified them as being among the best-of-the-best teachers in their respective schools. The team asked the teachers to individually reflect on their teaching and identify one or two areas they might choose if they could improve even more. Would they improve their classroom management skills? Testing skills? Motivational skills? For their module topics, teachers could choose an area of individual weakness, or they could choose to develop a model that focused on and would teach future teachers their greatest strengths.

To avoid duplication, the team made a comprehensive list of all identified areas and matched individual teachers with one of their top preferences. Each topic would become a learning module, which would immediately improve the skills of the teacher who developed it, and the grant writers would develop a dissemination plan to ensure these models would eventually impact teachers throughout the state. Any doubt that teaching is an art will quickly be dispelled by looking at the list of modules these teachers chose (Appendix 9.4).

After 6 months, news that their proposal had been selected for funding arrived. Unfortunately, Sandy was teaching a 3-week comparative education course in London, England. She returned on Saturday, checked her mail, and found both good and bad news. The good news was the proposal had been selected above all the competition for funding; the bad news was the program was to start full time at eight o'clock on Monday morning, leaving the team only 1 day to prepare! Naturally, all the writers panicked, and their naysayer voices spoke: "There's no way we can do this on such short notice." "We don't even have a meeting room." "Half these teachers have probably left town for the holidays; how will we reach them?" "We don't even have a program to follow."

An important and often overlooked advantage of grants is they provide opportunities to do things differently, things otherwise impossible. Another overlooked advantage is that every funded grant is loaded with learning opportunities. The common expression, "Every grant you write is easier than the one before" is true—at least, it is true for alert participants who note and record their successes and failures.

CURRENT ISSUES. Each graduate of the program was promised certification. The summer would be spent writing modules. Each teacher would carefully compute an estimate of the number of hours required to complete the module. The module would then be assigned a number of credits. For example, modules requiring 45 or more hours to complete would earn 3 credit hours of coursework.

Every grant you write is easier than the one you wrote before.

Some modules were required of all students because they were based on content either required for graduation or for teacher certification. For example, all students in this program had to successfully complete the module on classroom management and the module on testing. The state also required a minimum number of credits in pedagogy, so each student had to complete enough modules to earn the minimum number of credits. Having completed these required modules, the student could then choose the preferred modules to earn the remaining credits. This enabled the students to ESCAPE the normal routine on campus, thus the acronym ESCAPE (Elementary and Secondary Competency Approach to Performance Education).

DISSEMINATION. When grant money is appropriated by federal, state, or local governments, the evaluators look for *assurance that the funded programs will serve the largest number of individuals possible*. **Tip:** Knowing this, you

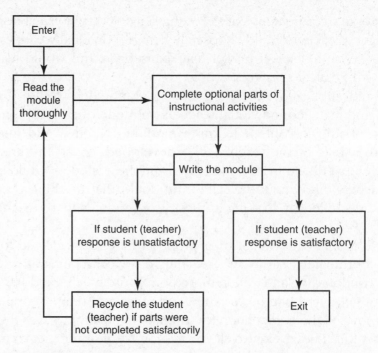

FIGURE 9.3   Sample Flowchart

can give your proposal a boost *by explaining how large numbers of people will benefit from your proposed program.* Wanting their project to benefit more teachers than the 50 who were directly involved in writing the modules, these granters put stipulations on each module they produced. Knowing that many teachers would be bored by a lot of reading assignments, they required each module to have a corresponding videotape. So that other teachers to tempt to use these modules, they required each module to have a flowchart, providing easy-to-follow steps for its application.

As seen earlier, Figure 9.3 is an example of the flowchart designed for one of the modules. Notice this particular flowchart provides its unsuccessful users an opportunity to recycle until they succeed. This is a strong quality that can be planned into any module. This module was designed to be the first module required of all students in Project ESCAPE. It served to prepare them to follow and use the other modules.

You must show how many students and other community members your program will impact.

A word that expresses the goal of dissemination is *impact.* You disseminate your grant so it will affect as many others as possible. Tahoe educator Cindy Brown wisely uses the concept of *impact* to get her proposals funded. "I approached the Foundation for the entire amount asking them to consider the impact the Freedom Writer would have on our community. I cited the gang activity, the segregated classes, the tension between races, and the kids who had just given up on themselves. The Foundation helped with most of the cost. The rest came from other service clubs in Tahoe. The whole event grew from the middle school to the high school and, finally, to a night presentation for families. All of the events were well attended and very moving."

Lessons Learned from Project ESCAPE

As mentioned previously, although you can never be guaranteed that a good proposal will be funded, the grant writer who uses the tips set forth in this book can significantly improve the probability of acceptance, and can learn from successes and failures associated with each proposal. Following is a list of **tips** that emerged from writing the grant titled Project ESCAPE:

- Flexibility is essential.
- The desires of the funder must take precedence over the proposal writer's needs.
- Grant writers should remain alert at all times, listening for new funding opportunities.
- The probability of a proposal's acceptance can be increased by including unique features in each proposal.
- Persistence can turn roadblocks into highways of success.
- The roles of collaborators should be spelled out clearly before the project begins.
- To be competitive, each proposal must have unique features.
- Citing current and recent references in books and journals can and will strengthen your proposal.
- Showing exactly how the product will be disseminated for the use of others enhances a proposal's success.
- Disagreement among collaborators can improve a proposal if the partners can express their differences and move onward.

PROPOSAL 4: THE SUMMER PHYSICS INSTITUTE

As discussed in Chapter 1, grant writing has many benefits, which differ from one grant writer to another, depending on the professional and personal goals of each. Successful grant writing requires knowing what benefits you most want to derive from each grant. A major benefit, perhaps even the most important of all, is the self-satisfaction grants can provide by enabling you to help others.

Having grown up in a rural area, Jack Rhodes attended a small, two-room elementary school with three grades in each room. His elementary schooling was second to none. The smallness of the classes, the integrated program, and outstanding teachers made a perfect combination.

By today's standards, the school Jack attended for his second 6 years of schooling was also small, with only 46 in his graduating class. Unlike his elementary school years, the smallness of his high school had a serious disadvantage—the curriculum was extremely limited. As a lover of both sports and music, Jack found the absence of a football team and a band at his small, rural school a major handicap. Later, in college, he would discover that for a student who preferred science and mathematics over other subjects, the absence of a foreign language, particularly Latin, was a major disadvantage. The proverbial straw was broken when, in his senior year, Jack was told that the limited curriculum offerings in his small high school would not allow him to take both advanced science and advanced mathematics. At the beginning of his senior year, he refused to choose between taking advanced science and advanced math, *and*, instead, transferred to a larger school with a more diversified curriculum.

After becoming a teacher of science and mathematics, and later returning to his home state to work as a teacher educator, Jack began writing grants to help improve the educational opportunities of others. Rumor was that his state, like all others, was passing legislation to provide block grants for universities to improve the knowledge and teaching skills of the state's high school teachers of mathematics, chemistry, and physics. Jack quickly contacted his dean of arts and sciences. Because his dean was a chemist, Jack proposed they collaborate on two grant proposals; his dean would take the lead and be the principal investigator on a chemistry grant proposal, and Jack would do the same on a physics proposal. Because each state was limited to only one grant in each discipline, winning either grant would require writing the best proposal in the state. The chemistry proposal was rejected, but their physics proposal was accepted.

Knowing they could not directly improve the knowledge and skills of all physics teachers in the state, they focused on those teachers who had little or no background in physics. They proposed to identify 10 very bright teachers who had taken little or no coursework in physics and yet had signed contracts to teach physics in the fall. The grant would enable them to bring these teachers to campus for summer institutes in physics. Their goal was to improve their knowledge of physics and their pedagogical knowledge and skills.

Many individuals are so discouraged because they know they have limitations that permanently dissuaded them from writing grants. But by looking at our limitations, we can often turn them into strengths, bringing substantial strengths to our grant proposals. Reflect on your own background, and identify some of your major limitations. Can you think of a way to use them to strengthen your future grant proposals?

While your competition is using buzzwords to make their proposal "talk to talk," you must take this process and make your proposal "walk the walk."

TALKING THE TALK. The fact that money was being provided to improve science and math teaching skills at a time when the nation's teachers were being criticized for students' low standardized test scores in science and math was no coincidence. The most common adjective found in the many education reform reports and articles was *rigor*. The writers were saying our teacher education programs preparing science and mathematics teachers lacked rigor. Jack used this knowledge and made the proposed program very rigorous. Each summer, each participant would take a full 12 semester hours of physics. This would be a heavy load, indeed, but these were especially gifted teachers. Instead of just "talking the talk" about rigor, this project turned the talk into real program improvements; this program would also "walk the walk."

UNIQUE FEATURES. Through having had previous proposals funded, Jack knew that to be seriously considered for funding, a proposal has to get the attention of the evaluators. Gaining their attention required a proposal to have one or more unique features. He reasoned that if one unique feature would help their proposal get funded, several would almost make it a shoo-in. This proposal would definitely have several unique features including (1) being highly rigorous, (2) having a special course taught by a special teacher, (3) having a very nontraditional and motivating weekly seminar, (4) being loaded with laboratory experiences requiring no expensive materials or equipment, and (5) having a special evaluation system occurring at a unique time.

A SPECIAL COURSE. Most of the coursework in this program would be standard physics courses, but the program would also have a very unique course on pedagogy for physics teachers. Instead of the common courses on generic teaching methods or science methods, this course would be a special treat for teachers who were faced daily with challenging physics problems at the end of each chapter in their high school physics textbooks. Even the textbook for this course would be special; unlike the books used in other college classes, it would not be a college text at all but would be the state-adopted textbook for high school physics classes. Once each week the participants in this summer institute would have the unusual opportunity of seeing an expert work the problems at the end of each chapter.

The physics department had 17 full-time faculty members, and any of them could have worked these problems with little effort, but the program developers decided to use none. The current literature had many articles on *master teachers*. To the layperson, and consequently to legislators, this term had a good ring. Of course, everyone should want all elementary and secondary classrooms staffed with master teachers. They took advantage of this knowledge and hired a local high school physics teacher who had earned the title *master teacher*. Each week this teacher would leave her school for 3 hours to come to the university and work the problems at the end of the chapters in her high school physics text. What a treat for inadequately prepared teachers who were struggling with many of these problems, trying to stay just one step ahead of their students. What a boost for a proposal!

As a sidebar, it is interesting that although the evaluators really liked the idea of using a *master teacher*, and although this unique feature undoubtedly played a major role in their decision to fund this proposal, after one summer they decided to replace this highly competent teacher because the program participants refused to give her the respect and cooperation they gave to college professors. If Jack and his team members were starting all over from the beginning, would they include the high school master teacher? Indeed, they would; using buzzwords of the day pays off. Another group of teachers might have responded differently. Anyhow, the first objective of grant writers must be to have a good idea, and the second is to always sell this idea to the evaluators. They believe the master teacher component was a major factor in getting this proposal accepted.

Chapter 7 advises that too much ill advice is given to grant writers regarding the need to use jargon and other unfamiliar language; yet, like the previously discussed teacher burnout proposal, this proposal is aimed at getting funds established by legislators, and legislators do pay an inordinate amount of attention to the buzzword language their constituents use. The one thing these writers did differently is they not only used the language, *master teacher*, but they also actually *used* a master teacher. Encourage your teachers to use plenty of unique strengths to capture the evaluators' attention. Suppose the evaluators had overlooked the fact that the program "walked the walk" with the use of rigor. The actual use of a master teacher was a second chance to get recognized for "walking the walk."

A WEEKLY SEMINAR. As discussed previously, effective grant writers learn to keep one eye on the RFP, being careful to respond to every part, while keeping the other eye on their own resources—what they have to offer that the competitors do not (or do not think about offering). Perhaps the most overlooked strength a university or school district has is its human resources. Because their university was large and diverse, it was rich with human resources. These grant writers wanted to bring these resources to the bargaining table, so they developed a weekly seminar.

Each Friday, the participants and the codirectors of the institute had lunch together in a dormitory cafeteria. After a leisurely hour-long period of eating and socializing, they all walked together to meet a special member of the university faculty who had volunteered to give them a special seminar. Jack was careful to invite professors who had topics he knew would have high interest for high school physics teachers. Among the many excellent speakers was a physics professor whose specialty was robotics. He brought to the seminar a robot he had designed and built. The robot performed tasks at each teacher's verbal command.

Another seminar session was conducted by a member of the physics department whose specialty was quasars. The guest speaker took the teachers to the observatory at night for lectures on quasars. Because only a few physicists in the entire country specialize in quasars, these teachers had an interesting story to share with their students the following fall.

Robots, quasars, and stories about the physicists' personal lives. Imagine the motivational power of these seminars. Imagine their influence on the proposal evaluators.

Another fascinating seminar session was conducted by a retired physics professor who had spent his career teaching physics and researching the personal lives of famous physicists. He talked at ease for 2 hours, keeping everyone mesmerized with his fascinating stories, using a catalog drawer of 3″ × 5″ cards. Each card told a story about a particular physicist, personal information unknown to most people. Imagine the high school students' reactions to their teachers' personal encounters with robots, quasars, and little-known stories on the personal lives of the physicists in their textbooks. The seminars were as entertaining as a high-quality serial movie. Throughout the summer, each guest speaker seemed to top the previous performance. Imagine the motivational power these experiences had on these teachers, and, in turn, on their students the following fall. Imagine the influence such a variety of unusual experiences would have on the proposal evaluators' ultimate decision.

Every grant proposal needs a unique feature to separate it from all of its competitions; and, as with this proposal, all grant writers bring this uniqueness to their projects by joining their colleagues at the workplace or elsewhere and using their expertise. Make a list of professional colleagues and their respective areas of expertise, including those with unusual or very high levels of expertise.

Lessons Learned from the Summer Physics Institute Grant

• Persistence pays. Whenever someone tells you it can't be done, it's time to shift into high gear.

• Grant writers can garner support by studying the mission and goals of potential funders simply by closely examining the goals set forth in the RFP.

• All proposals can be strengthened by adding one or more unique features.

• Grant writers can strengthen their grant-writing programs by making a list of colleagues with unique and/or exceptionally high levels of expertise.

• Flexibility is an indispensable trait for all grant writing.

• Serious writers must never trust others to write their grants.

PROPOSAL 5: A MILLION-DOLLAR TECHNOLOGY PROPOSAL

Apart from providing the means of improving existing and initiating new programs, perhaps the next greatest advantage to having a grant proposal funded is the opportunity it provides the authors to improve their grant-writing skills. Never was this more obvious to Ann Redlhammer than the experience of writing a million-dollar technology proposal.

When Ann arrived to assume the principalship of a very large high school, she was shocked to learn that the school had no policy to ensure its students completed their programs equipped with the technology skills they would need throughout their careers. Ann was equally shocked to learn this large school had only about half the number of computer labs most schools its size have, and these labs were woefully ill-equipped with dated computers. For years, the school's leaders had been slow to embrace technology. They were unwilling to commit to any innovations requiring recurring expenses because they understood that technology is money and energy hungry. The more money and time you spend on technology, the more you discover you must spend to keep your investments from becoming dated, or worse yet, obsolete.

Ann assembled a team that of faculty members who indicated they shared her concern. She placed the head of the school's computer department in charge and gave the team its assignment. The team was to write a grant proposal to correct the school's technology shortage. The team began meeting once a week to discuss this assignment. After a few weeks, the intervals between the meetings began to grow. Ann became concerned with the lack of progress and began nudging the team leader. Her nudging turned to prodding. A year passed without a finished proposal. It became clear to her that if a proposal was going to be written, she would have to draft it.

Ann began by investigating possible funding sources, learning that in recent years, to avoid investing in equipment requiring recurring expenditures, her school had resisted the purchasing of computers for its faculty and offices. It had, nevertheless, at some time and under a former administration, hired a major computer company to wire all the buildings to make computers available for students. Running the required amount of cables was an expensive project. Ann wondered if the company that had gotten this large bid would be a good place to submit a proposal to meet her school's current technology needs.

Ann asked her superintendent if his office might arrange for her to meet with one of this company's funding officers. The following week, she was told that two officers would give her 30 minutes of their time in one joint session. Ann had only one 30-minute shot, and she was determined to make the best of this unusual opportunity. She quickly researched the company's funding history and learned that it was a leader in funding distance education. So, she drafted a proposal that focused on distance education. Many of her students lost school days because of icy mountain roads. If anyone could benefit from a distance education grant, then it was surely this school. Distance education would enable teachers to take their classes to these students. Furthermore, the company to which she was targeting the grant was a proven leader in distance education; it seemed a perfect match.

Ann had heard that many grant writers fail by putting all their energy into one proposal and going for all or nothing. She was far too committed to improving her school to take that risk, so after drafting a distance education proposal, she drafted a second, very different, proposal, then another and another until she had five rough drafts for five distinctly different proposals. For each proposal, she made two or three PowerPoint slides with graphs, charts, and tables, enabling her to communicate her ideas clearly and quickly. After all, she would have an average of only 5 minutes to present each proposal; that would leave 5 minutes, and she had special plans for the remaining 5 minutes.

Ann arrived early, set up the PowerPoint program, and tested it. She arranged her frames so she could give her presentations without notes and stay within the allotted time for each. Twenty-five minutes had passed and she had submitted all 5 proposals (Ann thought to herself, "This must be a world record."). Now it was time for a showdown, so Ann played her final trump card. She had included one final frame on the screen showing the title and a one sentence description of every proposal. She asked the officers to rate them. A zero would be given to any proposal completely missing the target, 1 point to any that sparked an interest, and 2 points to any the officers found especially intriguing.

But her audience did not respond. It was obvious Ann had overplayed her hand. Finding her strategy excessive, the evaluators were reluctant to assign written numerical ratings to her proposals, but they were willing to discuss their reactions verbally, and the strategy paid off. Ann was shocked to learn that her favorite proposal, the distance learning proposal had sparked no interest. The officers' reaction was one of: "We've done distance education, so let's move on to something new." Only one proposal aroused the interest of both evaluators. She was shocked to learn that it was the one proposal that focused on the topic they knew nothing about, *learning communities*. But neither of these issues concerned Ann because she now had her direction and knew exactly what she had to do. She would focus all her energy in one direction.

As Ann carefully crafted this proposal, she planned to replace her school's severely dated computers with state-of-the art computers and add a server in each room. She also proposed two additional identically equipped computer labs. The school had a site-based decision committee, which was in charge of everything from discipline to curriculum decisions. Members of this committee would be connected electronically. The program would make use of the existing wiring and enable the mounting of a program on all or any designated number of computers throughout the school. Each department chair's office and each elementary grade-level chair's office would be connected to all computers within the respective department. This was a long-time dream of Ann's, and she knew of no school anywhere with such an ideal system.

Politics can play a significant role in grant writing. The success of this grant proposal can be attributed, at least in part, to the customer–client relationship Ann's school had with the funder. Put frankly, her school was a good

By examining your district's business activities, you can arrange for politics to have a positive and healthy role in your grant program.

customer. Think about your own workplace. Can you identify a company for which your school district has been a good customer? Now, try to identify a project topic that would benefit both your school and this company.

Results

When the proposal draft was completed, Ann researched the literature to find support for this program and to find data to convince the potential funders that, although her ideas were without precedence, they were pedagogically sound. First, she defined such concepts as *learning community* and *site-based, decision-making committee,* and then she reported research from the literature showing the effectiveness of each.

Ann made one point perfectly clear; by funding this proposal, the company would become an active partner with the school's learning community and its site-based, decision-making committee. This gave the company strong connections with the community.

In all, Ann had asked for a package of hardware and connections worth 1.1 million dollars. To her absolute astonishment, the company funded it in full; not one cent was negotiated. (This, in itself was a victory, for it was the only proposal Ann had ever heard about that didn't require negotiation.)

Lessons Learned from the Technology Grant

The technology project taught Ann that successful grant writing requires serious commitment, determination, and tenacity. It reinforced her belief that if you have a good idea, you investigate the market and carefully craft your proposal to make it fit the goals of a potential funder, and you are persistent, then you can get your proposal funded. Ann had already learned that *most fly-by-night proposals,* that is, *proposals written quickly to meet short deadlines, are rejected,* and, in contrast, *those proposals carefully written and rewritten are usually funded,* if not on their first submission, then on a resubmission.

You must craft each proposal so that it serves the goals of its intended funder.

This proposal also taught Ann that if you are really serious about grant writing, *never trust someone else to do your work.* She was the one who felt this burning need to update her school's technology. Her teachers had gone along for years, comfortable without this new equipment. They had adjusted well to the school's culture, which had no serious commitment to technology. Would she ever again collaborate on a proposal? Absolutely! But, from that time forward, she would *make certain each partner shared her level of commitment and passion for the proposal.* Would she ever totally entrust the leadership for the writing of a proposal she dreamed up to someone else? Absolutely not!

The proposal reinforced Ann's belief that *successful grant writers must remain flexible,* acknowledging that the first and most important goal is to carefully design a proposal that will meet the funders' goals at a level promised by none of the competing proposals. It also reinforced her belief that while establishing need is an important factor in persuading funding agencies to support your proposal, *need pales in comparison to the ability to convince the funder that you and your teachers are winners.* You must use your own unique strengths and the strengths of your school and community to persuade potential funders that you will do a better job than others would at reaching the funders' goals.

Summary

Grant writing is a highly competitive activity, and a high level of success demands a well-structured approach. Yet, by choosing potential funders whose goals parallel their own and carefully crafting their proposals to make them meet the funders' goals, grant writers can succeed at the level at which they are willing to work to achieve.

Districts serious about grant-writing either have their own staffed grant-writing office or they have a formally designated director of grant-writing. Most successful districts have both. These teams and programs are ongoing; the grant writers continuously listen and look for opportunities. They continue to build their grant-writing resources through staying current with the literature in their fields and maintaining ongoing lists of data, including their own strengths and weaknesses. Although they may carefully select colleagues to collaborate with them, these grant writers do not trust their grant-writing programs to others; so when they do choose to collaborate, they select partners who are self-motivated, self-starters—individuals who do not require prodding. Excellent grant writers are flexible, so flexible that they always put the funders' goals ahead of their own, sometimes even changing the major thrust of the proposal.

Grant writers can give all their proposals an advantage over that of the competitors by including unique features in each proposal. Two additional advantages can be gained by (1) making lists of strengths and weaknesses and learning to use both to strengthen their proposals, and (2) by seeking out grant proposal topics that can be advantageous in ways additional to the goals stated in the RFPs.

RECAP OF MAJOR IDEAS

- The funder's wants and needs always trump the grant writer's wants and needs.
- Flexibility trumps stubbornness.
- Having everyone understand your school district's culture is a valuable asset.
- Identifying your school district's business connections can increase the probability of getting your proposals funded.
- Understanding the funders' priorities is beneficial.
- For grant-writing teams, majority agreement is necessary, but unanimity is not.
- Having a plan for disseminating the benefits of the program to help others gives a proposal an advantage.
- Knowing and communicating your school district's strengths is important.
- Persistence is absolutely essential to successful grant writing.

LIST OF TIPS

1. Always put the funders' needs first.
2. Follow the RFP to a T.
3. Stay alert for new grant ideas and funding opportunities.
4. Know your strengths and limitations.
5. Don't be discouraged to learn that sometimes the best proposals are rejected.
6. Always be flexible in both your thinking and your practices.
7. Encourage your teachers to distance themselves from those who would discourage them from writing grants.
8. Be persistent.
9. Never completely trust others to write your proposals.
10. Help your teachers keep up with current trends and developments.
11. Ensure that everyone knows the district's goals and uses grant writing to reach them.
12. In each proposal, include unique features that will hook the evaluators.
13. Use the buzzwords of the day but make your proposals "walk the walk."

Reference

Henson, K. T. (2010). "Developing a learning community." In *Supervision: A collaborative approach to instructional improvement*. Long Grove, IL: Waveland Press.

Going to the Stars

INTRODUCTION

In their engaging book *Made to Stick*, brothers Chip Heath and Dan Heath (2007) report an abundance of research on why some ideas stick in our memories and others don't. They stress the need to focus on one mission and state it succinctly, offering as examples, Bill Clinton's successful 1992 campaign guide "It's the economy, stupid" and Southwest Airlines' successful phrase, "We offer lower fares." According to these authors, when you say something three times, you say nothing. My grant-writing motto is THE BEST IT CAN BE.

The theory that undergirds this book is if you are going to write grants, write grants that succeed. Don't settle for less. How do you do that? It's simple. **Tip:** *make every proposal you write far better than the evaluators expect it to be.* And you can do it! But it requires you and your teachers to develop your own personalized grant-writing program. Every chapter in this book has been designed to help educators turn out one excellent proposal after another.

Like everything else, some grant-writing days are better than others. But even rejection doesn't mean failure. The only failure in grant writing is not trying. The next time you are a little discouraged, remember the Oscar Wilde comment, "We are all lying in the gutter but some of us are looking up at the stars." This final chapter aims to leave you not lying in the gutter but always looking at the stars—and reaching them, one step at a time.

The only failure in grant writing is not trying.

KEEPING YOUR GRANT

Some of your teachers are still waiting for their first acceptance letters. Assure them that it will happen. Perhaps not on the first try or the second, but *quality plus persistence is a winning formula.* By following the advice laid out in this book, the chances are excellent that it will happen sooner than they expect. What next, then? What will you do when the big moment arrives and your team's grant has been funded? A bottle of champagne and a good Italian dinner would seem appropriate. But don't stop with the celebration.

Recall the song, "After the Loving?" The following words say it all, "I'm still in love with you." The author is suggesting that love should be more than a one-night stand. So should grant writing. Grant writing offers you a love that can grow better with age. After all, isn't that what love is supposed to do? But most successful lovers would be quick to say you have to work at love. Like a flower garden, to prosper, love must be tended and nurtured. Grant writing is no different. From the beginning, this book has said grant writing is something *you can do*, and indeed, you can even take it to the level you choose. But remember that *you can take your grant writing only to the level at which you are willing to work*. The good news is that *the more you cultivate it, the easier grant writing becomes until, for many grant writers, the work gradually turns into play*.

The book says you must commit to making each of your proposals, how good? "The best it can be." Right now, you should make a second commitment. **Tip:** *You should commit to getting every funded grant refunded*. This requires more than just a pledge; it requires planning. Here is more good news; getting a proposal refunded is much faster and easier than getting it funded in the first place. More exactly, you have more control the second time around and, for that matter, all subsequent times.

Getting a grant refunded is much easier and faster than writing another grant.

The Fortune 500 companies have learned that although they must continue their research and development activities and continue searching for new clients, above all, they must take care of their current clients. To stay a member of this elite group, the leaders of these companies have learned they must provide excellent services for their existing clients. So it is with grant writing. Of course you will want to write new grants to meet new goals, but only after taking steps to please your current donor. You can begin by developing a documentation process.

DOCUMENTING YOUR GRANT

Perhaps you recall from reading the Project ESCAPE grant that a big mistake was made in that the authors neglected to write articles to prove the grant even existed. You will also want this documentation to use as you begin developing a grant-writing track record. Fortunately, the Project ESCAPE program went on to win a national award, and all the hard work that went into it was eventually recognized through that award. Those grant writers were lucky. But you cannot and must not depend on being so lucky. You need a method of ensuring, from the get-go, that your grants and your team's grants will get documented. So, right now, even before your first (or next) grant is funded, you should *begin gathering documentation*.

Tip: *Consider asking for a press conference during your next school board meeting*. This is an excellent forum for announcing the grant award. But, be prepared. The district might just be facing crunch time. The upcoming vote on closing down one or more failing schools can easily emotionally charge the audience, shadowing your grant news and leaving minimal time on the program for your announcement. But if you have done the necessary planning, even such bad timing can work to your advantage. After all, during these worst of circumstances, the district would have an unusually high need for some positive news. The point here is that even during the busiest times and under the most negative climate, a well-planned announcement of a grant funding can be a welcome event.

You need an ongoing procedure for collecting news about your grants. *Create a publicity section in your three-ring binder.* Include in this section a copy of your proposal abstract. Next, *use this abstract to write a short news release.* Get your grant announcement added to the next school board meeting agenda. The main tip here is to *make the announcement now, make it exciting, and make it brief.*

Getting publicity for your grant is imperative, and it is your responsibility.

USING ACTION RESEARCH

It was said previously but bears repeating: *grant proposal evaluators love data.* Serious grant writers devise means of getting a steady stream of data to use to support their proposals. Unfortunately, few teachers share this love of numbers. Even fewer enjoy conducting research to gather data. But there is good news. If you are among the many who cringe when *research* is mentioned, then you will be glad to hear that we are not talking about your father's research. Remember the ad: "This is not your father's Oldsmobile." Well, this is not your father's research. Unlike your father's research, which was stiff, demanding, time consuming, and laden with statistics and rules, the type of research required to keep a fresh supply of grant-writing data is friendly, easy, fast, and yes, it can even become fun. Commonly known as *action research*, this is research you initiate to improve your working world, research over which you have control, and research that works for you, not vice versa. *One of the best action research tools is the one-page questionnaire.* The questionnaire is a fast and easy tool for gathering the data needed to substantiate the needs of your classroom, school, or district. Once your proposal is accepted, the questionnaire can be used to quickly gather the evidence that you will need to support your claim that your program is working even better than you implied it would. Following is a strategy for conducting questionnaires. Share this news with your teachers.

Grant writing has a quality that requires taking risks. First, be completely honest and candid with your faculty. Tell them there is no guarantee they will get an acceptance, certainly not the first time they send a grant forward. Be honest. Grant writing is a little risky.

Different people react differently to activities involving risks. Some run away. Looking over their shoulders, they seem to scream out, "I'm not afraid to do it. I don't fear rejection. I want to write grants, but I just don't have time for it!" Or, "I'm not a researcher or a grant writer; I'm a teacher. I want to spend my time preparing for my classes." Such comments as these imply that grant writing and good teaching are somehow mutually exclusive. Those people who say they choose teaching over research don't explain how they are able to stay current in their field while remaining so detached from research and grant writing. Other people react just the opposite. Like moths drawn to a flame, they find the risk and the challenge irresistible.

Although some people find grant writing scary, others find it stimulating.

Of course, grant writing is not the only behavior that scares some and stimulates others. Research has the same effect on people. Like grant writing, research is just a paper tiger—if you master a few basic skills and select the right type of research.

Because there is one type of research that is quick, easy, and nonthreatening, and yet is a valuable tool to those grant writers who learn how to use it, encourage your teachers, including beginners, to use it. Of course, the subheading for this section is a dead give-away as to which type of research this refers, *action research*. As stated previously, action research is easy to conduct. In contrast to the theses, dissertations, and other major research challenges many of us faced in college, action research does not require the investigators to master complex research designs or complicated statistical designs. Rather, it enables researchers to use the skills they already possess.

In a sense, everybody is a researcher. Anyone who ever prepares food and experiments with spices by measuring and tasting is a researcher, and, in fact, our home kitchens are perfect examples of research laboratories. Every time we go shopping, if we try even one product or brand for the first time and systematically record the results, then we are conducting research. When the vacuum cleaner stops picking up debris and we check to see whether the bag is full, we are performing an investigation. When golfers select new clubs or adjust their swings, or when anglers selects new lures or casting methods, these athletes are using action research. When they begin recording the results, they are initiating action research.

Out home kitchens are perfect examples of research laboratories, and conducting action research at work is just as easy as conducting it at home.

Although these examples may appear trite, they deliver an important message; everyone uses research skills. Conducting action research at work is just as easy as conducting it at home. We should be a little more formal and write down our problems, our predictions, and our results, but that, too, is very elementary and possesses no serious challenge to anyone.

Sometimes aspiring grant writers say they want to write grants but they don't know how to begin. Others say they would write grants, but they don't believe they know enough about the current developments in their field. They know that for their proposals to succeed, they must first convince evaluators that they are on the cutting edge of the research and best practices in their profession.

The solutions to these concerns can be found in the use of surveys, and each survey requires only a well-constructed, one-page questionnaire. At this point, I want to share with you a simple, one-page questionnaire that has worked well for over two decades. See Figure 10.1. This simple tool has power! By revising this questionnaire each time it is used, this one-page questionnaire has enabled its investigator to share the results of these surveys with over 1 million readers.

Tip: *Encourage your teachers to reflect on their professional goals, as well as on their school's and district's missions, and to select topics that can help them reach these goals.* My purpose for using this questionnaire is to stay current in the field of publishing so that I can help others become more successful, published authors. I want to help them avoid those common mistakes most frequently leading to rejection.

As noted previously, success for all grant writers depends on them knowing their own goals. Some participants bring ideas or dreams to my workshops and quickly use the workshops to learn how to fulfill those dreams. Others bog down at the beginning because they don't believe that they have

EDITOR'S INFORMATION FORM

Name of Editor _____

Name of Journal _____

Address _____

1. a. _____ Approximate number of subscribers.

   b. Your primary audience is _____

2. _____ % of the contributors are university personnel.

   _____ % are graduate students, and _____% are K-12 classroom teachers;

   _____ % are K-12 administrators; _____% specialists; _____% other:

3. Refereed 10 yrs ago? _____ Refereed now? _____ If yes, nationally? _____, or in the office? (by the editor and/or the editorial staff) _____ If refereed, is it anonymous? _____ Other? _____

   Please explain _____.

   Do you provide the referees with a rating instrument? _____

4. _____% of the articles in your journal report research data, i.e., what percent of the articles report the results of a study conducted by the author(s)?

5. _____% of the total number of articles published in one year relate to a particular theme or issue.

6. _____% of all manuscripts received are accepted for publication.

7. _____ days lapse before we answer query letters. (please estimate)

8. _____ days lapse before we acknowledge receipt of a manuscript.

9. _____ weeks lapse before we make the publishing decision.

10. _____ months lapse between acceptance and actual publication.

11. _____ manuscript pages is our preferred article length. Our max. length is _____ pp. Our min. length is _____ pp.

12. In addition to the original, how many photocopies do you require? _____

13. Required style: APA ____, MLA ____, Chicago ____, Other ____.

14. Accept dot matrix? _____ Letter quality? _____ Photocopies? ___.

15. Good black & white photos would enhance acceptance in this journal? none _____, possibly _____, likely _____.

16. To inquiries about possibly submitting a manuscript, do you welcome query letters? _____, phone calls? _____ Which do you prefer? _____.

17. Some common mistakes made by contributors.

18. Recommendations to contributors:

This simple one-page questionnaire has enabled the author to reach over 1 million people.

FIGURE 10.1 Sample One-Page Questionnaire to Editors

the knowledge or skills they need to really help others. The questionnaire is a tool that quickly fulfills this need for these reluctant participants. Let your teachers know that they, too, can develop a questionnaire that will quickly gather the data needed to write a convincing grant, a grant that will support and fulfill their desire to help others.

Reexamine the personal goals you identified and listed in Chapter 1. Align these goals with your school's or district's mission statement. Now, examine your professional work and identify a topic you can research to move you nearer to your goals and your school's goals.

This book has a section on action research because of its practicality to grant writing. Put simply, *action research works.* Actually, this is an understatement; not only does action research work, but it also has a high rate of return for the modest amount of energy and time required to develop and use it. To illustrate the effectiveness of action research, I want to return to the one-page questionnaire I have used for 20 years. I mentioned that this simple questionnaire has enabled me to communicate with over 1 million people, but I neglected to emphasize I added one thing to this questionnaire that made it effective, hard work—hard, not in the sense of being difficult, but in the sense of having the commitment to take time to design and conduct it correctly.

As a result, this questionnaire has provided the data required to write many manuscripts, no less than a dozen in a single journal, the *Phi Delta Kappan,* a premiere journal that rejects about 95% of the manuscripts it receives. The same one-page questionnaire has provided data to write several book chapters and conduct some 300 workshops on grant writing and writing for publication. I have also used these same data to teach a course on writing for publication and to convince grant proposal evaluators to accept several grants.

These successes are a joint product of the survey and hard work. By itself, the act of developing a questionnaire and mailing it to potential funders is totally inadequate and will likely produce little success. Let me explain how a good work ethic can make all the difference. Individuals who have worked with questionnaires know an important prerequisite to their success is getting an acceptable return rate. This could mean anywhere from 20–40%. Over the years, the return rate for this questionnaire has averaged just over 90%. (The exact return rate for each mailing is clearly documented in each article.) The quality of the data reported is equally high. By using the following advice, you can experience this same level of success.

DEVELOPING QUESTIONNAIRES

Target each questionnaire to an audience who will benefit from it. Then point out how each recipient will benefit from completing it.

You must select an appropriate topic; determine the types and number of questions to use; test the questionnaire; and write preliminary, cover, and follow-up letters. Developing an effective questionnaire is a multistep process. Carefully share the following advice with your teachers. As you read it, think about your next grant topic and your next questionnaire and its accompanying letters, and how you will use this advice to design them. Grant writing is a game of probability, and omitting any of these steps will likely diminish both the rate of return and the quality of the responses.

Selecting a Topic

Begin developing your questionnaire. **Tip:** *Always select a topic you believe not only you but also the respondents will consider important.* People will be much more likely to take the time to respond to your questionnaire if they consider it important. This is easy if you choose a topic that meets the needs of the respondents. By completing such questionnaires, the respondents are helping themselves. Notice that the Questionnaire to Editors, shown in Figure 10.1, is designed to help writers prepare better manuscripts and target those manuscripts to appropriate editors. From my own editing experience, I knew these two topics were major problems at publishing houses: Far too many manuscripts are poorly written and far too many are sent to the wrong journals. By helping me help writers prepare better manuscripts and target them to the right journals, the respondents would actually be *helping themselves.*

Because you are using this questionnaire to gather data to use in your grant proposal, you might also consider the needs of the potential funders. This means that before choosing a survey topic, you might want to survey the current funding opportunities. Finding a request for proposal (RFP) on a topic that fits your interests is an important step in your grant-writing program.

Now that you have begun thinking about your own professional goals, list two or three of them and two or three goals for your school and district. As you continue to explore grant opportunities, try to tie some of the funders' goals you see in RFPs to some of your district's goals and to some of your own.

LENGTH OF QUESTIONNAIRE.   The rate of return of questionnaires drops dramatically when they are longer than one page. **Tip:** *Limit the length of each questionnaire to one page.* This can be difficult when you have a lot of questions you need to ask. I have found three ways to squeeze in additional questions.

When the length of a questionnaire spills over to a second page, the percent of returns plummets.

Thanks to the availability of computers, you are no longer limited to a finite number of words on each page. By *selecting a slightly smaller type*, you will be able to ask a few additional questions. However, do not use type smaller than 10 points. You can also add about 2 more questions by *using a legal-size page*. One final suggestion for getting in more questions: *keep each question short.*

Types of Questions

When using questionnaires, you can choose from open-ended questions, closed questions, or both. I recommend the last choice. **Tip:** *Use several closed questions and only two or three open-ended questions.* The reason for limiting the number of open-ended questions is that they require more space and threaten to expand the length of your questionnaire beyond one page. The reason for including open-ended questions is that they have the power to discover insights of the respondents, often important insights that would otherwise go unnoticed by the investigator.

ARRANGING THE QUESTIONS.   Once you have determined how many items to use, the next job is to decide their sequence. **Tip:** *Look ahead and try to picture your grant proposal.* Will it begin by showing a need? Most proposals do. If so, seek out those questions that will gather data you can use to convince the funder that the need you claim for your school or district is, indeed, real.

Next, your proposal must convince the funder that you are the best prepared grant writer to meet this need. At this point, you may want to refer to Chapter 4, which contains the model known as The Triangular Method. Review your strengths. Then focus on your weaknesses and try to think of a few questions to turn your weaknesses into strengths.

Tip: *Arrange your questions in the same sequence you envision for your proposal.* Having them in this order will make the data more accessible as you proceed with developing your grant.

Now return to your research topic and write a few quick-answer questions to gather the data you need to convince a funder to sponsor your project.

ADMINISTERING THE QUESTIONNAIRE

Testing the Questionnaire

Once the draft copy of your questionnaire is complete, it is time to test it. Put yourself in the role of a recipient and answer the questions. When you find ambiguity, rewrite the question. One thing you cannot afford to have in your questionnaire is ambiguity. If the question isn't totally clear to you, rewrite it.

Tip: *Ask a colleague to complete the questionnaire in your absence and without your explanations.* And ask your colleague to be candid. If the colleague finds any question to be less than crystal clear, you need to know about it. If the respondent suggests ways to improve either the entire questionnaire or an individual question, *listen and thank your colleague.*

But as tempting as it may be, *don't ask for suggestions for ways to remove the ambiguity.* You can figure this out. If you lean too heavily on your readers, they may respond by rushing over your questionnaire. Their pointing out of the ambiguity alone is priceless because you can be certain others would have noticed this ambiguity.

Some grant writers are reluctant to share their unfinished work with others. If you don't have a colleague with whom you feel comfortable sharing your questionnaire, *put each proposal aside for a few days.* This will enable you to see some of the duplications, omissions, and ambiguities you were unable to see while working closely with the instrument.

Sending the Questionnaire

Prior to actually sending the questionnaire, w*rite a short letter to alert the recipients that soon they will receive the questionnaire.* See Figure 10.2. *Always enclose a self-addressed, stamped envelope.*

Dear

Within the next few days, you will be receiving a short, one-page questionnaire about_____. The purpose of this survey is to_____. I have kept the questions short and easy to make the job easy and fast. I hope you will take a few minutes to complete and return this short questionnaire. Thank you.

Sincerely,

Kenneth T. Henson
[title]

FIGURE 10.2 Preliminary Questionnaire Letter

Dear

Enclosed is the short questionnaire that I promised to send. By completing this form, you will [here I make a promise statement telling the respondents how their completing this form will actually serve them].

Please check the box below if you want to receive a copy of the results of this survey.

Thank you very much for your assistance.

Sincerely,

Kenneth T. Henson
[title]

___ Yes, I would like to receive a copy of the results of this survey.

FIGURE 10.3   Sample Questionnaire Cover Letter

Your teachers must decide whether to use all, some, or none of these suggested steps. Remind them again that grant writing is a probability game, and each of these steps can actually raise the probability your questionnaire will be completed and returned. Now, draft a short preliminary questionnaire letter for your project. Your two main goals in this letter should be clarity and brevity.

Preparing a Cover Letter

When you mail the questionnaire, *always enclose a cover letter*. See Figure 10.3. So far, I have suggested you begin each action research project by

A cover letter gives you an opportunity to remind the respondents how the survey benefits them.

- Selecting a topic of importance to your recipients
- Devising a short, one-page questionnaire
- Completing the questionnaire yourself, as though you were a recipient
- Correcting any ambiguous items
- Asking a colleague to complete the questionnaire
- Devising a short cover letter
- Mailing the cover letter, questionnaire, and a self-addressed, stamped envelope

After about 10 working days, check your return rate. From all this work, don't expect a return of more than 40–50% of the questionnaires. But if you want an even higher return rate, don't stop yet.

Tip: *Prepare and mail a follow-up letter* such as the one shown in Figure 10.4. Remember the purpose of the follow-up letter is to make the recipients understand that by completing and returning the questionnaires, they will be helping themselves.

The follow-up letter *does not blame* the respondent. It *emphasizes the brevity* of the questionnaire (only a few minutes are required to complete this form). Finally, it *expresses gratitude* and is accompanied by a self-addressed, stamped envelope.

> Dear
>
> Recently, I mailed a short, one-page questionnaire to you [here, I insert the purpose of the questionnaire to show how completion of the questionnaire will benefit the recipient]. Because that letter may have been lost in the mail, I am enclosing a copy of the questionnaire. By taking a few minutes to respond to these quick questions, you will help [here, I restate the benefits].
>
> Thank you for your time.
>
> Sincerely,
>
> Kenneth T. Henson
> [title]

FIGURE 10.4   Sample Questionnaire Follow-Up Letter

Wait another 10 working days. By now, if you are lucky, your total return rate has reached 60–70%; so, it's time to make your final play. **Tip:** *With a stack of blank questionnaires before you, each with the name of one of your missing recipients, begin phoning.* Your conversation should follow this path:

> Hello Mr./Ms./Dr. _____
> This is Ken Henson (no need for titles or other formalities here) in Charleston, South Carolina. Recently, I attempted to send you a short questionnaire. You may not have received it.

At this point, I pause briefly. Often the recipient openly acknowledges having received the questionnaire and apologizes for failing to complete it. (This always reminds me that we live in a very hurried and demanding world.) My intent here is to remain positive and enthusiastic, so I quickly explain that I understand and it doesn't matter because I have a copy of the form in front of me, and, if I might have just 5 minutes, I can jot down the answers. I have never been refused this request. The results usually take the total return rate into the low 90th percentile. Understand that you will never reach the remaining 10% because people are so active and so mobile. Realizing how busy the respondents are, I respond to their cooperation by *moving through the questionnaire very quickly.*

For studies such as this, which return to the same respondents year after year, do one other thing. *Return their completed questionnaires from the year before*, along with a letter such as the one shown in Figure 10.5. Each year, several respondents will report no changes. Some will mark only one or two changes. Seldom will the respondent change the majority of the answers.

Dear

Thank you for participating in my biennial survey 2 years ago. I am repeating that survey and would like to invite you to participate again this year.

To make this job easier and faster, I am returning a copy of your previous responses. Will you please use a colored pen and cross out any responses that have changes and enter the new data. If no changes have occurred, just mark NO CHANGES across the top of this form.

Thank you again for your assistance.

Sincerely,

Kenneth T. Henson
Professor of Education
The Citadel

ENC: Last year's completed questionnaire
S.A.S.E.

FIGURE 10.5 Revised Questionnaire Cover Letter

Summary

This concludes the process I use to handle questionnaires. Many colleagues consider my efforts excessive because they assume the whole purpose in them is to get a high return rate, which they also consider excessive. In addition to a higher return rate, I believe the extra attention results in more accurate data.

WORKSHOPS

This book has provided the tools you will need to help your teachers craft one excellent proposal after another. As you and your teachers continue to collect data and use them over and over, your grant-writing knowledge base will grow, making the grant-writing process easier. Grant-writing workshops can be a rich source of additional tips. So encourage your teachers to take any opportunity they may have to attend grant-writing workshops given by speakers who have written successful proposals and can offer first-hand advice. You might give your teachers the following advice:

Getting useful information while attending workshops and connecting it to your grant writing program is both your right and your responsibility to ask questions.

   Tip: *When you arrive at the workshop, this is no time to be shy and sit quietly in the back row.* Arrive early and get a front-row seat on the 50-yard line. A notepad and pencil will likely be provided. But just in case they are not, take along a pencil or pen and a good, lined 8 ½ × 11 inch pad. After the workshop, you will want to punch holes in your notes and add them to your binder. When the speaker says something you don't understand, ask for clarification. Even if you are given a copy of the PowerPoint presentation, take copious notes. These will reinforce the major points in your long-term memory.

   Information that you don't know how to apply to your personal program is useless information. Throughout the workshop, ask yourself, "What implication does this have for *our* grants? How can *we* use each fact, box, and tip to enrich *our* proposals?" If you still don't know, ask. Regardless how good the speaker and the presentation are, without questions from the audience, no speaker can make the workshop work for everyone.

Summary

Experienced grant writers know that once you reach the point of having a proposal funded, it is much easier to get *re*funded than to start all over and write another proposal and try to get it funded. Therefore, it will behoove you and your team to get your proposals refunded again and again. This takes planning, and the time to begin planning is right now.

You need to spend some time thinking about how you are going to publicize your grant, and you need to begin this publicizing process now. Yes, even *before* it is funded. Use your proposal abstract to write a short news release to give to your local newspaper, radio, and television news agents. While you are preparing this release, begin planning a strategy for evaluating your program. Develop a one-page questionnaire. Include both essay and short-term questions. Fill three-fourths of the page with short-answer questions asking for numbers and percentages. Remember, proposal evaluators prefer quantitative data. Using the data you collect, replace such needs statements as "We really need this money" and "Our program has been very successful."

You have taken time to learn how to help your school use grant writing effectively. Use these tips and you will not have to depend on Lady Luck. Keep reminding your teachers that if they continue applying these steps, they will succeed.

RECAP OF MAJOR IDEAS

- Getting a proposal refunded is faster and easier than starting over and writing a proposal from scratch.
- The writer has more control over the fate of a proposal that has already been funded.
- A steady supply of data is needed to get proposals funded and refunded.
- A one-page questionnaire is an invaluable tool for gathering data quickly and easily.
- Some school districts have highly skilled and continually successful grant-proposal committees.
- Many volunteer groups do more talking than writing.

LIST OF TIPS

Remind your teachers to:

1. Limit the length of their questionnaires to only one page.
2. Use clear and simple language when developing a questionnaire.
3. Ask their colleagues to read their questionnaires and give them feedback.
4. On questionnaires, use mostly short-answer questions that call for numbers and percentages.
5. Start planning to get each of their proposals refunded before their project is accepted.
6. Create a publicity section in their three-ring binder.
7. Continue building their grant-writing skills.
8. Every time your team meets, make sure it has an agenda and that the meeting immediately gets to agenda, moves steadily through it, and completes it on time.

Reference

Heath, C. & Heath, D. (2007). *Made to stick*. New York: Random House.

APPENDIX 3.1

Extended Glossary

Abstract: Brief summary description of the entire proposal.

Block grant: Federal funds given to a state, city, or county for broad purposes, the amount based on population.

Boilerplate: General statement that is used repeatedly in different grants.

Budget justification: Explanation of the need for each and all budget items.

Budget narrative: Description of each and all budget items.

CEO: Chief Executive Officer. The top officer.

Collaboration: Two or more individuals or groups working together to gain a mutual goal.

Cost sharing: Costs met mutually by the grantor and the grantee, but usually not on an equal basis.

Cover letter: Letter that accompanies a grant submission.

Direct costs: Costs of all items that directly support a proposal, including such items as salaries, materials, supplies, and travel.

Dollar-for-dollar match: Cost sharing between the grantor and grantee on an equal basis.

DUNS Number: Number assigned to organizations that apply for grants. All federal grants and an increasing number of other government funders require organizations that apply for their grants to have a DUNS Number on file.

External evaluation: Appraisal of a funded program conducted by an external, impartial party.

Federal Register: Government publication that contains the RFPs for all government-funded grants in a given year.

Formative evaluation: Short assessments that occur intermittently during a program.

Foundation: Private or public charitable funding source.

Funder: Source of grant funds.

Funding cycle: Period in which foundations make grants (annual, semiannual, etc.)

Funding guidelines: Descriptions of forthcoming grants, including eligibility, announcements, and directions for applying.

Grant: Gift for performing a job.

Grantee: Institution or individual who is awarded a grant.

Grantor: Organization that awards a grant.

Grants administrator: Individual charged with directing or overseeing a funded program.

Indirect costs: Percentage of total program costs a nonprofit institution can take to pay for overhead.

In-kind contributions: Noncash donations to a particular funded program, including salaries, space, heating, and electricity.

Input goals: Goals that focus on resources provided.

IRS Form 990: Internal Revenue Service form whose completion is required if the organization is to be exempt from paying income tax.

Jargon-free proposal: Proposal that avoids the use of unfamiliar or unintelligible language.

Letter of inquiry: Request for permission to submit a proposal.

Letter of intent: Letter informing a foundation or government agency of the intent to submit a proposal.

Letter of support: Letter of testimony from an individual, sometimes representing a group, offering support for the proposed program.

Matching budget or matching grant: Grant whose funding is contingent on the grantee paying a specified percent of the total cost.

Memorandum of agreement (MOA): Also known as Memorandum of Understanding (MOU). Statement signed by two parties that spells out the responsibilities of each party in a collaborative project. The MOA or MOU serves as a legal contract.

Mirror test: Comparison between the budget list and the budget narrative to ensure that no item is accidentally being left off either list.

Mission statement: Brief statement of an organization's purpose.

Needs statement: Written description of an organization's problems and shortcomings the proposal purports to overcome through the grant.

Output goals: Goals that focus on outcomes.

Partnerships: Collaboration of a combination of two or more individuals, schools, school districts, and universities to achieve a common goal, benefiting all parties.

Principal investigator: Senior member of a proposal writing team.

Proposal rating form: Form that assigns a specific number of points to each part of a grant proposal.

Project summary statement: Required summary statement whose parts are specified by the funder.

Query letter. See Letter of Inquiry.

Quotable quote: Short quote expressing an important concept with unusual clarity.

Request for proposals (RFP): Announcement of a funding opportunity including eligibility criteria and directions for applying for one of these grants.

Review of literature: Investigation to determine what is currently known about a field of study under investigation.

Smokestack theory: Premise that funding agencies are partial to proposals that are developed locally (within the shadows of their smokestacks).

Source map: Tool to ensure that the applicant's institution is eligible to receive grants from any funding agency being targeted.

Sustainability plan: Written strategy to ensure continuation of a project beyond the funding period.

Timeline: Schedule showing when major steps in a program will be accomplished.

Triangular model: Grant-proposal writing model that puts the funding agency's goals first and uses the grantee's individual, school, and school district strengths to convince the grantor that the grantee will do a better job than the competition in reaching the funder's goals.

APPENDIX 6.1

Enhancing Education Through Technology Grants

PROGRAM SUMMARY

West Ashley High School (WAHS) is applying for the At-Risk Student Innovative Grant in the amount of $200,000. The first initiative CATS (Continuous Advancement Toward Success) will serve students in a range of programmatic options using the following key elements: initial credit, credit recovery, units of instruction recovery, HSAP preparation and remediation, and EOC test preparation for traditional day students in both regular and special education categories. Currently, 675 students are served in the CATS model. We anticipate serving 700 students during the 2009–2010 academic year with CATS. The second initiative WRAP (Wildcats Redirection and Prevention) will serve 50 students who are at-risk for recommendation for expulsion. We will use the key elements of the CATS model paired with intense physical education activities, individualized career preparation, and practical work force readiness. Both groups will be provided with extensive supports from guidance, teachers, administrators, career specialists, parents, and the West Ashley community support system. The goal for CATS and WRAP is to empower, encourage, and educate all students to become confident, self-directed, lifelong learners, and provide career opportunities paired with academic success in partnership with parents and the community. The academic objectives focus on measurable data collected from reviewing the number of students progressing toward on-time graduation, suspension, retention, and drop-out rates. The social objectives will focus on students' success collected by surveys, career-based assessments, work samples, and testimonies. The primary outcome of these initiatives is to ensure that at-risk students will graduate on time with a career pathway established and a work ethic characterized by honesty, integrity, self-respect, and respect for others.

SECTION 1: STATEMENT OF NEED

West Ashley currently has 136 repeating 9th graders, a 12.6% school retention rate (source: 2007–2008 School Report Card), and 670 out-of-school suspensions (source: August 08–April 09), which translates to 1,114 days of lost instructional time. Without academic and social intervention, the potential for an increased drop-out rate is looming for our future graduates.

West Ashley needs to continue the CATS model using computer-assisted instruction to support our at-risk population by giving them a chance to recover credits lost, acquire credits for courses not attempted due to movement between high schools on different schedules (4 × 4, traditions day, A/B block), and take courses that accelerate the time of graduation. After focusing on academic support, our attention was drawn to an additional variable: suspension rates. The suspension component adversely affects students deciding to drop out after they are unable to meet the challenges of the traditional school. Data collected reflect that 47% or 3,462 referrals stem from incidences that occurred in the hallways (source: Educators Handbook). Our WRAP initiative

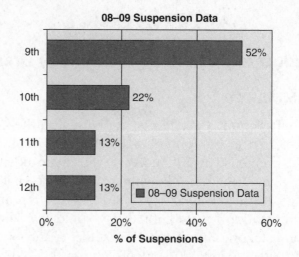

would modify hallway movement for these at-risk students and redirect them toward positive behaviors and positive self-regard. WRAP would reduce the loss of instructional time and cultivate a culture that meets the needs of the workforce by surrounding these students with extensive supports that redirect behaviors and prevent suspensions, truancy, and dropping out.

An analysis of the school's At-Risk Alert System (ARAS) report reveals that that 30% of next year's projected 10th graders, 23% of 11th graders, and 9% of 12th graders are considered "high risk," with scores of 15 or higher on a scale of 24 points. These at-risk indicators apply to 64% of the student population, which impacts the work of teachers, administrators, and support personnel daily, dealing with attendance, discipline, and academic failure.

The following two charts display ARAS data that documents the at-risk factors. This same data drove WAHS to create CATS and emphasize the need for this EEDA At-Risk Student Innovative Grant to continue. The ARAS report looks at school attendance, age for current grade, current grades, and previous test performance. For example, the rising 10th graders risk factors for overage for grade was 60%.

The current CATS model has demonstrated a high degree of effectiveness over the past 15 months of implementation. The initiative can be credited with increasing performance of the 2007–2008 West Ashley School Report Card.

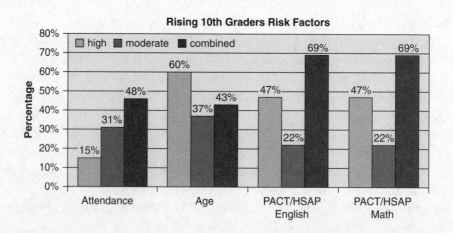

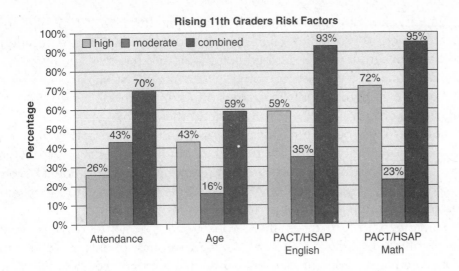

The Absolute Rating at WAHS moved from At-Risk to Average. Moreover, the Growth Rating at WAHS moved from At-Risk to Excellent. WAHS has served 427 students with the current CATS model earning 219 credits, and 208 credits are in progress as of April 2009. It appears that the conservative spending exercised, due to concerns for the SC Department of Education budget constraints, will reflect approximately $40,000 remaining in the grant account. Extraordinary support for CATS from our dedicated faculty facilitated service to this large number of students. In addition, Charleston County School District (CCSD) recognized the value of the model. CCSD contracted with APEX Learning for online courses, which reduced the need for WAHS to purchase site licenses from a different vendor. SC Virtual High School (SCVHS) was used as a secondary source by students for initial credit. Likewise, the A+ Learning System was used by many of the students seeking credit recovery. No funds had to be expended for A+ Learning System. WAHS was used as a model site for the vendor TE21. The tutoring component will be funded during 2009–2010 by the WAHS vending account.

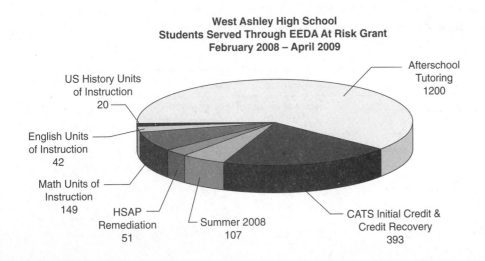

The urgency of continuing CATS and adding the new WRAP program is unprecedented; West Ashley High School acquires a significant addition of at-risk students from our feeder middle schools and receives additional NCLB students from across the district (currently serving 150 NCLB). It is noteworthy that there are 13 high schools in Charleston County School District, and 2 are designated to receive NCLB. WAHS is one of these two.

Students must be able to advance toward graduation and complete the graduation requirements in a 4-year window of time. Students must be able to recover units of instruction to ensure that retention rates and students overage for grade will decrease. Many of WAHS students have social and familial circumstances that impact school performance.

Students who face disciplinary consequences, such as expulsion, and negative affect thinking, are not well served through expulsion. The district has one alternative program that serves students through age 16. Students who are approaching 17 or older have only two legitimate educational options—adult education or GED preparation. Frequently, these students do not have the required 12 units of credit, including the 2 English and 2 math units, to matriculate into adult education and thus pursue a high school diploma.

The redesign of programmatic efforts (WRAP) to better serve these at-risk populations will enhance their opportunities to graduate from high school and take with them the skills and capacities to move into postsecondary settings such as Trident Technical College, South Carolina colleges and universities, the military, and/or employment. The model will instill in these at-risk students a renewed confidence by capturing a sense of hope and direction that reinforces their internal locus of control and path toward adulthood. It provides the ultimate opportunity to capture a positive high school experience that is rooted in preparation for life.

SECTION 2: PROJECT DESIGN

The current program used to address credit recovery (initial credits and recovered credits) is based on the Union Alternative Model (Utilizing Computer-Based Instruction and Reconnecting Youth [RY] for Life Skills). The WAHS initiative already in place is called CATS. The CATS model will be used to address the academic course components of WRAP, which will serve students identified as at-risk for suspension and/or may lay toward expulsion. The data in the At-Risk Factors data chart addresses the effectiveness of the initiative in place from February 1, 2008 to June 2008.

At-Risk Factors	2005–06	2006–07	2007–08
Retention	12.2%	14.5%	12.6% (due to CATS intervention)
Graduation rate	58.4%	48%	63.2% (due to CATS intervention)
Drop-out rate	3.7%	4.1%	1.4% (due to CATS intervention)
Poverty rate	51.9%	56.37%	56%

At-Risk Factors	2005–06	2006–07	2007–08
Students older than usual for grade	14.2%	7.1% (due to intervention programs)	14.7% (need to continue CATS and start WRAP)
Attendance rate	95.1%	94.2%	95.1%
SC report card absolute ratings	Below average	Unsatisfactory	Average (significant targets met due to CATS)
% of Out-of-school suspensions or expulsions for violent and or criminal offences (SC school report card)	1.6%	1.8%	4.3% (need WRAP)
% of Individual graduation plan	n/a	n/a	9th: 100%

The data clearly indicate measures must be taken to reduce retention rates. By recovery units of instruction, increasing graduation rates, and stabilizing and reducing drop-out rates, students can become more productive. CATS will effectively address these needs. Students have authentically embraced the CATS model and depend on it for progress toward graduation and career pathways.

Student Testimonials

Year in School	Grade Level	Gender	Quote
3	10th	Female	"I was ready to drop out of school and never look at a school again. My guidance counselor encouraged me to be a part of CATS. I love it and without it I would not have any hope in graduating June 2010. I need this diploma to support my baby."
4	12th	Male	"I have completed 6 credits in CATS. My behavior and grades were horrible and I fathered a child. My guidance counselor led me to CATS and it has been my salvation. I lack two electives to graduate and will take them at Trident Tech as dual credit beginning in September 2009. I will complete my high school diploma and my first year of college by May 2010."

(*continues*)

Year in School	Grade Level	Gender	Quote
3	9th	Female	"After my father's tragic death, I came to Charleston crushed and in deep academic trouble. I came from a 4 by 4 schedule and was so far behind I thought I would never catch up. I come to CATS every day Monday-Thursday and Saturdays. I have earned 4 credits through CATS and must continue on this path with CATS so I can graduate in June 2010."
3	12th	Female	"I have supported myself for 3 years and need to graduate and attend Trident Tech full time. My father suffers from an addiction and my mother is suicidal. CATS will allow me to graduate a year early and achieve my goal of becoming a Pharmacy Technician as soon as possible."

The suspension data demonstrate an immediate need to implement an effective intervention to begin in August 2009. Student participation for the WRAP initiative will be selected from the 2008–2009 school year, discipline data, and age. Recommendations for the initial WRAP group will be selected through the CORE team, guidance counselors, parent recommendations, administrators, and the principal.

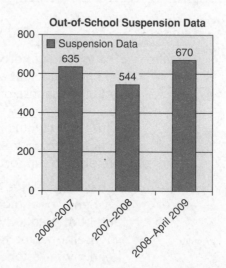

To continue the CATS initiative and add WRAP, WAHS would require the much needed funds provided by the At-Risk Innovative Grant. At West Ashley, 64% of the students for the 2008–2009 academic school year are identified as at-risk. The students served in the WRAP initiative will receive extensive supports to modify behaviors, increase positive regard for academic success, and prepare themselves to be successful in career pathways.

Enhancing services for this particular student population will decrease drop-out rates. The need to service this population underscores the need to build on an effective model. The students participating in WRAP will be identified and served on a semester-by-semester basis. This will ensure that they will be transitioned back into the general student population or matriculate into a myriad of program pathways.

The key elements of WRAP include those listed here.

WRAP Initiative Components

Student Selection	Type and Duration of Services	Physical Education	Parent/ Guardian
• CORE team recommendation • Recommendation from administrators, guidance, and/or parents • Discipline data from SASI/ Educators Handbook	• Self-contained classroom using CATS • 1.0 FTD Certified Employee • 1.0 FTD Teaching Assistant • Individual Achievement Plan tied to level system • Semester by semester	• 1st period daily (over 18 weeks) • Health and fitness • Brain-based research model • John Ratey, MD, from Harvard and author of *Spark: The Revolutionary New Science of Exercise and the Brain* • Will use the role of exercise to optimize mental and physical health	• Bimonthly conferences • Required classroom visits • Coordination between home, school, and career behavioral expectations • Parent Link on Internet for grades, attendance, and discipline

Career	Academics	Behavior Modification	Guidance Support
• Work KEYS measurement to each student • KUDER • SCOIS • Internship • Community service • College tour • Guest speakers	• CATS • APEX Learning System • Weekly progress report tied to level system	• Level system based on Positive Behavior Intervention System • Passes to athlete events • Privileges to take drivers' education or other desired courses	• You Can Program by National Guard • Peer mediation • Anger management • Problem solving • Drug/alcohol counseling

Long-Term Goal

- To empower, encourage, and educate all students to become lifelong learners and provide career opportunities paired with academic success.

Short-Term Goal

- WAHS will use the CATS and WRAP models to increase graduation rate, reduce drop-out rate, and reduce suspensions and expulsions.

Objectives:

1.1: Graduation rate will increase from 63.4% to 68% by allowing students to earn units of credit and receive supports daily.

1.2: The number of students who are retained (due to failing one or more core course) will decrease by 10% by recovering instructional units and units of credits.

1.3: The number of students recommended for expulsion will decrease from 14 to 7 by participating in WRAP.

1.4: Individual graduation plans (constructed by guidance counselors, students, and parents) will reach 100% for grades 9, 10, 11, and WRAP students.

Strategies/Activities	Evidence Base	Link to Objectives
Guidance counselors will identify students for CATS (Credit Recovery, Initial Credit, WRAP)	Union Alternative Model, Reconnecting Youth Model, and current CATS data	Objective 1.1
Teachers will identify students in need to recover units of instruction and submit this roster of students to guidance	Current CATS model	Objective 1.2
The CORE team program administrator, guidance will identify students for WRAP	2008–09 Suspension Data	Objective 1.3
Individual Achievement Plan will be developed for all CATS and WRAP students	Current CATS model	Objective 1.1, 1.2, 1.3
WRAP students will take the following assessments: KUDER or Work Keys, ASVAB, and/or SCOIS, and develop a relevant Individual Graduation Plan	EEDA and 2008–09 Suspension Data	Objective 1.4

Coordination with Other Programs

Career and Postsecondary Programs	Academic Programs	WAHS and CCSD Initiatives
You Can—National Guard	PLTW	Internships for WRAP students
Work Keys, KUDER	HSTW	APEX purchased through CCSD
ASVAB	School of Maritime Science	A+ Learning System funded by WAHS
APEX	School of Health Science	
A+	New coursework, i.e., Turf Management	
Trident One Stop	Culinary Arts Courses (beginning 8/09)	
Trident Tech	Home Systems Technology	

Other Funding Contributions

Local	State	Federal
• Donations of exercise equipment and funds by community	$7,500—Teen Lead Project	None
• National Guard donation of backpacks, calculators, pencils, and other incentive items		
• Businesses for WRAP's physical education component		
• Palmetto Gold funds awarded $21,956 for new computers and printers for CATS labs		
• Tutoring component of CATS funded by WAHS vending account ($4,500)		

CATS Timeline

Activity to Achieve Objectives	Start and End Date	Related Objective and Goal	Evidence/Data Collected from Activity	Persons/Agency Responsible
Identification for CATS	August 2009–May 2010	1.1, 1.2	Student rosters and CATS application packets	CATS guidance counselor, CORE team, and administrators
CATS orientation	August 2009–June 2010	1.1	Parent link call system	CATS guidance counselor
Students begin CATS courses	August 2009–June 2010	1.2	Data collection	CATS guidance counselor and CATS teacher
Progress reports	August 2009–June 2010	1.2	Daily and weekly	CATS teacher
Recognition and celebration	October 2009, January 2010, March 2010, May 2010	1.1, 1.2	CATS/WRAP recognition reception	WAHS Parent Teacher Student Association

WRAP Timeline

Activity to Achieve Objective	Start and End Date	Related Objective and Goal	Evidence/Data Collected from Activity	Persons/Agency Responsible
Review of discipline data	April 2009–June 2010	1.3	Grades, suspensions, truancy, discipline data	CATS guidance counselor
Identify WRAP students	April 2009–June 2010	1.3	Grades, suspensions, truancy, discipline data	CORE team
Interview teacher candidate	July 15, 2009	1.3	Interview process and certification letters	Principal, CATS guidance counselor & CORE team
WRAP parent/ student orientation	August 2009 and January 2010	1.2, 1.3	Student WRAP schedule disseminated	Guidance counselors and assistant principal

(continues)

Activity to Achieve Objective	Start and End Date	Related Objective and Goal	Evidence/Data Collected from Activity	Persons/Agency Responsible
Students begin WRAP courses	August 18, 2009–January 19, 2010	1.1, 1.3	Data collection	WRAP teacher
Bimonthly parent conferences	April 2009–June 2010	1.3, 1.4	Parent conference, IGP	WRAP teacher
Student folders	August 2009–June 2010	1.3, 1.4	Progress reports, Individual Achievement Plan, IGP, discipline, attendance data	WRAP teacher, CATS guidance counselor
Transition to traditional school day	December 2009–May 2010	1.3	CATS credits, discipline, and attendance data	CORE team authorization and CATS guidance counselor
Recognition and celebration	October 2009, January 2010, March 2010, May 2010	1.1, 1.2, 1.3	WRAP recognition reception	WAHS Parent Teacher Student Association

SECTION 3: MANAGEMENT AND SUSTAINABILITY

Management

The management for CATS/WRAP is critical to effectively meet our goals and objectives at West Ashley High School. By embedding CATS into the school structure, we create a culture of care and concern for student achievement and on-time graduation. The WRAP initiative will constitute a school-within-a-school model to support students with social/discipline issues. It will provide them with an opportunity to connect their academic work with career pathways in a nurturing and supportive environment using behavioral techniques.

Chain of Command and Time Allocated to CATS/WRAP	Personnel	Job Title and Description
Principal (5 hr week)	Mary Runyon	Principal, 2 years Assistant Principal, 7 years Direction of Special Education, 4 years Instructor for Classroom Management (1999–Present, College of Charleston) Ensure the curriculum is supporting the current instructional needs of the students

Chain of Command and Time Allocated to CATS/WRAP	Personnel	Job Title and Description
Project Manager (8 hr week)	Dale Metzger	Assistant Principal, 1 year Certified Mathematics Teacher, 10 years –Assigned administrative duty by principal –Clearly communicate the goals of the program to all staff members –Facilitates transportation Monday–Thursday for CATS students
Assistant Principal CORE Team Chair (8 hr week)	Daniel Ilagan	Assistant Principal, 21 years –Certified in Secondary Counseling –Social Studies, Administration, Candidate for –PhD in School Leadership
CATS Guidance Counselor (40 hr week)	Nicole Johnson	Secondary School Counselor, 3 years GCDF –Complete CATS/WRAP application, including parent/student signatures, check transcript, attendance, discipline, IEP/504 status, and track placement of all students in the program
CATS Certified Teacher (40 hr week)	Ashlyn Anderson	Language Arts Certified Teacher, 14 years –Communicate with the Site Administrator on a regular basis
CATS Certified Lead Content Part-Time Teacher (12–15 hr week)	Ryan Cumback	Language Arts Certified Teacher, 3 years
WRAP Certified Teacher (40 hr week)	Pending Funding Approval	South Carolina Certification in a Core Content Area with strong skills in behavior management and physical education –Communicate with the Site Administrator on a regular basis

The professional development will be provided at no additional costs related to this grant for the CATS/WRAP initiative. Components include (1) technology-related information for APEX and A+ Learning Systems; (2) behavior modification strategies provided by Mary Runyon, Principal; (3) brain-based research related to physical education by CCSD Team Associate; (4) career components by Global Career Facilitator, Nicole Johnson; and (5) character education provided by WAHS National Certified Counselor, Elizabeth Dorris.

The CATS/WRAP Advisory Team includes the guidance director, assistant principals, guidance counselors, department chairs, and CATS/WRAP teachers.

Sustainability

The CATS initiative has become such an important part of the daily routine and culture of WAHS that it would constitute a "culture shock" to abandon these opportunities for students. It is our belief the WRAP initiative will be a compelling activity that will likewise support student success and become an essential option for at-risk students. The West Ashley CATS Advisory Board and CORE team are committed to seek funding sources, community support, and district support to sustain the models beyond the grant funding. The values and principles of the CATS/WRAP initiatives embody the core foundation of the WAHS mission. We are committed to promoting a culture of academic and social success for all students. WAHS supports activities that define and promote career pathways, increase community and parent involvement, and implement the 10 keys practices of High Schools That Work.

SECTION 4: EVALUATION AND DISSEMINATION

Evaluation

The following evaluation measures are indicators of the desired outcomes. They are based on the objectives that will drive the CATS/WRAP initiatives for the 2009–2010 school year.

Evaluation Measures	Objective	Window of Time	Data Manager
Truancy	1.1, 1.2, 1.3	August 2009–June 2010	CATS/WRAP teachers, guidance, and project manager
Absenteeism	1.1, 1.2, 1.3	August 2009–June 2010	CATS/WRAP teachers, guidance, and project manager
Discipline	1.3	August 2009–June 2010	CATS/WRAP project managers
Retentions	1.2	August 2009–June 2010	CATS guidance counselor
% of Population on grade level	1.1, 1.2	August 2009, January 2010, and June 2010	CATS guidance counselor
% of Population who stay in school	1.1, 1.2, 1.3	August 2009–June 2010	CATS guidance counselor
% of Target population who complete an IGP	1.4	August 2009–June 2010	CATS guidance counselor, WAHS guidance counselors
% of Target population earning Carnegie Units for graduation	1.1	August 2009, January 2010, and June 2010	CATS guidance counselor, WAHS guidance counselors

Evaluation Measures	Objective	Window of Time	Data Manager
Attitude of target population toward school and learning	1.1, 1.2, 1.3, 1.4	August 2009–June 2010	CATS/WRAP teachers and CATS guidance counselor administering student surveys
% of Target population who graduate on time	1.1, 1.2, 1.3	June 2010	CATS guidance counselor

Dissemination

The CATS/WRAP initiative will be disseminated through several vehicles. These include, but are not limited to,

- Presentations at the Business and Education Summit in June 2009
- Presentations at future HSTW conferences
- Presentations at the Chamber of Commerce Education Coalition
- Presentations at local Business Education Summit
- Extension of invitations to other schools to visit WAHS to see the models in action

Program artifacts including forms, flowcharts, data collection, and curriculum components will be available on request. Within the Low Country Area, we would share our program with the Charleston, Dorchester, and Berkley School Districts through the Education Foundation and EEDA Regional Education Advisory Board monthly meetings.

Competitive Priorities

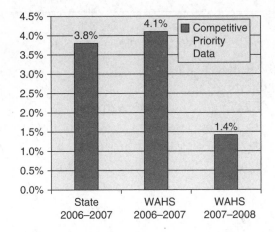

The CATS intervention model was the catalyst for significantly decreasing the WAHS drop-out rate. It fuels our passion and motivation to continue the CATS initiative and add the WRAP initiative on behalf of our students.

SECTION 5: BUDGET

West Ashley needs a total of $200,000 to operate the CATS and WRAP initiatives. The line items and formulas for calculating costs are reflected here:

Budget Summary

Object Category	Instructional Series (100)	Support Services Total (200)	Total
Personnel (salaries) (100)	$148,436	0	$148,436
Employee benefits (200)	$38,532	0	$38,532
Purchased services (300)	0	$13,032	$13,032
Supplies and materials (400)	0	0	0
Capital outlay (500)	0	0	0
Other (600)	0	0	0
Total	$186,968	$13,032	$200,000

Entries are based on Charleston County average salaries by position or actual salary of CATS employees.

Personnel	Salary	Health and Dental	Retirement	Social Security	Total
CATS guidance counselor	$44,600	$3,441	$5,749	$3,411	$57,201
CATS teacher	$43,953	$3,441	$5,666	$3,362	$56,422
WRAP teacher	$39,464	$5,001	$5,051	$3,410	$52,926
Afterschool teachers @ $35 hr	$20,419	0	0	0	$20,419
				Total	$186,968
Transportation	$13,032	0	0	0	$13,032
				Total	$200,000

The funds cover the following items:

- 1.0 FTE CATS certified teacher
- 1.0 FTE WRAP certified teacher
- 1.0 FTE CATS/WRAP guidance counselor
- After school CATS Teachers (one or two, depending on number of students)
- Monday–Thursday from 2:30 pm–5:30 pm and Saturdays from 8 am–12 pm

APPENDIX 6.2

Kathy Haven's TWI Bilingual Grant

CASH AND IN-KIND DONATION APPLICATION WINTER 2009/10

1. Name of Nonprofit Organization: Two-Way Immersion Program,
                                          Bijou Community School,
                                          Lake Tahoe Unified School District

2. Federal Tax Exempt No.: See attached info about public schools

3. Contact information:
   Name: Kathy Haven
   Title/Position: Parent/TWI Volunteer Coordinator & Grant Writer
   Address: 3501 Spruce Ave., South Lake Tahoe, CA 96150
   Email: _____
   Phone: _____
   Fax: _____

4. *Mission and purpose of the organization (please list any relevant statistics including number of people served, etc.):*

Bijou Community School is a socioeconomically disadvantaged school in South Lake Tahoe, CA (Lake Tahoe Unified School District). Whereas 87.5% of the students at Bijou are on the free and reduced breakfast and lunch program, the school has a spirit among its students, staff, and family that is rarely found. Bijou is truly a community school. Besides educating about 500 elementary aged students, it also hosts the Boys and Girls Club every day after school, is used extensively on the weekends and weeknights by community families and organizations, and is used by our city's parks and rec. dept. to host softball and soccer leagues (see #7 for more info specifically about the Two-Way Immersion program and visit our website at www.tahoetwowayimmersion.com).

5. *Type of contribution requested:*
   ✘ Cash Contribution: $4,315
   ☐ In-Kind Product:

6. *In which area(s) is the contribution?*
   ✘ Youth—Education
   ☐ Youth—Recreation/Sports
   ☐ Youth—Other
   ☐ Environment

7. *Briefly describe the project or activity that is seeking support.*
   ■ *Who will benefit, and what numbers will be served?*
   ■ *What need(s) is being addressed?*
   ■ *What differences will this project, program, activity make in the community?*

In 2007, LTUSD began South Shore's first Two-Way Immersion (TWI) program at Bijou Community School. TWI is an all-inclusive, educational program that creates bilingual, bicultural, and academically strong students. The TWI program teaches an equal number of English-speaking students and Spanish-speaking students all academic subjects in two languages, English and Spanish. The program also promotes cultural equality and acceptance. Students enter the program in kindergarten and continue on each year until 5th grade. Bijou Community School currently has a 2nd-grade class, a 1st-grade class, and 2 kindergarten classes. Each year, we will add another grade for the oldest students, and as of this year, we will start adding a second class per grade as the program has gotten so popular with families in our community, that we implemented a second kindergarten class to accommodate everyone. Thus, when the program reaches 5th grade, we will be directly serving 240 students and their families.

The TWI program also benefits Bijou Community School in its entirety. The TWI program is an incredible program because everyone—students, teachers, staff, and parents—is very involved. The TWI parents who sign their children up for this program agree to volunteer at Bijou in return for the extra education their children are receiving. Half of their volunteer time (20 hours a year) goes directly to their child's class. The other half of their volunteer time (another 20 hours a year) goes to Bijou Community School. This year, with about 80 families in the TWI program, Bijou Community School has created 8 volunteer committees to "deal" with all this help. Parents are now helping in classrooms, in the work room, at recess, at lunchtime, in the library, and even after school with clubs they have started. Basically 80 extra hours a week are being given to Bijou Community School by parents of the TWI program. Obviously, every child, the staff, and the Bijou community are benefiting from these volunteers!

The long-term benefits of TWI are incredible. For one, the students in the TWI program will help connect families of different cultures throughout our town. Thus, as we are already seeing, more families will become more involved in education, in community affairs, and in local governing. Second, the students themselves will become better prepared for working in a global economy as they will have the benefit of true bilingualism. Lastly, and perhaps most importantly, if only half of the TWI students return to South Lake Tahoe as adults, our community will become a better place to live! Because of their bilingualism, these students will become the communicators and leaders of our community. They will reach across cultural lines, language barriers, and even socioeconomic levels to create a more united and close-knit South Lake Tahoe.

8. *How will the contribution specifically be used? Please indicate target timeline for associated program/project implementation.*

Every year, until our program reaches the 5th grade, we are looking for additional funding to help offset the extra costs of the Two-Way Immersion Program. Basically, the extra costs consist of buying materials, books, and supplies in two languages rather than just one. We do not want to impact any other classrooms in our district by using more funds for our program than any other, so we look for outside sources to help cover the one-time costs of setting up classrooms for the TWI program. We have written for over 25 grants in the past two years and will continue to do so to make sure the TWI program gets all the supplies and books it needs to run successfully, all the while not creating an undue burden on LTUSD and its other students.

Currently, we are seeking funding for the leveled reading books in Spanish that are needed in every classroom. There are three sets of books we need to buy for the TWI classes: the Santillana leveled readers, the National Geographic readers, and the Wright Group leveled books. These sets are all inclusive. They come with 10–15 levels of books (about six books for each level), a teacher's guide, supplementary teaching materials like CDs, and software. We have broken down our figures so that this Echo Grant could fund any portion of the $4,315 that we need. All three of these leveled reader sets are instrumental in the continued growth in literacy for our students.

The Santillana leveled reader set costs $1,495.
The National Geographic readers set costs $1,801.
The Wright Group leveled books set costs $1,019.
The total for all three sets equals $4,315.

Any and all funding toward these books would be so very appreciated. We are very excited about the progress our program has made, and will do anything and everything to ensure its continued success for our children. Thank you in advance for the time and effort your organization puts into our children and our families.

9. *Please outline total budget of the project requested contribution supports.*

Since we are starting up two new TWI classes every year for the next three years, and then one more classroom for two more years, I have outlined our expenditures per classroom. In other words, every year, the TWI program costs about double the total below. Yet, it is a little misleading, because any new class would cost about $12K to start up . . . thus a TWI class costs about $12K extra [I have bolded the extras], until the classes reach 5th grade. After 5th grade, we will have only normal expenditures for replacement of used materials.

Budget for a New TWI Classroom

Budgetary Items	Description	Cost
Textbooks	Classroom set of textbooks in English and Spanish for reading, math, science, and social studies, plus teacher materials/editions	$3,000
Reading program supplies	**Leveled Readers (sets): Santillana; National Geographic, Wright Group, Rigby, Hampton Brown**	**$6,000**
Classroom set of computers	3 sets of HP computers and the hardware and software for student use—$675 each	$2,000
Desks/chairs	Classroom set of student desk and chairs, plus one teacher desk/chair	$3,000
Miscellaneous supplies	Rugs, bookshelves, posters, manipulatives, overhead, writing materials, etc.	$3,000

(continues)

Budgetary Items	Description	Cost
White boards	Two large white boards with necessary tools (pens, etc.)	$1,000
Teacher extra service	Research and develop materials, meet with TWI teachers, and visit TWI sites outside of paid time	$2,500
Spanish Immersion Program for Teachers	Two teachers attended a 2-week Spanish program to practice and improve Spanish skills	$3,500
TOTAL		$24,000

10. *What is the total annual budget of the organization?*

LTUSD budget information is in the millions of dollars and is available online at www.ltusd.org. Total revenues are projected to total $31.9 million for the current year. (This is a decrease of approximately $610,000 over June's budget.) The state substantially reduced LTUSD's funding by $252 per pupil, which translates into a loss of approximately $1 million that is being offset by Federal Stimulus Funding. Expenditures are projected to total $35.1 million—an increase of $1.6 million. The majority of expense increases are the result of balances carried forward into the new year. So, in essence, with a transfer in of $400,000, the deficit will be approximately $2.8 million in 2009/10.

And, as expected, LTUSD pays for all the startup costs of a normal classroom. But since we are in a time where the budget is being whittled away by the state, and most programs are downsizing, rather than growing (like TWI), we just try to supplement the extras for the Spanish materials with grants and fundraisers so that we do not impact other classrooms in the district by taking funds from their regular programs.

11. *Please list other major donors/contributors to (1) this project and (2) the organization's general operations. Please list both in-kind and cash contributors.*

Most of the costs incurred by the TWI program are being covered by LTUSD. We are working hard to make our program the best it can be with multiple grants from our community. In the past few years, we have received grants from the El Dorado Community Foundation, Lake Tahoe Educational Foundation, the Rotary Club of South Lake Tahoe, Parasol Foundation, Barton Health Foundation, and the Bessie Minor Foundation. Every year, we proceed to find the funding for the extras of the new TWI classrooms that we are setting up. We expect to continue this search for another 5 years at which point our program will be complete from kindergarten to 5th grade—benefit for 240 children, their families, our school and our community!

APPENDIX 7.1

Grammar Exercises

PART 1: COMMAS

The best way to write a powerful sentence is to use a concrete noun and place it at the beginning of the sentence. But when you do put words or phrases ahead of the subject, always set these off with commas. Following are some sentences you can use to practice this rule.

1. Gradually she improved her grammar.
2. Hopefully she will continue to improve.
3. Gradually improving she met her goal.
4. Gradually improving makes you feel better.
5. Paying attention to every word he carefully completed every part of the RFP.
6. Paying attention to every word pays off.
7. Without hard work wishing is of little value.
8. Without hard work is how he wants to get through school.
9. Working not wishing brings success.
10. Seeking help she improved her grammar skills.
11. Seeking help improved her grammar skills.
12. Improving his grammar improved his grant success.
13. Improving his grammar he became increasingly successful at his grant writing.
14. Practicing her comma usage improved her grants.
15. Wishing without working is of little value.
16. Wishing hard she dropped the proposal in the mail.
17. Eventually the good proposals will be funded.
18. Weighing every day he eventually lost ten pounds.
19. Weighing every day helped him lose ten pounds.

PART 2: NUMBER AGREEMENT

Perhaps the most common yet damaging error is disagreement in number.

1. The school board closed five of their lowest-scoring schools.
2. The English department takes pride in their use of grammar.
3. The family brought their dog to the picnic.
4. Every teacher should guide their students careers.
5. Every student has a subject that they like best.
6. Floridas coach wanted their team to beat Alabama.
7. The analysis of data and using it to improve test scores is their goal.
8. Usually woman has a set of theories that determine how they feel.
9. A dozen donuts are too many.
10. Twelve donuts are too many.
11. Once one learns to read they can educate themselves.
12. The senior class said their final farewell.
13. Studying math and applying it is my favorite pastime.
14. Most curricula our district uses is set up for individual work.

15. Knowing and using good grammar pays off.
16. Not knowing and using good grammar is often embarrassing.
17. The data I saw is incorrect.
18. The parade of cars had their headlights on high beam.
19. The tenth grade needs to get their act together
20. The high school held their senior prom last Saturday night.

PART 3: ITS

Perhaps only second to number disagreement errors, the misuse of this small word distracts from grant evaluators' attention to each proposal.

1. The stray cat lost its way.
2. Its a quarter past two.
3. It's the principals call.
4. Its not my fault.
5. Madison School District gave it's teachers a raise.
6. That dog knows its time for its bath.
7. I think its a Johnny Mercer tune.
8. I can tell by its actions that its really hungry.
9. Its hard to drink enough water when its this hot.
10. Its a cold day.
11. The eagle will build its nest here.
12. Its my job to help our faculty improve its grant record.
13. The storm is in its worst hour; its almost over.
14. Ultimately Its your reputation that really matters.
15. Its too bad its too wide to fit in its case.
16. Is ten its length or its width?
17. Its washing its paws.
18. Its time to write another proposal.
19. The abstract is perhaps its easiest but most important part.
20. Is it its budget or its narrative that should reflect the other?

PART 4: APOSTROPHES

1. The Cook County students scores were the highest.
2. Which countrys 2007 TIMSS average scores were the highest?
3. Most teachers children are well behaved.
4. Our band leaders children are good kids.
5. Most preachers sermons are getting shorter, but not my preachers.
6. Tomorrow is todays youths futures.
7. In our district, is discipline the facultys responsibility or the students?
8. I think it's the facultys responsibility not the students.
9. You can't miss John Hancocks signature.
10. Listen to your school boards advice.
11. Theres room for only one in the winners circle.
12. The two parents ideas were the best.
13. Its the fault of its mother.
14. Its is a possessive word.
15. Shes the music teachers pet.
16. Uncertainty is part of our youths life.

17. Most of todays youths are self reliant.
18. shes a principles image of an up to date teacher.
19. Hes a well behaved kid not it behaved but well behaved.
20. Hard work leads to most peoples self improvement

PART 5: HYPHENS

When self precedes another word, it's hyphenated. Example: self-concept. When a collection of words form a concept, they are hyphenated. Example: up-to-date. When a word describes an adjective, that word and the adjective are hyphenated. Example: third-grade teacher.

1. Some first grade teachers are very creative.
2. Some teachers loose their passion for teaching
3. Good counselors help students develop positive self concepts.
4. Sometimes twelfth grade students feel too self confident.
5. He is a self made man.
6. She is one computer smart teacher.
7. Don't go self righteous on me.
8. Lets grab a ready to eat dish at that fast food restaurant.
9. Did he really make a hole in one?
10. Lets go one on one from the free throw line for ten minutes.
11. Do you mean we will shoot a ten minute round of free throw shots?
12. Has your district gone over board over high test scoring?
13. NCLB requires the use of data based methods.
14. Is your classroom fire proof?
15. That's a half baked idea.
16. Do you like hip hop dancing?
17. He is one down in the mouth principle.
18. Her self confidence is improving.
19. She is a self confident, self assured, self fish person.
20. Our make up test puts you on your honor.
21. His motives are self serving.
22. She serves only top of the line brands.
23. Self confidence and self initiative are traits of a self made woman.
24. Self dedication insures success.

PART 6: TECHNOLOGY TERMINOLOGY

Data is always a plural word. Internet is always spelled with a capital i. PowerPoint and SMART Board are tricky.

1. All students must make power point presentations.
2. She uses the internet everyday.
3. I believe that data is flawed.
4. Soon all teachers will use smart board.
5. Its time to use more power point.
6. Hopefully, data will stand on its own.
7. Thankfully he picked up smart board skills quickly.
8. Secondly she praised smart board and lastly she praised power point.
9. Does your principle favor the internet?

10. My favorite technology is power point.
11. He uses smart board every day.
12. Data is something you must get used to using.
13. It's the data that gives your proposal credibility.
14. Did you find this data on the internet?
15. Eventually all faculty will use the smart board and the internet.
16. Whose data is that on the smart board?
17. More data was used in my bachelors degree program than in my masters degree program.
18. The baby saw its picture on the internet.
19. Check your data and tell me if its correct.
20. All educators should know power point and smart board.
21. The internet is full of errors.
22. With or with out data power point is motivating.
23. That data in your power point presentation seems to be its best part.
24. The Charleston school board were impressed by all of that data.
25. Hopefully your school board will support the use of internet.
26. Finally we began using all that data that we find on the internet everyday.

PART 7: EDUCATION TERMS

1. That principle has a life long passion for helping others.
   Correction: That principal has a lifelong passion for helping others.
2. Is that data correct?
   Correction: Are these data correct?
3. Lets get a smart board for every classroom
   Correction: Let's get a SMART Board for every classroom.
4. Lets make power point a life long habit.
   Correction: Let's make PowerPoint a lifelong habit.
5. Does technology really effect learning?
   Correction: Does technology really affect learning?
6. Does technology effect change?
   Correct as is.
7. Where's the data?
   Correction: Where are the data?
8. Her life long dream is to become a counselor.
   Correction: Her lifelong dream is to become a counselor.
9. What effect if any did that data have?
   Correction: What effect, if any, did these data have?
10. The data and the presentation was impressive.
    Correction: The data and the presentation were impressive.
11. The data was convincing enough to make me a life long believer.
    Correction: The data were convincing enough to make me a lifelong believer.
12. Whose affect was greatest in the countys scores, the teachers or the principles?
    Correction: Whose effect was greater in the county's scores, the teachers' or the principal's?
13. Shes the principle that improved the most.
    Correction: She's the principal who improved the most.
14. Hes the principle thats good to have on your side.
    Correction: He's the principal who's good to have on your side.

15. I feel that walking the walk is better than talking the talk.
Correction: I believe that walking the walk is better than talking the talk.

16. Don't you feel that good counselors can effect their students self concepts?
Correction: Don't you believe that good counselors can affect their students' self-concepts?

17. Shes the one thats got the beat.
Correction: She's the one who has the beat (Or, She's the one with the beat).

18. Hes the teacher that wrote the best proposal.
Correction: He's the teacher who wrote the best proposal.

19. Its time to clip its wings.
Correction: It's time to clip its wings.

20. Regretfully its my poor grammar and not my lack of effort that hurts my grant writing the most.
Correction: Regretfully, it's my poor grammar and not my lack of effort that hurts my grant writing the most.

21. Its my poor punctuation and my mediocre spelling that challenges me the most.
Correction: It's my poor punctuation and my mediocre spelling that challenge me the most.

APPENDIX 7.2

Grammar Exercises

PART 1: ANSWERS

Following are corrections to the flawed sentences found in Appendix 7.1.

1. Gradually she improved her grammar.
   Correction: Gradually, she improved her grammar.
2. Hopefully she will continue to improve.
   Correction: Hopefully, she will continue to improve.
3. Gradually improving she met her goal.
   Correction: Gradually improving, she met her goal.
4. Gradually improving makes you feel better.
   Correction: Gradually improving makes you feel better. (Gradually improving is the subject and, therefore, needs no comma.)
5. Paying attention to every word he carefully completed every part of the RFP.
   Correction: Paying attention to every word, he carefully completed every part of the RFP.
6. Paying attention to every word pays off.
   Correction: Paying attention to every word pays off.
7. Without hard work wishing is of little value.
   Correction: Without hard work, wishing is of little value.
8. Without hard work is how he wants to get through school.
   Correction: Without hard work is how he wants to get through school.
9. Working not wishing brings success.
   Correction: Working, not wishing, brings success.
10. Seeking help she improved her grammar skills.
    Seeking help, she improved her grammar skills.
11. Seeking help improved her grammar skills.
    Correct as is.
12. Improving his grammar improved his grant success.
    Improving his grammar improved his grant success.
13. Improving his grammar he became increasingly successful at his grant writing.
    Correction: Improving his grammar, he became increasingly successful at his grant writing.
14. Practicing her comma usage improved her grants.
    Correction: Practicing her comma usage, she improved her grants.
15. Wishing without working is of little value.
    Correction: Wishing without working is of little value.
16. Wishing hard, she dropped the proposal in the mail.
    Correction: Wishing hard, she dropped the proposal in the mail.
17. Eventually the good proposals will be funded.
    Correction: Eventually, the good proposals will be funded.
18. Weighing every day he eventually lost ten pounds.
    Correction: Weighing every day, he eventually lost ten pounds.
19. Weighing every day helped him lose ten pounds.
    Correct as is.

PART 2: NUMBER AGREEMENT

Perhaps the most common yet damaging error is disagreement in number.

1. The school board closed five of their lowest scoring schools.
   Correction: The school board closed five of its lowest scoring schools.
2. The English Department takes pride in their use of grammar.
   Correction: The English teachers take pride in their use of grammar.
3. The family brought their dog to the picnic.
   Correction: The family brought its dog to the picnic.
4. Every teacher should guide their students careers.
   Correction: All teachers should guide their students' careers.
5. Every student has a subject that they like best.
   Correction: Every student has a favorite subject.
6. Floridas coach wanted their students to beat Alabama.
   Correction: Florida's coach wanted its students to beat Alabama.
7. The analysis of data and using it to improve test scores is their goal.
   Correction: The analysis of data and using them to improve test scores are their goals.
8. Usually a woman has a set of theories that determine how they feel.
   Correction: Usually, a woman has a set of theories that determines how she feels.
9. A dozen donuts are too many.
   Correction: A dozen donuts is too many.
10. Twelve donuts are too many.
    Correction: Twelve donuts are too many.
11. Once one learns to read they can educate themselves.
    Correction: Once individuals learn to read, they can educate themselves.
12. The senior class said their final farewell.
    Correction: The seniors said their final farewells.
13. Studying math and applying it is my favorite pastime.
    Correction: Studying math and working math puzzles are my favorite pastimes.
14. Most curricula our district uses is set up for individual work.
    Correction: Most curricula our district uses are set up for individual work.
15. Knowing and using good grammar pays off.
    Correction: Knowing and using good grammar pay off.
16. Not knowing and using good grammar is often embarrassing.
    Correction: Not knowing and using good grammar are often embarrassing.
17. The data I saw was incorrect
    Correction: The data I saw were incorrect.
18. The parade of cars had their headlights on high beam.
    Correction: The parade of cars had its headlights on high beam.
19. The tenth grade needs to get their act together
    Correction: The tenth grade needs to get its act together.
20. His high school held their senior prom last Saturday night.
    Correction: His high school held its senior prom last Saturday night.

PART 3: ITS

Perhaps only second to number disagreement errors, the misuse of this small word distracts from grant evaluators' attention to each proposal.

1. The stray cat lost its way.
   Correction: The stray cat lost its way.

2. Its a quarter past two.
   Correction: It's a quarter past two.

3. Its the principals call.
   Correction: It's the principal's call.

4. Its not my fault.
   Correction: It's not my fault.

5. Madison School District gave it's teachers a raise.
   Correction: Madison School District gave its teachers a raise.

6. That dog knows its time for its bath.
   Correction: That dog knows it's time for its bath.

7. I think its a Johnny Mercer tune.
   Correction: I think it's a Johnny Mercer tune.

8. I can tell by its actions that its really hungry.
   Correction: I can tell by its actions that it's really hungry.

9. Its hard to drink enough water when its this hot.
   Correction: It's hard to drink enough water when it's this hot.

10. Its a cold day.
    Correction: It's cold.

11. The eagle will build its nest here.
    Correct as is.

12. Its my job to help our faculty improve its annual grant record.
    Correction: It's my job to help our faculty improve its annual grant record.

13. The storm is in its worst hour; its all most over.
    Correction: The storm is in its worst hour; it's almost over.

14. Ultimately its your reputation that really matters.
    Correction: Ultimately, it's your reputation that really maters.

15. Its too bad its too wide to fit in its case.
    Correction: It's too bad it's too wide to fit in its case.

16. Is ten its length or its width?
    Correction: Is ten its length or its width?

17. Its washing its paws.
    Correction: It's washing its paws.

18. Its time to write another proposal.
    Correction: It's time to write another proposal.

19. The abstract is perhaps its easiest but most important part.
    Correction: The abstract is perhaps its easiest, but most important, part.

20. Is it its budget or its narrative that should reflect the other?
    Correction: Is it its budget or its narrative that should reflect the other?

PART 4: APOSTROPHES

1. The Cook County students scores were the highest.
   Correction: The Cook County students' scores were the highest.

2. Which countrys TIMSS average scores were the highest?
   Correction: Which country's TIMSS average score was the highest?

3. Most teachers children are well behaved.
   Correction: Most teachers' children are well behaved.

4. Our band leaders children are good kids.
   Correction: Our band leader's children are good kids.

5. Most preachers sermons are getting shorter, but not my preachers.
   Correction: Most preachers' sermons are getting shorter, but not my preacher's.

6. Tomorrow is todays youths futures.
   Correction: Tomorrow is today's youths' futures.

7. In our district is discipline the facultys responsibility or the students?
   Correction: In our district, is discipline the faculty's responsibility or the students'?

8. I think its the facultys responsibility not the students.
   Correction: I think it's the faculty's responsibility, not the students'.

9. You can't miss John Hancocks signature.
   Correction: You can't miss John Hancock's signature.

10. Listen to your school boards advice.
    Correction: Listen to your school board's advice.

11. Theres room for only one in the winners circle.
    Correction: There's room for only one in the winner's circle.

12. The two parents ideas were the best.
    Correction: The two parents' ideas were the best.

13. Its the fault of its mother.
    Correction: It's the fault of its mother.

14. Its is a possessive word.
    Correction: Its is a possessive word.

15. Shes the music teachers pet.
    Correction: She's the music teacher's pet.

16. Uncertainty is part of our youths life.
    Correction: Uncertainty is part of our youths' lives.

17. Most of todays youths are self reliant.
    Correction: Most of today's youths are self-reliant.

18. Shes a principles image of an up to date teacher.
    Correction: She's a principal's image of an up-to-date teacher.

19. Hes a well behaved kid, not ill behaved but well behaved.
    Correction: He's a well-behaved kid, not ill-behaved but well-behaved.

20. Hard work leads to most peoples self improvement
    Correction: Hard work leads to most people's self-improvement.

PART 5: HYPHENS

When self precedes another word, it's hyphenated. Example: self-concept. When a collection of words form a concept, they are hyphenated. Example: up-to-date. When a word describes an adjective, that word and the adjective are hyphenated. Example: third-grade teacher.

1. Some first grade teachers are very creative.
   Correction: Some first-grade teachers are very creative.

2. Some teachers loose their passion for teaching
   Correction: Some teachers lose their passion for teaching.

3. Good counselors help students develop positive self concepts.
   Correction: Good counselors help their students develop positive self-concepts.

4. Sometimes twelfth grade students feel too self confident.
   Correction: Sometimes, twelfth-grade students feel too self-confident.

5. Hes a self made man.
   Correction: He's a self-made man.

6. She is one computer smart teacher.
   Correction: She is one computer-smart teacher.

7. Don't go self righteous on me.
   Correction: Don't go self-righteous on me.

8. Lets grab a ready to eat dish at that fast food restaurant.
   Correction: Let's grab a ready-to-eat dish at that fast-food restaurant.

9. Did he really make a hole in one?
Correction: Did he really make a hole-in-one?

10. Lets go one on one from the free throw line for ten minutes.
Correction: Let's go one-on-one from the free-throw line for ten minutes.

11. Do you mean we will shoot a ten minute round of free throw shots?
Correction: Do you mean we will shoot a ten-minute round of free throws?

12. Has your district gone over board over high test usage?
Correction: Has your district gone overboard over high-test usage?

13. NCLB requires the use of data based methods.
Correction: NCLB requires the use of data-based methods.

14. Is your classroom fire proof?
Correction: Is your classroom fireproof?

15. That's a half baked idea.
Correction: That's a half-baked idea.

16. Do you like hip hop dancing?
Correction: Do you like hip-hop dancing?

17. He is one down in the mouth principle.
Correction: He is one down-in-the-mouth principal.

18. Her self confidence is improving.
Correction: Her self-confidence is improving.

19. She is a self confident, self assured, self fish person.
Correction: She is a self-confident, self-assured, selfish person.

20. Our make up test puts you on your honor.
Correction: Our makeup test puts you on your honor.

21. His motives are self serving.
Correction: His motives are self-serving.

22. She serves only top of the line brands.
Correction: She serves only top-of-the-line brands.

23. Self confidence and self initiative are traits of a self made woman.
Correction: Self-confidence and self-initiative are traits of a self-made woman.

24. Self dedication insures success.
Correction: Self-dedication ensures success.

PART 6: TECHNOLOGY TERMINOLOGY

Data is always a plural word. Internet is always spelled with a capital i. PowerPoint and SMART Board are tricky.

1. All students must make power point presentations.
Correction: All students must make PowerPoint presentations.

2. According to her, she uses the internet everyday.
Correction: According to her, she uses the Internet every day.

3. I believe that data is flawed.
Correction: I believe those data are flawed.

4. Soon all teachers will use smart board.
Correction: Soon, all teachers will use SMART Board.

5. Its time to use more power point.
Correction: It's time to use more PowerPoint.

6. Hopefully, this data will stand on its own.
Correction: Hopefully, these data will stand on their own.

7. Thankfully he picked up smart board skills quickly.
Correction: Thankfully, he picked up SMART Board skills quickly.

8. Secondly she praised smart board and lastly she praised power point.
   Correction: Second, she praised SMART Board, and last, she praised PowerPoint.

9. Does your principle favor the internet?
   Correction: Does your principal favor the Internet?

10. My favorite technology is power point.
    Correction: My favorite technology is PowerPoint.

11. He uses smart board everyday.
    Correction: He uses SMART Board every day.

12. Data is something you must get used to using.
    Correction: Data are something you must get used to using.

13. It's the data that gives your proposals credibility
    Correction: It's the data that give your proposals credibility.

14. Did you find this data on the internet?
    Correction: Did you find those data on the Internet?

15. Eventually all faculty will use the smart board and the internet.
    Correction: Eventually, all faculty will use the SMART Board and the Internet.

16. Whose data is that on the smart board?
    Correction: Whose data are those on the SMART Board?

17. More data was used in my bachelors degree program than in my masters degree program.
    Correction: More data were used in my bachelor's degree program than in my master's degree program.

18. The baby saw its picture on the internet.
    Correction: The baby saw its picture on the Internet.

19. Check your data and tell me if its right.
    Correction: Check your data and tell me if they are correct.

20. All faculty should know power point and smart board.
    Correction: All teachers should know PowerPoint and SMART Board.

21. The internet is full of errors.
    Correction: The Internet is full of errors.

22. With or with out data power point is motivating.
    Correction: With or without data, PowerPoint is motivating.

23. That data in your power point presentation seems to be its best part.
    Correction: Those data in your PowerPoint presentation seem to be its best part.

24. The Charleston school board were impressed by all of that data.
    Correction: The Charleston School Board members were impressed by all those data.

25. Hopefully your school board will support the use of internet.
    Correction: Hopefully, your school board will support the use of Internet.

26. Finally we began using all that data that we find on the internet everyday.
    Correction: Finally, we began using all those data that we find on the Internet every day.

PART 7 EDUCATION TERMS

1. That principle has a life long passion for helping others.
2. Is that data correct?
3. Lets get a smart board for every classroom
4. Lets make power point a life long habit.
5. Does technology really effect learning?
6. Does technology effect change?

7. Where's the data?
8. Her life long dream is to become a counselor.
9. What effect if any did that data have?
10. The data and the presentation was impressive.
11. the data was convincing enough to make me a life long believer.
12. Whose affect was greatest in the countys scores, the teachers or the principles?
13. Shes the principle that improved the most.
14. Hes the principle thats good to have on your side.
15. I feel that walking the walk is better than talking the talk.
16. Don't you feel that good counselors can effect their students self concepts?
17. Shes the one thats got the beat.
18. Hes the teacher that wrote the best proposal.
19. Its time to clip its wings.
20. Regretfully its my poor grammar and not my lack of effort that hurts my grant writing the most.
21. Its my poor punctuation and my mediocre spelling the challenges me the most.

APPENDIX 8.1

List of Kappa Delta Pi Awards by State

State	Award
IL	Victoria will be purchasing books for her school's small and outdated library.
NC	Melissa will purchase math manipulatives for her classroom of 26 students.
NY	Hope-for-Hispanic students will affect 75 students by providing them with English books on CD.
DC	Katherine will purchase Spanish books for ELL students at her largely minority and free/reduced lunch school, affecting over 300 elementary students.
CA	Carol will purchase PE equiment that students can use both in gym class and during recess.
MN	Fitting Kids and Keyboards Together will affect 300 students when Patricia purchases child-size keyboards to help them learn to type.
NJ	Patricia will purchase age-appropriate magazines to allow 47 students access to current events, theatre, sports, entertainment, and short stories.
LA	In a Heartbeat will affect 125 alternative school students by training them to use CPR.
NY	Thirty of Mary Jo's at-risk students will be affected by this grant when she purchases math manipulatives and games to help them learn.
CA	Alice will purchase math manipulatives for her classroom of 20 students in a Title 1, majority ELL school.
NY	Francine can continue her listening center project that affects 100 students. She will replace products purchased with the teacher grant a few years ago.
GA	Robin will purchase a classroom set of calculators to be used by 100 Title 1, ELL, ESS, and other disadvantaged students.
OH	Christina will purchase books to begin a reading buddy program in her school.
PA	Sing, Move, Read will affect 300 students by incorporating literature and music with movement.
FL	Nine hundred gifted students will be affected by this grant. Krisi will purchase copy paper and highlighters for teachers to print and copy handouts to help prepare students for testing.
OK	Fifty to seventy-five special education students will be affected each year by the use of white boards in the classroom.
NY	Medically fragile and special needs pre-K students will be able to use books, art supplies, toys, puzzles, and other items in their school.

(continues)

State	Award
MI	Let's Document Math in Our Environment will affect 140 students. Digital cameras will be purchased so that students can document geometry in our environment.
NY	Painting Like Michelangelo will affect 48 students. Students will paint underneath tables in their classroom to study Renaissance art and gain empathy for Michelangelo painting the Sistine Chapel.
NJ	The Used Battery Collection will affect 1,000 students. Students will institute a school-wide battery recycling program to help them understand the harmful effects of chemicals and to make a positive impact in their community.
IN	Earthworms, Nature's Recyclers will affect 24 pre-K students. Students will care for and feed the earthworms while learning the worms' necessary place in the world.
AL	"The play's the thing." Hamlet Act 2 Scene 2 will affect 12 highly special needs students. Students will visit an opera house, where they will watch Hamlet and then travel to the mall to learn of community opportunities.
OH	This butterfly project will affect 47 students. Students will document the transition of a caterpillar to a butterfly in their classroom.
MA	Italian Pen Pals and ePals Culture DVD Project will affect up to 140 students. Students in this classroom will create DVDs to send to Italian classrooms that document their everyday lives.
FL	Fun Reading Every Day will affect 200 students, most who are reading at or above their expected reading level.

APPENDIX 8.2

Phi Delta Kappa International
Regional Project Application

_____   _____
NAME   DATE

_____
PROJECT TITLE

_____ or _____
CHAPTER NAME   MEMBER NAME

_____   _____
CHAPTER NUMBER   MEMBER ID NUMBER

_____   _____
REGION   REPRESENTATIVE

Leadership / Research / Service

PHI DELTA KAPPA INTERNATIONAL
408 N. Union Street, Bloomington, IN 47405-3800
www.pdkintl.org
Ph. 812-339-1156 • 800-766-1156
Fax 812-339-0018
E-mail: customerservice@pdkintl.org

Regional Project Application   FORM 112 (10/09)

PROPOSAL NARRATIVE FORMAT

Please answer the following questions about your project and attach to the application.

What do you expect to happen? Outcomes sought? Project goal(s)?

What are your objective(s)? How will you accomplish your goals?

How will the success of the project be evaluated?

For additional guidelines and assistance, visit the PDK website at **www.pdkintl.org** or contact your Chapter/Member Liaison, Region Representative, or PDK International.

Regional Project Application

REGIONAL PROJECT PROPOSAL
PHI DELTA KAPPA INTERNATIONAL

A. Project Title _____

B. Sponsoring Chapter _____ Chapter No. _____

    or Sponsoring Member _____ Member ID _____

C. Statement of Project Objective (supported by attached narrative)

D. Project Personnel

    Director _____ Title _____

    Address _____ E-mail _____

    _____ Business Phone (   ) _____

    _____ Home Phone (   ) _____

    Co-Director* _____ Title _____

    Address _____ E-mail _____

    _____ Business Phone (   ) _____

    _____ Home Phone (   )

    Chapter Treasurer or Financial Agent**

    Title _____ E-mail _____

    Address _____ Business Phone (   ) _____

    _____ Home Phone (   ) _____

    *For chapter-sponsored projects, a chapter officer must be identified as director or co-director. For member-sponsored projects, a regional chapter/member liaison must be identified as co-director.

    **For chapter-sponsored projects, the chapter treasurer must be identified as the financial agent. For member-sponsored projects, an approved agency named in the project proposal must be identified.

E. Beginning Date _____ Ending Date _____

F. Amount of Regional Project Funds Requested (supported by attached budget)

G. Signatures

_____ _____
Project Director Co-Director

_____ _____
Treasurer or Financial Agent Chapter/Member Liaison

_____
Chapter President (chapter-sponsored only)

Project Approval: _____ Yes _____ No _____ **Conditional (explanation below)**

Regional Representative _____ **Date** _____

Regional Project Application

REGION PROJECT PROPOSAL BUDGET

Project Title: _____

Sponsoring Chapter or Member: _____

BUDGET ITEM	Phi Delia Kappa Regional Support	Chapter Support		Other Support		Total
		In-Kind	Real Money	In-Kind	Real Money	
1. Speakers, Other Personnel						
2. Miscellaneous Supplies						
3. Support Services a. Office Supplies						
b. Clerical Services						
c. Phone						
d. Postage						
e. Printing						
f. Other						
4. Equipment Rental (Include Computer Services)						
5. Travel						
6. Other (Please see "Budget Explanation" statement below.) a.						
b.						
c.						
TOTAL						

Current Balance in Chapter Treasury _____
(for chapter projects only)

BUDGET EXPLANATION

Provide at least one sentence of specific information for each budget item. Please use a separate sheet. Also identify sources of "other support."

Regional Project Application

EVALUATION CRITERIA
REGIONAL PROJECT APPLICATION

Name of Applicant _____

Chapter Number _____   OR   Member ID Number _____

Title of Project _____

Date Submitted for Review _____   Date of Project Implementation _____

The following are criteria used in evaluating Regional Project applications. These criteria collectively will be used in making a final decision about funding your project submission.

The scale ranges from 1 (lowest) to 5 (highest).

1.	Significance of activity to PDK	1	2	3	4	5
2.	Clarity of project description	1	2	3	4	5
3.	Soundness of procedure/methodology	1	2	3	4	5
4.	Ratio - "in-kind" to direct dollar support	1	2	3	4	5
5.	Cost Effectiveness	1	2	3	4	5
6.	Evidence of funding support	1	2	3	4	5
7.	Evidence of member involvement	1	2	3	4	5
8.	Project impact on recipients	1	2	3	4	5
9.	Quality of project - genuine benefit	1	2	3	4	5
10.	Application complete and thorough	1	2	3	4	5

Total Points (50 potential)_____

Other considerations:

Is the application the first one from the chapter or member?   Yes / No

Is the application a repeat of a previously funded project?   Yes / No

Has the chapter or member ever been funded?   Yes / No

Is the chapter or member eligible for regional support?   Yes / No
(e.g. good-standing, reports filed, etc.)

Evaluator's Name: _____   Date Reviewed: _____

Regional Project Application

APPENDIX 8.3

Beating to a Different Drum

SECTION B: PROPOSAL NARRATIVE

1. Summary of Project

The *Beating to a Different Drum* project was designed as a partnership between the United Way of Metropolitan Atlanta and The Third Circle to increase out-of-school time activities for youth through music. This project enables our United Way to engage in a collaboration that serves a diverse group of youth in neighborhoods we have be unable to reach in DeKalb and Fulton counties. In addition to six public performances, our 30-week project will include skill-building sessions focused on keyboarding, drumming, dance, and drill/step. Through active participation in these sessions, our vision is that youth will be empowered to choose at least one form of music, improve their skills and knowledge about that form, and be excited about performing their skills in front of an audience. The *Beating to a Different Drum* project was designed to achieve four main outcomes: youth will feel confident in their new skills to enjoy performing publicly, school attendance will increase, academic performance will improve, and youth feel that they mastered at least one new musical skill.

2. Description of United Way Organization

The United Way of Metropolitan Atlanta connects people, resources, and ideas to build a stronger, safer, more vibrant community across our 13-county area. The community we serve is characterized as both urban and rural encompassing over 3.6 million citizens. Our mission is to measurably improve the human condition in our community. In order to achieve our mission, we have strategically designed 13 key indicators with measurable targets. We invest in over 300 programs that fall under four main outcome areas: nurturing children and youth, strengthening families, increasing economic self-sufficiency, and encouraging citizen involvement. One of our key indicators is *"safe, productive, structured group activities outside school hours."* There are currently 413,500 children, ages 6 to 17, in working-parent families in our 13-county metro area. A 1997 needs assessment revealed 70,500 spaces in five-day-a-week, structured afterschool programs. We lack five-day-a-week structured afterschool program spaces for 343,000 children and young people. Our current target is to increase quality, out-of-school time activities for 136,250 more children and youth in the 13-county metro Atlanta area by the end of the 2003–04 school year. Achieving this goal means that 50% of children in working parent families will have access to safe, productive, structured activities outside school hours.

The accomplishments of our afterschool initiative to date demonstrate our capacity and readiness to successfully implement and sustain our proposed project. The following highlights just *a few* of our strengths:

- Concerned Black Clergy, AT&T, GA Council for the Arts, GA Parks and Recreation, American Business Collaborative, Eastman Kodak, among many others.

- 12 school systems. With growing foundation support and United Way investments, we have a grantee network of more than 107 programs in 80 plus organizations working on youth development and afterschool (YMCA, YWCA, Boys & Girls Club, Girls Inc., etc.).
- We now have 118 out-of-school time activities partners in metro Atlanta, including University of GA, 10 school systems, Quality Care for Children, Partnership for After-school Education, and GA School Age Care Association. Superintendents have committed to make afterschool a focus area in their districts with the United Way.
- United Way brought four school districts together to potentially leverage $12 million in federal dollars for the 21st Century Learning Centers initiative to create more afterschool slots; three school districts already have 21st Century grants. United Way is working with a consortium of school districts to design a sustainability plan for these federal grants.

3. Project Design/Plan

The proposed project, *Beating to a Different Drum,* will enable United Way's afterschool initiative help reach our goal of ensuring at least 50% of metro area youth have enriching out-of-school time activities. Most important, the project will serve as a catalyst to create a new partnership with a "nontraditional" partner in our area, The Third Circle. This organization works to increase the National School Age Care Alliance (NSACA) capacity to have a positive impact on the quality of programs serving low-income communities. The Third Circle was selected because of the program's ability to incorporate music into afterschool activities and target youth, particularly Hispanic, Asian, and African American, from neighborhoods in DeKalb and Fulton counties we have been unable to reach.

The goals of *Beating to a Different Drum* include the following:

- Goal 1: Build beginning and advanced skills in keyboarding, dance, and drumming in an out-of-school time environment for youth.
- Goal 2: Increase youth opportunities to perform in front of their peers and family members, in addition to audiences that include people of other cultures at "sister" centers.
- Goal 3: Empower youth to work as a team to learn about music and to plan and deliver public performances.

The *Beating to a Different Drum* project recognizes the fact that the key to performance is experiencing success and that success is always a motivator. Children are natural music lovers and because of this love, they want to experience all phases of music and are determined to master the experience. This project will transfer this "determination to master" to their classroom experiences. Our youth will have the opportunity to engage in skill development that will empower them to play the keyboard and drums, and learn the movement skills needed to perform dance and drill patterns. Enrichment sessions will teach the children about the types of drums and sounds of other multicultural instruments dances.

Many of our students are not involved in the social aspects of their schools and, because of this, they find school dull and boring. The school systems in our area have cut back on music education; therefore, youth are not consistently introduced to these opportunities. However, when summer music programs are introduced, 50% of the students joined band at their local school the following year even though they did not have an interest previously.

The target population includes approximately 225 youth between the ages of 5 and 12 in DeKalb and Fulton counties in metro Atlanta. Youth participants will include those who attend afterschool programs from 3 to 6 p.m. at three agency sites (YMCA, Decatur Recreation and Parks, and The School Kids Club) where the project will be implemented. Our targeted youth for this project are 50% African American, 40% Hispanic, and 10% Caucasian.

Over 70% of these youth are from single-parent homes, and 80% are on free or reduced lunch. The project will be implemented by three professional Site Coordinators trained in youth development. Please see attachments for detailed resumes. In addition, our key partners will serve as the music specialists for each session. These include university music departments (Morris Brown, Morehouse, Clark, and Spelman), DeKalb County School Music Department, and the South DeKalb Conservatory of Dance. An Advisory Committee will meet on a monthly basis to monitor and evaluate our progress. Members will include a parent, a music specialist partner from the university, three project staff, a youth participant, director of The Third Circle, and our United Way Director of Community Investments for Afterschool. A local Best Buy representative will also be invited to serve on the committee. In addition, Best Buy employees and their families will be invited to performances and to serve as volunteers.

Our 30-week project will include sessions focused on keyboarding, drumming, dance, and drill/step. The project includes the following three phases:

Phase 1 (mid-September to mid-October) *Introduction:* The first 5 weeks of the project will allow youth participants to participate in all 4 musical sessions listed above. The purpose of this phase is to assure that participants learn the history of music and the advantages the music industry has to offer. These enrichment sessions will also give our youth an opportunity to discover which form of music is interesting to them by seeing, hearing, and touching different instruments. In addition, innovative craft sessions will enable children to learn how to make their own instruments and write their own lyrics. Children will rotate to all 4 sessions so they will learn the basics for each and become better equipped to choose the focus area(s) they wish to continue learning.

Phase 2 (mid-October to mid-December) *Developing a Skill:* During the next 10 weeks of the project, youth can choose which sessions they want to continue to experience. Keyboarding and drumming will have 2 1-hour classes that meet twice a week. Dance and drill/step will have 2 1-hour sessions that will meet three times a week. This phase will include an initial "practice" performance at the beginning of November for peers only so youth can get used to being in front of an audience. A second "formal" performance will be conducted at the end of November for parents, family, and friends at each site. A holiday "exchange" concert will then be conducted in mid-December in collaboration with all three sites. In addition to public performances, youth participants will also be involved in learning how to set up sound equipment, video cameras, staging, special effects, and decorations as a team.

Phase 3 *(January–May) Mastering a Skill:* The final 15 weeks of the project will further develop the musical skill(s) youth chose to develop. Skill-building sessions will continue to meet as in Phase 2. In addition, the four different groups (keyboarding, drumming, dance, drill/step) will collaborate together to practice, set up, and deliver three public performances (February–Black History Month, April–Spring Fever, May–Final Drumdown) at community sites such as a local high school, Maranatha Academy Complex, and a local mall. The keyboarding and drumming participants will play the music for the dance and drill/step routines. The following highlights our intended outcomes and measures of *Beating to a Different Drum* project.

Outcome Measure Activities to Lead to Outcome

Youth will feel confident in their new skills to enjoy performing publicly.

Collect anecdotal information from parents after each performance about youth's confidence level; youth show up to perform publicly; staff will record observations and compare confidence levels from the first to last performance.

Youth learning, choosing musical activity, and practicing each week; performing in front of peers first, then parents and friends; working as a youth team.

School attendance will increase.

Compare school attendance records before and after the project is implemented.

Access to special music activities is contingent on going to school; interest in continuing to develop new music skill will spark youth to access and participate in opportunities at school.

Academic performance will improve.

Compare academic performance record (grades, discipline referrals, etc.) before and after the project is implemented; parents will present report cards to staff as "proof" of academic performance.

Learning about the history of music, making instruments, listening to other youth perform, and setting up public performances will stimulate youths' ability to think creatively, problem solve, work as a team, etc., all of which contribute to academic performance; recognize youth for grade improvements.

Youth feel that they mastered at least one new musical skill.

Collect anecdotal information about participants; staff observe youth individually and how they work as a team; survey youths before they begin the project and after to determine if their attitudes have changed; determine number of youth who engage in school day musical programs.

Youth learning, choosing musical activity, and practicing each week; performing publicly.

The United Way of Metropolitan Atlanta and The Third Circle are excited about the potential our *Beating to a Different Drum* project will have in our community. With your help, we will continue to build a stronger, safer community for our youth.

SECTION C: PROPOSAL BUDGET

Total Project Costs: $49,150
Total In-Kind: $29,600*
Total Requested from Best Buy: $19,550

Budget Category/Narrative Requested Funds
In-Kind Support
Total Cost

I. PERSONNEL
   a. *Site Coordinators*—to implement the project at each site: 3 sites @ $1,500 each = $4,500
   b. *Program Staff*—to assist site coordinators in supervision and project coordination: 3 sites @ $1,000 each = $3,000
   c. *Van Drivers*—to transport children from school to project site: 3 drivers @ $400 each = $1,200

   Subtotal Personnel $8,700

II. CONTRACTUAL
   a. *Keyboard Specialists*—to provide specialized sessions: 3 sites @ $1,320 each = $3,960
   b. *Drummer Specialists*—to provide specialized sessions: 3 sites @ $1,320 each = $3,960
   c. *Dance Specialists*—to provide specialized sessions: 3 sites @ $1,980 each = $5,940
   d. *Drill/step Specialists*—to provide specialized sessions: 3 sites @ $1,980 each = $5,940
   e. *Building Rental*—3 sites × $1,000 each = $3,000

   Subtotal Contractual $22,800

III. EQUIPMENT
   a. *Keyboards*—15 keyboards × 3 sites × $53.33 per keyboard = $2,400
   b. *Drum Sticks*—15 stick sets × 3 sites × $6.66 each set = $300
   c. *Drum Pads*—15 pads × 3 sites × $26.66 per pad = $1,200
   d. *Storage Cabinet*—3 sites × $300 per AV cabinet = $900
   e. *Utility Carts*—3 sites × $200 per AV cart = $600
   f. *Rental Fees*—for stage/platform for performances: 6 performances × $250 per rental = $1,500
   g. *Sound Equipment*—DVD, speakers, converters, etc.: 3 sites × $1,333.33 equipment costs = $4,000

   Subtotal Equipment $10,900

IV. SUPPLIES
   a. *Educational*—music software, books, posters: 3 sites × $500 = $1,500
   b. *Audio Visual*—tapes, video, film: 3 sites × $200 = $600
   c. *Arts* and *Crafts*—paints, brushes, skins, bamboo: 3 sites × $150 = $450

---

*In-Kind costs are provided by the three sites involved in this project—YMCA, Decatur Recreation and Parks, and The New Kids Production and Design.

d. *Food/refreshments/invitations*—for 6 performances × $100 each = $600
e. *Costumes*—t-shirts, flags, streamers: 3 sites × $600 = $1,800

Subtotal Supplies $4,950

V. TRAVEL

a. *Local Travel*—to exchange performances at each site, includes gas, van = $1,800

Subtotal Travel $1,800
TOTAL PROJECT COSTS $49,150

Subcontracts: The United Way of Metropolitan Atlanta has designed this project in collaboration with The Third Circle. This organization coordinates the project with the three sites involved in the project. More information about The Third Circle can be found in Attachment F. Additional Funders/
Sustainability: This project will be able to sustain and continue by establishing relationships with other lenders of art programs, including

• DeKalb Extension Services
• Woodruff Arts Center
• Hyde Museum

APPENDIX 8.4

Reach for the Stars

PROJECT ABSTRACT

Reach for the Stars is a program that will reach more than 630 students in grades K–6 at Petersburg Elementary School* and their families. This program will train teachers, provide opportunities for student experimentation, involve participation by parents and utilize partnerships with community experts.

Through Reach for the Stars teachers and community partners will be trained to fully utilize the existing optical telescope that was purchased with grant funding and housed at Petersburg Elementary School. Once this training has been established students and parents will be invited to participate in learning workshops one evening each month. Local astronomers and teachers will conduct workshops. These sessions will provide hands-on opportunities for students, along with their parents, to explore the stars and planets of our solar system. Reach for the Stars will also provide opportunities for our students to experience first hand, various careers in space science through visits to the National Radio Astronomy Observatory in Green Bank, West Virginia, as well as the planetarium at Frostburg State University.

The natural progression of Reach for the Stars will include the formation of an astronomy club with members of all ages. This organized, student-driven, teacher-guided instruction will provide ongoing, extended hour learning opportunities to all grade levels.

GOALS AND OBJECTIVES

The primary goal of Reach for the Stars is to help to prepare students to live and work in a world that is increasingly scientific and technical in nature. Reach for the Stars will provide training and support for teachers as well as increased opportunities for inquiry-based science instruction. The use of speakers, field trips, and hands-on activities will provide students with the opportunity to aggressively explore the link between space science and technology. Reach for the Stars students' activities will address, at the appropriate grade levels, the West Virginia Instructional Goals and Objectives, National Education Goals, National Science Education Standards and the International Society for Technology in Education Standards. Teachers will be provided with resources to supplement their current curriculum through WVU/NASA Ames IV & V Facility offerings and trainings provided by the staff at Greenbank National Radio Astronomy Observatory. Internet-based resources will be identified, compiled and presented to staff by Project RIGHT2 (Reaching Instructional Goals with Hi-Tech Tools) coordinator.

Reach for the Stars will involve parents and community members as partners in the education process by utilizing their skills and knowledge to support the development of a junior astronomers club. Community leaders have

---

*Petersburg Elementary School, located in Grant County is designated as a 100% rural county. More than 60% of students at Petersburg Elementary School receive free or reduced lunch.

committed to provide leadership and support in this exciting endeavor to help our students "Reach for the Stars" both literally and figuratively.

METHODS TO IMPLEMENT PROJECT

In the fall of 2000, Green Bank National Radio Astronomy Observatory staff will provide teachers, parents and community partners with multifaceted training. The first phase of staff development will prepare participants to fully utilize the existing optical telescope at Petersburg Elementary School. Secondly, *STARLAB* training will be the focus of attention so that our students can utilize the STARLAB during school hours. In this way, we can ensure that all students will have the opportunity to explore the vast expanse of our universe in an exciting and meaningful manner. Finally, *Hands-On Universe* training will be provided to interested teachers throughout our county. Software necessary to support trained teachers will be purchased as part of this project.

[Name omitted] and [Name omitted], prominent members of the community who have volunteered their time and expertise to support this project, have both agreed to come into the classroom and provide astronomy-related, hands-on activities. [Name omitted] and [Name omitted] have agreed to assist with the astronomy club and provide expertise to enhance this project. Julia Colaw math/science/technology instructor and Project RIGHT2 coordinator will provide technical support and assistance to all staff in utilizing the STARLAB, telescope, and computer software. Mrs. Colaw will also serve as the teacher supervisor for the astronomy club.

A star party will be held as a kick-off activity to encourage participation in the astronomy club. Students and their families will participate in an evening of star-related activities and have the opportunity to hear knowledgeable guest speakers. Learning stations including the STARLAB and the optical telescope will be staffed and available for exploration.

PROJECT EVALUATION

Evaluation of Reach for the Stars success will be trifold. The first component of this evaluation will be the completion of planned professional development activities. Once trained, teachers will be able to utilize the STARLAB, Hands on Universe Curriculum, and telescope. Each teacher who participates in this project will document classroom activities utilizing the digital camera, video camera or media coverage. This documentation will be compiled and presented at the WVTEAMS conference and at state level science conferences.

The second part of this evaluation will be to measure the extent of parental involvement in this project. Currently there are no academic clubs or activities meeting after school hours. Through this project we will increase parental involvement and provide extended learning opportunities for students. The facilitator will log participation in after-school activities by students, parents and community partners.

The third aspect of evaluation will occur by an examination of standardized test scores of 3rd–6th grade students for the 2000–2001 school year. A successful project will show an increase in science test scores for students involved in this program.

PROJECT TIMELINE

September 2000	Training for teachers and community partners
October 2000	Star Party
November 2000	Astronomy club kick-off
December 2000	Field trip to Frostburg Planetarium
January 2000	Astronomy club meeting and activities
February 2000	Astronomy club meeting and activities
March 2000	Astronomy club meeting and activities
April 2000	Astronomy club meeting and activities
May 2000	WV TEAMS presentation
August/September 2000	Field trip to Green Bank

NRAO

Astronomy club meeting and activities

Evaluate test scores and other data

Year-long activities will include:

* Use of Hands-On Universe software by trained teachers
* Documentation of Reach for the Stars activities
* Media coverage of classroom and schoolwide activities
* Presentations to Grant County Board of Education by students

BUDGET

* Field trip to Frostburg Planetarium

  9 buses @ $.50 per mile (140 miles) = $630

  9 drivers @ $100 per day per driver = $900
* Field trip to Green Bank National Radio Astronomy Observatory

  9 buses @ $.50 per mile (140 miles) = $630

  9 drivers @ $100 per day per driver = $900
* Hands-On Universe Software 8 teachers @ $200 per trained teacher = $1,600
* Astronomy Star Guide Books—30 books @ $15 = $450
* Supplies for Star Party activities; miscellaneous items to conduct a variety of hands-on experiments = $500

  Total Requested Budget $5,610

IN-KIND SUPPORT

* Professional development provided by NRAO staff

  3 days of training @ $800 per day = $2,400

  STARLAB rental 1 week @ $300 per week = $300

- Community partner volunteers

  Approximately 75 hours @ $20 per hour = $1,500
- Travel/accommodation

  Expenses for presentation of Reach for the Stars at conferences; approximately 5 days @ $150 per day = $750

Total In-Kind Budget $4,950

PROJECT COORDINATORS

Background Information

[Name omitted] Math/Science/Technology Instructor

Project RIGHT2 coordinator

B.S. Elementary Education/Edinboro University of Pennsylvania

County Technology and Curriculum Team Member

Astronomy enthusiast

[Name omitted] Physician, Astronomer, and Community Partner

Graduate of University of Cincinnati

Undergraduate of The Ohio State University

Lifelong interest in astronomy

Started designing his own telescope mirrors at age 9

Taught astronomy lessons to fourth- and fifth-grade students in Loudin County, VA (5 years)

[Name omitted] Community Partner and Astronomer

Professor of Physics and Mathematics/Davis & Elkins College 1955–1989

Planetarium Director/Davis & Elkins College 1973–1989

Taught Introduction to Astronomy/Davis & Elkins College 1965–1986

Taught Introduction to Astronomy/Alderson Broaddus (two summers)

APPENDIX 8.5

Ronald McDonald House Charities
Grant Application Form

Funding Source: **Ronald McDonald House Charities grants@rmhc.org**

Ronald McDonald House Charities funds grants aimed at improving children's health. Elegibility requirements include being a nonprofit organization. All grants must be for programs that can be duplicated in other locations.

Grant Application Form

1. INFORMATION ON ORGANIZATION
   Name of Organization: **Edmunds Elementary School**
   Address: **299 Main Street**
   City/State/Zip: **Burlington, VT 05401**
   Contact Individual: **Paul Schreiber**
   Title: **Principal**
   Phone Number(s):
   Specific Amount Requested from RMHC: **$11,350**
   Specific Date Funds are needed: **No specific date**
   Title of Project/Program: **Edmunds Elementary Technology Upgrade Project**

2. RONALD MCDONALD HOUSE CHARITIES INFORMATION
   Have you received RMHC or RMCC funding in the past?
   No
   If so, please explain how that funding was used:
   Please name the nearest McDonald's restaurant location in your organizations area:
   1125 Shelburne Road, South Burlington, Vermont
   To what extent, if any, have you worked with a McDonald's representative?
   None
   If you are working with a McDonald's representative, complete the following:
   McDonald's Contact:
   Title/Position:
   Address:
   City/State/Zip:
   Telephone Number(s):

(Be assured that your request will receive the same consideration with or without an affiliation with McDonald's)

3. BRIEF HISTORY OF YOUR ORGANIZATION:
   Edmunds Elementary School draws kindergarten through fifth-grade students of various socioeconomic backgrounds from across Burlington's center. Sixteen academic classrooms with specials in Spanish, physical education, art, library/technology, and music serve 325 students. The school's mission statement is, "To educate all students for the present and for the future. To help prepare students to participate in, influence, and shape their own future."

4. Summary of the specific project/program for which RMHC Funding is requested:
   The Edmunds Elementary Technology Upgrade Project ties directly to the school mission statement in preparing students for the future. The uses for the requested technology range from adding video clips to the classroom homepages, allowing faculty/students to video and play back demonstrations, integrating the Internet into classroom lessons, creating art and music and much more.

The projects long-term goal is to provide a document camera (or Elmo) with LCD projector, Smartboard and associated technology such as Flip cameras and digital cameras to each classroom.

Due to the capital investment required and to ensure that the technology is embraced by faculty and students prior to such a large expenditure, we have adopted a phased approach. Phase One, for which we are requesting funding from RHMC, will provide one Elmo, one LCD and one Flip camera for each grade level. The Smart Board would be housed in the computer lab for use by all faculty/students.

Please check the category that best describes your project/program:

_____	Civic and Social Services
___X___	**Education and the Arts**
_____	Healthcare and Medical Research

5. TARGET AUDIENCE (i.e. who will specifically benefit from your project, the number served, age(s), socioeconomic and geographic group(s), etc.)
Currently, there are 325 students grades K–5 enrolled at Edmunds Elementary school. These students live in the center of Burlington and represent the diversity of the city, spanning the socioeconomic spectrum and speaking 24 primary languages. Approximately 30% of Edmunds Elementary students qualify for free or reduced price school meals. Access to technology in elementary classrooms will positively impact not only current students but be available for future students as well.

6. BUDGET for specific project/program (including the amount requested and an itemized budget of your program in the space below or attached as an addendum.)
As mentioned, the long-term goal is to have an Elmo, LCD, Smartboard and associated technology installed in each classroom to aid teachers in daily instruction.

The itemized phase 1 technology list and prices are included below. The budget is below.

Phase 1 Technology Needs	Number	Price	Subtotal	Shipping	
Elmos & LCD Projectors (package)	6	$ 1,300.00	$ 7,800.00	$ 100.33	
Smart Board	1	$ 3,000.00	$ 3,000.00		
Flip Cameras	6	$ 75.00	$ 450.00		
		Total	$ 11,250.00	$ 100.33	$ 11,350.33

Amount Requested from RHMC: **$11,350**

7. ADDITIONAL FUNDING—RHMC of Burlington, VT evaluates each grant application and makes final determination in one of four possible ways:
   - Approve the full amount as requested
   - Approve partial funding for the program/project
   - Table the decision to await further information or clarification, which will then be reviewed at an upcoming meeting of the Grant Review Committee; or
   - Deny request

If your organization received partial funding for this project, will additional funding be sought from external sources, or will organization make an internal funding commitment?

Please explain:

Neither the school nor the PTO currently has resources in the budget to purchase the technology requested in the grant. However, the administration and PTO are researching other fundraising and grant opportunities to purchase the requested items and fund subsequent phases of the project.

8. PERMISSION TO USE YOUR NAME—If your organization receives funding from RHMC, will you allow us to use your organization's name and other details about your specific project in promotional material published by RHMC (which may include but is not limited to in-store signage, tray liners, direct mail, radio, newspapers, TV, etc.)?

       ___X___   Yes   _____ No

Signature of Authorized Individual:

Paul Schreiber
Title: **Principal Edmunds Elementary**

Date of Submission:

APPENDIX 9.1

Cullman's Community Awareness Emergency Response Grant Project Narrative

1. **Need for the project**
   a. **The magnitude of the need for the services to be provided or the activities to be carried out by the proposed project**

   Cullman County's Community Awareness/Emergency Response Partnership addresses a wide variety of safety issues prevalent in Cullman County. The proposed plan will assist schools, communities, and partnering agencies in becoming proactive instead of reactive when safety issues or emergencies develop.

   Cullman County's school system consists of 28 separate school campuses located throughout the county. In addition, most of these campuses house other buildings such as gymnasiums, lunchrooms, band rooms, field houses, libraries, and bus barns that are not physically connected to the main campuses. Quick and effective communication with all of these facilities becomes a primary concern in the event that regular means of communication fail due to a natural disaster or other emergency situations.

   A recent weather situation provides a perfect example of shortcomings in the current means of communication used by the Cullman County Board of Education. On April 10, 2003, a severe weather front was moving toward Cullman County. The Emergency Management Agency informed Superintendent Nancy Horton of the developing conditions and advised early dismissal of students from schools to avoid buses being on the road during possible tornadic conditions. The Director of Transportation immediately began contacting bus drivers in order to get the buses back to the schools and to get students at the Child Development Center and the Career Center back to their home schools as quickly as possible. The Central Office staff began attempting to contact all local schools with the correct dismissal times and the procedures that should be followed for students who drive their own vehicles or who are picked up by their parents or designated person. A major problem arose when local schools could not be reached due to blocked telephone lines. Many schools received information over the radio or from parental calls before they received Central Office notification. Conflicting dismissal times due to lack of communication led to mass confusion at many of the schools. Although all students arrived home safely, the confusion could have been eliminated if a more direct and timely form of communication had been used.

   This situation has caused Cullman County Schools to reevaluate its safety and emergency response plans and to identify the areas of specific need listed below:

   - Effective means of communication between local schools and the Central Office
   - Versatile surveillance equipment that can be linked to the Sheriff's Department

- Accurate identification procedures for all children should an emergency situation arise
- Community awareness of school procedures in the event of an emergency situation or natural disaster
- Identification of all Cullman County School personnel and related visitors, such as construction teams, when on school campuses
- Extensive staff development concerning safety concerns and emergency procedures

When emergency situations ranging from tornadoes to chemical spills occur, communication radios located at each school that are linked to the Central Office will be instrumental in notifying all schools immediately. Principals and resource officers will then be able to effectively evaluate the situation and follow the appropriate emergency plan. Should a problem like an intruder on campus occur, the Central Office can be notified immediately and the appropriate agencies contacted to assist in bringing the situation to a safe and speedy resolution.

Surveillance equipment that is linked to the Central Office will provide an excellent method of monitoring the conditions on each school campus. Cameras will be strategically placed throughout each campus to assist in the monitoring of all activity. If an emergency situation occurs, the superintendent or her designee will have the capability of observing the situation first-hand and can communicate with the school immediately using the communications radios. A future link is planned with the sheriff's department that will provide an added measure of protection for our children.

When emergency situations occur, the primary concern of all school personnel is getting all students to a safe location. Depending on the situation, the need for immediate action may result in lack of ability to account for all students. A laptop computer at each site that contains student information and class schedules for each period will assist in accurate accounting for all students. This computer will be taken by a designated person to where the students are located whether outside the building during a fire or to another physical location due to a bomb threat or chemical spill. This computer will also be used to keep track of students in the case of severe weather situations that are often accompanied by power outages that shut down regular means of accountability.

Creating an extensive community awareness network is another area of need that will be addressed by the Cullman's Community Awareness/Emergency Response Partnership. Cullman County Schools will partner with participating agencies to provide community meetings that address a variety of issues pertinent to school safety including drug awareness and prevention, emergency situations, public health, and school safety. Newsletters will also be sent home with students each month addressing different topics and areas of concern.

Identification badges for all Cullman County School employees will provide an added measure of security in our schools that is currently missing. All employees will be required to wear identification badges while on any school campus. Furthermore, all vendors and visitors such as contractors will be required to wear visitor passes. This will help to eliminate unidentified people on campus that could pose a risk to students.

Extensive staff development will be conducted on a wide variety of topics dealing with school safety and crisis situations. Guest speakers from partnering agencies and government representatives will conduct in-service meetings to educate teachers and staff on possible risks and ways to deal with these risks. Teams will be formed to reevaluate current school safety plans and to make suggestions for improvement. Representatives from local schools will be encouraged to attend workshops or conferences dealing with school safety. Information gained at these meetings can then be shared with other teachers at the local level.

b. **The extent to which specific gaps or weaknesses in services, infrastructure or opportunities have been identified and will be addressed by the proposed project, including the nature and magnitude of those gaps or weaknesses.**

The breakdown in communication experienced during a recent tornado warning emphasized our need for a direct line of communication when emergencies occur. Although this weakness has been identified previously by our principals, Cullman County Schools has not had the funds available to provide the communication radios necessary to meet this need. This grant will assist the system in placing direct communication radios in all schools. These radios will be used in all emergency situations including severe weather, intruders on campus, chemical spills, and bomb threats.

Surveillance equipment that is linked to the Central Office and will later be linked to the Sheriff's office will provide an additional source of security on school campuses. If a dangerous situation occurs, administrators and teachers may be unable to reach a phone for assistance. Using this surveillance equipment, a system will be developed that will alert the Central Office if an emergency situation arises. The appropriate agencies will then be contacted to rapidly resolve the situation.

In the event of emergencies due to fire, severe weather, bomb threats, chemical spills, etc., it is essential that all students be accounted for as quickly as possible. A laptop computer at each campus containing complete student information will assist in implementing an accurate accountability system. Even if a power outage occurs, records stored on the laptop will be available. The laptop can be transported with the children to a safe location where students can be identified. This rapid identification will assist teachers and administrators in locating any students who might be missing as quickly as possible.

The response plan developed through this grant will include a schedule for community awareness events that will focus on school procedures in emergency situations as well as strategies for keeping children safe at home. Information will be disseminated through Open House meetings, PTO meetings, parent/teacher conferences, monthly newsletters, and brochures. Partnering agencies will be instrumental in providing speakers who will share current information on topics such as automobile safety, health issues, severe weather action plans, etc. Local television and radio stations as well as newspapers will also provide safety updates.

As the number of school campuses continues to increase, identifying people on the campuses is becoming increasingly difficult. Cullman County Schools would like to implement an identification system that requires every person employed by Cullman County Schools to wear a plastic identification badge. Funds from this grant will be used to purchase an identification badge machine and the materials to make the badges. All visitors will also be required to wear an identification badge. People not wearing badges will be escorted to the office to receive a badge or be removed from campus. Future plans for this system include creating student badges to be used on field trips and at athletic events.

Staff development will play an integral role in developing a successful emergency response plan. Funds from this grant will be used for stipends for teachers to work with administrators and partnering agencies in the summer to review current safety and emergency response plans. Needs assessments will be utilized to identify strengths and areas that need improvement. Plans will then be developed that will address these needs. Speakers from the Office of Safe and Drug Free Schools will be invited to speak at in-service meetings to provide current information to employees of Cullman County Schools and partnering agencies.

Funds from this grant will be used to send members of the Community Awareness/Emergency Response Team to seminars and conferences that focus on school safety, drug-free schools, and crisis management/emergency response. The Superintendent and her designee will also attend all meetings required in the grant guidelines.

2. **Significance: In determining the significance of the proposed project, the following factors are considered:**
   a. **The likelihood that the proposed project will result in system change and improvement**

   The development of the Cullman County Community Awareness/ Emergency Response Partnership will provide a platform for systemic change. A network of partners will be formed that will coordinate a variety of services available to our schools and communities. Parents, students, and teachers will be made aware of possible crisis/emergency situations and will be provided with effective methods of dealing with these situations.

   County-wide drills will be implemented to insure the development of effective response strategies. These random drills will also provide insight into areas that need improvement. Partnering agencies will assist in evaluating the drills and will help develop and implement plans that will increase the effectiveness of the response plans. Continuing communication with the community through PTO meetings, parent/ teacher conferences, and newsletters will keep parents updated as the response plans evolve to meet the needs of the community.

b. **The extent to which the proposed project is likely to build local capacity to provide, improve, or expand services that address the needs of the target population.**

The purchases made with grant monies will serve as the foundation for a network of services that will be expanded as the school system's needs grow and change. The comprehensive approaches proposed in Cullman County's Emergency Response/Crisis Management Plan will identify vulnerabilities and present methods of addressing these areas of weakness. The Cullman County Community Awareness/ Emergency Response Team will address the four phases of crisis planning in the following manner:

- **Mitigation/prevention**—Although an actual emergency may not be prevented, it needs to be dealt with as quickly and efficiently as possible. With 28 school campuses dispersed throughout the county, Cullman County Schools are vulnerable due to a number of risk factors. Four major thoroughfares—I 65, Highway 278, Highway 31, and Highway 157—traverse the county. A railroad system runs in close proximity to many of the schools. We are also located 45 miles from Brown's Ferry Nuclear Plant and within 50 miles of the Arsenal in Huntsville.

    Although a chemical spill or a natural disaster cannot be prevented, a well-developed plan that is familiar to the community needs to be in place. If parents know the procedures for evacuation in the event of an emergency, much confusion can be eliminated. For example, if a chemical spill necessitates the evacuation of a school, parents need to be aware of the school's evacuation plan. Alternate routes to the predetermined evacuation site need to be familiar to parents in case of road closings. Providing parents with as much information as possible before a situation arises will eliminate much of the confusion and panic that follow most emergency situations.

    Equipment purchases such as communication radios and surveillance systems will assist schools in communicating with partnering agencies in order to provide the safest method of dealing with a wide variety of emergencies. Laptop computers will assist schools in keeping accurate records of student locations.

- **Preparedness**—Developing and implementing an effective emergency response/crisis management plan is the first step in being prepared for emergency situations. Even a well-developed plan can only be implemented effectively if all the parties involved are aware of the steps of implementation. Teachers can be made aware of current risk factors through in-service meetings and attendance at conferences and workshops. PTO meetings and newsletters can provide parents with current information on emergency plans and can notify them when changes are necessary. Students can be familiarized with proper emergency response procedures through frequent drills. Partnering agencies will provide the most current information available to the schools and will assist in reevaluating plans when necessary.

- **Response**—The response of the schools and the community will be appropriate to the situation. Each school will develop a multifaceted plan with a number of options designed to meet the needs of that school. Close contact among the schools, the Central Office, and partnering agencies will assist the schools in choosing the best plan for each situation. Communication radios and surveillance cameras linked to the Central Office and the Sheriff's Department will provide immediate feedback when emergency situations arise.

- **Recovery**—An integral part of any emergency response and crisis management plan is the steps for recovering from the disaster. Health and mental health partners will play an essential role in developing an effective recovery plan. Once the EMA and Sheriff's Department have the emergency situation under control, the Health Department and Child Advocacy Center will assist with any physical and emotional problems that arise. Local government agencies will assist with clearing roads, repairing electrical and water systems, and participate in minor building repairs. Once the initial crisis has been dealt with, partnering agencies will continue to provide assistance to restore balance to the community.

The Cullman County Community Awareness/Emergency Response Partnership will provide a much needed forum for the schools, community, and partnering agencies to develop a comprehensive plan that will best meet the needs of all involved.

3. **Quality of the project design: In determining the quality of the design of the proposed project, the following factors are considered:**

a. **The extent to which the proposed project is designed to build capacity and yield results that will extend beyond the period of Federal financial assistance**

The Cullman County Community Awareness/Emergency Response Partnership will evolve to meet the ever-changing needs of the community. Cullman County Schools will depend on its partners to share current information on violence prevention, drug awareness and use prevention, health issues, weather-related information, and a host of other topics that impact the safety of our schools and communities. This partnership will meet for regularly scheduled meetings twice a year and will call special sessions whenever circumstances dictate. Information shared at these meeting will be taken back to the local schools and incorporated in their local safety plans. Updates will be shared with parents through PTO meetings and newsletters.

The equipment and materials purchased with grant funds will serve as the foundation of a program that will continue to expand to meet the needs of the schools. The communication radios and surveillance systems will be put to immediate use in the local schools. As the need to expand these systems arises, we will use local funds, donations from partners, and other monies that can be secured to meet these needs. The local technology team will assist in maintaining both systems. All people employed by Cullman County Schools will be given photo identification badges this fall. The county will be responsible for maintaining the machine and replenishing supplies as needed.

As part of the Cullman County Schools Safety Plan, all schools will be required to reevaluate current safety plans with the entire faculty on a yearly basis using the cycle for crisis planning—mitigation, preparedness, response, recovery. Revised plans will be turned in to the Central Office and will be reviewed by members of the Community Awareness/Emergency Response Team. Suggested changes will be forwarded to the schools for inclusion in their safety plans. An emergency procedures checklist will be posted in each school office for easy access in case of an emergency. Once the situation is resolved, the principal or his/her designee will fill out an emergency procedures report procedures report and submit it to the Central Office. This will provide another method of evaluating emergency procedures and making changes as needed.

b. The extent to which the design of the proposed project reflects up-to-date knowledge from research and effective practice

Members of the Cullman County Community Awareness/Emergency Response Partnership will pool their resources to integrate the most current information available in its emergency response/crisis management plan. The four elements of the cycle of crisis planning—mitigation, preparedness, response, and recovery—will be used to develop an emergency response/crisis management plan that will meet the diverse needs of all Cullman County Schools.

Mitigation/Prevention: Local schools will conduct incident frequency surveys to identify incidents that have occurred previously on school campuses such as natural disasters, severe weather, fires, bus crashes, bomb threats, medical emergencies, and student/staff deaths due to accidents or natural causes. Team members and school staff members will review current procedures for dealing with these incidents and will make suggestions for improving current plans. Needs assessments will also be conducted at each campus on a yearly basis to identify emerging risks and to develop action plans for effectively dealing with these risks.

Members of the Community Awareness/Emergency Response Partnership will assist in conducting yearly safety evaluations on each campus. Findings from these evaluations will be shared with all campuses to be incorporated in safety plan revisions. Specialists at the state and national level will also be asked to evaluate safety/response plans, determine weaknesses, and suggest improvements. These specialists will be asked to share their findings with faculty members and to answer any questions that may arise as a result of these evaluations.

Cullman County Schools currently conducts routine drills for tornado warnings, fire, and bomb threats. Partners from the Community Awareness/Emergency Response Team will be present for some of these drills in order to evaluate their effectiveness and to make suggestions for improvement. Furthermore, partners will be responsible for initiating surprise drills to more accurately duplicate an emergency situation. Results from all these drills will be evaluated and used to improve emergency procedures.

Local school counselors will use the findings of the incident frequency surveys to develop lesson plans that address commonly reoccurring issues. Local law enforcement, government, health, mental health, and other emergency service partners will provide guest speakers and additional materials to assist schools in reducing or eliminating the frequency of these occurrences.

When emergency/crisis situations occur, parents are understandably concerned for the welfare of their children. Phone lines become flooded with calls, often making phone contact with the schools impossible. The communications radios connecting the Central Office to all school campuses will provide an open line of communication in the case of an emergency. These radios may also be placed in the offices of partnering agencies to insure that the most current information will be shared and dispersed as quickly as possible. Parents will also be given a list of radio stations to listen to and television stations to watch for continual updates when emergency situations arise.

Preparedness: All Cullman County Schools have a safety plan currently in place. These plans will be evaluated for effectiveness by each school's faculty and staff as well as community partners. Evaluations will be used to modify and strengthen plans to meet the current needs of each school. Parents will also assist in this evaluation and modification process.

Roles and responsibilities of all staff members, partners, and parents will be clearly defined. Each faculty member will receive a copy of the emergency action checklist to keep in his/her grade book. Although the master copy will be kept in the school office, an emergency situation could necessitate other options. Each emergency action checklist will contain a list of duties and the person responsible for carrying out these duties in the case of an emergency. A backup for each position will also be listed. The principal of each school, the superintendent, and a contact person for each partnering organization will also have a copy of this list. In addition, an emergency folder will be kept at the Central Office with maps of each school campus, water, electrical, and gas shutoff points, and evacuation routes. Each plan will be revisited annually to insure that new faculty members and staff are familiar with emergency plans and that new or renovated structures have been added to the plan.

Emergency supply kits will be placed in each school office and at strategic points throughout each campus. These kits will include medical supplies, a copy of the emergency action checklist, and updated student rosters. A complete school roster will be kept on a laptop and will be carried to a safe place by the designated person who will then begin accounting for all students.

Partners will provide the Central Office with a contact person who will be notified in the case of an emergency situation. This person will then initiate the predetermined emergency response plan that lists the services that will be provided by each agency.

Parents will be provided with a copy of emergency procedures at Open House each school year. They will also receive a newsletter listing evacuation routes and safe points of pickup for their children in case an evacuation is necessary. All printed material will be translated into Spanish to meet the needs of non-English speaking students and their parents. Furthermore, each student with a special need will be assigned to a faculty or staff member to insure the student's safety in an emergency situation. A list of students with special needs will also be in the emergency supply kits.

Response: Immediate response to an emergency situation is essential. Once the type of crisis is identified, school personnel and partnering agencies can implement the appropriate emergency action plan. Constant communication among all parties involved is necessary for a smooth emergency plan implementation.

Once the crisis has been identified, the need for evacuation, shelter-in-place, or lockdown will be determined. Communication radios and surveillance systems will play an integral part in identifying the crisis, determining the course of action to be taken, and keeping all partners informed.

Once parents and the community learn of an emergency, panic often follows. Law enforcement and medical partners will play an important role in minimizing fear and keeping the situation under control. Parents who have been well-informed beforehand will have more confidence in the system. Likewise, parents who see that the situation is under control and that the school and partnering agencies are working together effectively will have more confidence in the school's emergency system in the event of future crisis situations.

An important aspect of any crisis management plan is to expect the unexpected. No one plan will be able to foresee all possible circumstances that will arise in an emergency situation. Student safety is always the top priority. If teachers and other emergency responders keep lines of communication open and address each situation as it occurs, the crisis plan will be implemented effectively. An effective plan is one that keeps all students safe with as little confusion as possible.

A detailed list of steps taken during the emergency should be completed immediately following the incident. This list will be used to evaluate the effectiveness of the plan. A list of damages also needs to be developed shortly after the incident occurs. This list will be used for insurance purposes and as a basis for determining a timeline for restoring the regular educational routine at the school.

Recovery: Although the actual length of the recovery process will differ depending on the situation, restoring the regular routine to the school day should be accomplished as quickly as possible. Once students have a sense of normalcy restored, problems that develop can be more easily identified. School personnel will be able to identify students who are having difficulty coping with the aftermath of the situation and can provide appropriate assistance. School counselors will work closely with teachers and partnering agencies such as mental health partners to adequately meet the needs of all students.

A parent meeting should be held soon after the crisis situation. This will give parents the opportunity to ask question and voice concerns. Representatives from partnering agencies will attend this meeting to answer questions and assist in any way necessary.

Once the initial shock of the crisis is over and order is restored, the crisis management team will meet to evaluate the effectiveness of the emergency action plan. This evaluation will determine which strategies were successful. It will also identify areas that need improvement. The plan will then be revised to help prevent future problems and to lessen the impact of a crisis when it occurs.

c. The extent to which the proposed project encourages parental involvement

Parents will be actively involved in all aspects of the Community Awareness/Emergency Response Partnership. Parents will serve as team members on the emergency action planning team and crisis intervention team. A copy of each school's safety plan will be available in the school's office for parents to view at any time. A copy of each school's safety plan will also be available at the Central Office.

Parents will be provided with frequent safety updates through a variety of methods. PTO meetings and newsletters will be one method used to communicate with parents. Parents can also check for safety updates on the Cullman County Board of Education Website. Local television stations, radio stations, and newspapers will also assist in disseminating information in a timely manner.

At the end of each school year, parents will be asked to complete a safety survey. This survey will evaluate their perception of the effectiveness of the school's safety plan. This will also provide parents with another opportunity to make suggestions for improvement to current safety plans.

4. **Quality of the project evaluation: In determining the quality of the evaluation, the following factor is considered:**

a. **The extent to which the methods of evaluation include the use of objective performance measures that are clearly related to the intended outcomes of the project and will produce quantitative and qualitative data to the extent possible**

The following methods will be used to evaluate the effectiveness of each school's emergency response/crisis management plan:

- **Annual Partnership Evaluations**—Partnering agencies will visit each school campus to identify potential safety problems. Suggestions provided from these visits will be incorporated in each school's individual safety plan. The Central Office Safety Coordinator will check each school's plan to be sure that these suggestions have been utilized effectively.

- **Safety Needs Assessment**—Each school will conduct an annual safety needs assessment. Information derived from these needs assessments will be shared with the Community Awareness/ Emergency Response Team. The team will then determine how partnering agencies can assist schools in meeting their needs.

- **Parental Safety Survey**—Parents at each school will complete a safety survey at the end of each school year. The results of this survey will be used to improve the school safety plan.
- **Student Incident Reports**—Each school will keep a student incident report that lists all incidents involving students that require disciplinary measures. These incidents will be categorized by level of severity. Action plans will be developed to decrease the number of students requiring disciplinary measures.
- **Emergency Response Reviews**—Each school will conduct periodic drills for tornadoes, fires, bomb threats, etc. Partners will also initiate surprise drills. Reports will be kept to record response times of all parties involved. These reports will be used to improve school safety plans.

5. **Quality of the management plan: In determining the quality of the management plan, the following factor is considered:**
   a. **How the applicant will ensure that a diversity of perspectives is brought to bear in the operation of the proposed project, including those of parents, teachers, the business community, a variety of disciplinary and professional fields, recipients or beneficiaries of services, or others, as appropriate**

   The Cullman County Community Awareness/Emergency Response Partnership provides the platform for a comprehensive safety plan that involves all areas of the community. Members of the Community Awareness/Emergency Response Team will meet twice a year to evaluate the roles of each partner plays in creating a successful safety system and to revise the plan to meet the evolving needs of the schools in Cullman County. Other groups such as the Cullman Area Chamber of Commerce and the Industry/Education Alliance will assist in developing and implementing a safety plan that benefits the entire community.

   The partnering agencies will provide the following services to Cullman County Schools:

   - **Sheriff's Department**—The Cullman County Sheriff's Department will provide resource officers on every school campus. These officers will teach drag awareness/prevention classes to students of all ages. They will assist with discipline problems that require outside intervention and will assist with traffic flow when necessary. The Sheriff's Department will provide speakers for PYO meetings, Open House meetings, and school assemblies. They will also dispatch units immediately to school campuses when emergency situations occur.
   - **Emergency Management Agency**—The EMA will notify the Superintendent when dangerous weather conditions are possible and when severe weather warnings are issued for our area. The EMA also has the responsibility of notifying the Superintendent in case of a biological or chemical threat. The EMA will provide speakers for PTO meetings and in-service meetings at the local schools on proper procedures to be followed when an emergency situation occurs.

- **Cullman County Health Department**—The Health Department assists Cullman County Schools by providing immunizations necessary for students to enter school. The Health Department also provides pamphlets and brochures on a variety of topics to parents, students, and school personnel. The Health Department provides speakers for health classes at local schools and will provide speakers for PTO meetings. It also provides frequent updates to school nurses on communicable diseases. Local doctors provide drug use/prevention and AIDS classes for local schools. Furthermore, the Health Department conducts food safety evaluations at all local schools.
- **Child Advocacy Center**—The Child Advocacy Center provides individual, group, and family counseling services for students and their families. The Center will also provide speakers for PTO meetings and for faculty in-service meetings on how to deal with students when crisis situations occur. The Center also partners with Cullman Caring for Kids to provide workshops on topics such as developing parenting skills, teen parenting, conflict resolution, etc.
- **County Commission**—The County Commission provides a variety of services that benefit the students of Cullman County. The Commission provides office space, utilities, and supplies for the County Board of Education. The Commission partners with the Board of Education to develop safe pedestrian crosswalks at schools and assists with developing traffic flow plans for school campuses. The Commission also provides equipment to keep roads and walkways cleared when campuses are damaged by severe weather.

Teachers at each local school will develop safety plans to meet the unique needs of their school environment. Safety information will be shared with parents through Open Houses, PTO meetings, parent/teacher conferences, newsletters, and radio, television, and newspaper announcements. Parents and teachers will reevaluate their school's safety plan annually to identify strengths and areas for improvement. The areas identified for improvement will be incorporated in the yearly revision of the school safety plan.

APPENDIX 9.2

Classrooms for the Future

ABSTRACT

What are your (1) expectations for this program's impact on how teachers and students will work in your high school (including changes in instructional strategies and practices and in student performance and learning) and (2) anticipated successes and challenges at the teacher and student levels?

The educational goals of the Classrooms for the Future Project are to a) improve student achievement in content area reading, mathematics, and science; b) create a comprehensive system of student and teacher laptop acquisition; c) initiate a program of staff development that promotes a working knowledge of classroom technology; and d) provide opportunities for parents to gain greater awareness of student achievement as it relates to involvement in technology related activities. Increasing student achievement through full integration of technology in the areas of content area reading, mathematics, and science is the primary intent of the Classrooms for the Future Project. It is expected that students and teachers will achieve greater success in the classroom as defined by improved PSSA reading and math results, extended use of computerized learning tools, and improved technological integration. By providing every mathematics and science student and teacher in grades 7–12 with a laptop computer and supportive peripheral devices, the Classrooms for the Future Project will make technology "as accessible as all other tools" for learning. Embedded within the goal of improving student achievement are supportive resources as outlined in Greenville Area School District's Technology Plan. The committee specifically endorsed the use of mobile technology to increase opportunities to use software to provide developmentally appropriate personalized instruction in conceptual mathematics. The school district has already successfully implemented the use of mobile technology at the elementary school level. Extending mobile computing to the high school will fill a void by expanding our instructional focus and staff development to include grades 7–12. This will enable students to gain access to a powerful learning tool that will provide personalized instruction (including remediation and enrichment) while teachers gain a technological advantage when designing lessons that simulate, motivate, and monitor progress toward mastery of Pennsylvania's Academic Standards. Challenges the school district has encountered when implementing the new technology-based initiatives are many, but not insurmountable. Lessons learned include the following: 1) Improving student achievement over time requires a systemic approach that is driven by data that is accurate and presented in formats that can be quickly interpreted into plans of action. 2) Training teachers to effectively teach to the academic standards and use technology-based assessments requires staff development efforts that inform, involve, and create changes in behavior. The Pennsylvania System of School Assessment has forced schools to explore ways to link testing, curriculum, and professional development with clearly articulated ideas about what students should be able to do. In some cases, we have asked teachers to change what they teach and how they teach it. Altering ways teachers have always done things is difficult for some educators. For this reason meaningful professional development programs that provide hands-on opportunities are needed for teachers to use technology to support student learning. 3) Implementing integrated learning software programs within the existing structure of a school program requires carefully thought out reasons for purchases, selection of vendors, and planning of training sessions. Acquisition and control of this process is accomplished differently and at varying rates depending on the styles and capabilities of each learner. The need exists within Greenville schools to expand opportunities for students to learn at individual levels appropriate to their age and development. Research has shown that acquisition of integrated software programs can help our students acquire needed content area reading and math skills in ways that are relevant, meaningful, and results driven. 4) Educating parents and community members about new technology-based approaches to learning requires multiple opportunities to inform, involve, and invite the entire school community. Reaching full integration from using technology in the classroom requires a major paradigm shift in how teachers deliver instruction in their classrooms. Teachers and administrators at Greenville High School are like many other segments of the population with respect to proficiency in technology. Some are "early adopters" who were "born ready" to teach with technology. Others need additional time to learn the mechanics and envision the possibilities that laptop computers and peripheral devices afford themselves and their students. This plan responds to all high school educators, in that it provides a differentiated approach to professional development that appropriately supports early adopters, novices, and everyone in between.

What are your expectations for organizational changes (such as the way you manage staff and administrative and communications tasks) and your proposed activities to promote best practices and incorporate lessons learned?

Increased access to information through new technologies, and the need to prepare students to compete in an emerging information-based economy, promises to fundamentally reshape school practice as we move into the next century. Despite increased attention for using educational technology in the classroom, Greenville High School is experiencing difficulty in effectively integrating these technologies into existing curriculum.

According to the U.S. Congress, Office of Technology Assessment, lack of teacher training is one of the greatest roadblocks to integrating technology into a school's curriculum. That same report revealed that most schools need financial assistance to adequately provide the level of training and development necessary to embrace new and promising technologies.

The Greenville Area School District recognizes that for projects where adequate funding exist, effective staff development is an essential part of its success. The school district believes that if technology is to be used by students, then teachers must possess the confidence, understanding, and skills to effectively incorporate technology into their teaching practices. This will only occur by providing adequate training and sustained development of teachers in a variety of formats.

To help teachers properly engage in an on-going series of professional development, Greenville High School will provide sustained staff development rather than merely introductory one-time training. This training will be coupled with on-the-job encouragement and on-site support. Staff development will occur during district in-service days, scheduled release times, and/or during summer classes. Instruction will be designed to provide teachers an exploratory view of technological possibilities in addition to advanced classes for the veteran technology user. Furthermore, school administrators recognize the need to create forums that encourage teachers to share their experiences through writing articles, presenting at conferences, or leading workshops.

Greenville High School has only three computer laboratories. The labs are very busy, leaving little opportunity for teachers and students to schedule computer time. Expectations include reclaiming the computer laboratories for research and individual student and teacher use. By "un-tethering" students in reading and mathematics courses from computer labs, the computer labs can serve as the supervised environment for which they were intended. This will mean more opportunity for professional development during the school day and greater centralization of resources such as printing and facilitation of long distance education for students enrolled in online courses.

Learning opportunities will increase dramatically when students and teachers acquire portable laptops that permit technology to play a larger and immediate role within the classroom. For example, teachers have repeatedly requested funds to purchase classroom white/SMART Boards that enable the creation of technology-laded interactive lessons. To date, the school district has been unable to fund these requests. It is expected that the Classrooms for the Future Project will provide the impetus for greater use of technology when teachers deliver instruction in ways that are effective, meaningful, and stimulating to the learner.

NEEDS ASSESSMENT

Describe how technology is currently being used in instruction, communication, and administration (or current plans for technology integration in these areas).

The Greenville Area School District has a wide variety of technology that is used for instruction. Teachers are expected to daily model the use of technology through interactive presentation skills and use of peripherals in the classrooms. However, a limited number of desktop computers are available in every classroom for student and teacher use. Increased computer use has created a need for greater bandwidth to ensure productivity from our recently upgraded fiberous network. Integrated learning software packages are used in several core-curriculum areas to provide curricular enhancements and perscriptive learning frameworks. Greenville High School currently has several distance learning classes in the areas of mathematics and foreign language. An interactive video distribution system resides at the high school along with VCRs and DVD players and satellites. Teachers can access the equipment through the phone system for classroom use. We will continue to expand in these areas as teachers are encouraged to utilize technology within their classrooms and when designing cross-curricular projects.

Technology is used across the entire school district for communication in many ways. The school district equips all teachers and classrooms with a telephone, voice mail, and e-mail account. This technology is used on a daily basis for educational communication. A satellite broadcasting system is used to update and inform community and parents of school happenings and events. In addition, the school district continues to update and maintain an extensive Web presence for posting school and community information, lesson plans and student grades. The technology department uses a district Web site for problem reporting and maintenance.

The district uses technology in administration in several ways. Currently, two databases are utilized to store information on local and state assessments. These databases allow teachers and administration to compile disaggregated reports on testing data to reallign curriculum and identify intervention areas. The Greenville Area School District currently has a student information database for attendance, grading, No Child Left Behind data calculations, and academic scheduling. The technology department uses several administrative software packages to ensure a safe and productive network including internet blocking and monitoring tools, firewalls, secure data connections, and virus protection software.

Describe your school's participation in programs that use teachers to help coach other teachers on technology use in instruction. This may include PDE's Keystones Technology Integrators program (see www.pde.state.pa.us/ed_tech for a description of this program). Enter N/A if not applicable.

In 2004, a classroom teacher at Greenville High School was nominated and selected as a Keystone Technology Integrator. The teacher is a Technology Education teacher that utilizes the many benefits technology by offering technology infused instructional practices. The teacher does not focus on the technology itself, but on student learning as a tool to support the instructional process. In addition, plans are underway to nominate another deserving classroom teacher as a Keystone Technology Integrator when the selection process opens again in February 2007. These teachers have routinely lead discussion groups and conducted presentations during school district in-service days. Their willingness to share their success from using technology in the classroom has been a great asset to the school district's staff development efforts.

The school district's Teacher Induction Plan is designed to provide a series of activities to help orient beginning teachers to the Greenville Area School District throughout their first year. Essential to that purpose is development of a working knowledge of technology coupled with an acute understanding of Greenville's unique personalized standards-based education. Furthermore, it is the intent of the Teacher Induction Program to provide learning opportunities via teacher mentoring, summer course work, and in-service instruction that position the teacher as a technological role model for students.

Describe any other current programs that train and/or assist your teachers in technology skills. Enter N/A if not applicable.

Teachers are offered technology training and assistance on a regular basis. Several vendors of products and software that are used annually are involved with professional development. The school district also utilizes resources from local and regional Intermediate Units to assist with technology integration and training of staff. As an integral part of the Greenville staff, the school district employs a team of trained technology support personnel. These individuals are available for in-service training, summer instruction, and provide technical support and inter-action. For example, interactive hands-on classes promoting proper use of the Internet and use of computerized technologies have been offered for the school community. A program sponsored through Mercer County Juvenile Probation will be offered next school year to Greenville teachers to promote awareness of inap-propriate use and potential abuse when using interactive technologies. A similar program will also be offered to the general public during the fall of 2006.

Describe how your school uses students to support technology skills and technol-ogy use in teaching and learning (e.g., student mentors, students who help with tech problems, computer fairs). Enter N/A if not applicable.

Greenville High School has a Computer Club that publishes a monthly newslet-ter, offers technical assistance, and promotes the use of technology through a variety of activities. Students from the Computer Club recently entered a contest where students earned recognition for demonstrating their programming skills. Greenville High School also has a Web Design Team that supports the school district's Web site and creates Web designs for school related organizations.

Describe any other current programs that train and/or assist your students in technology skills. Enter N/A if not applicable.

Microsoft Certification courses have become a mainstay within our computer education classes. Students enrolled in these classes enroll in online courses that provide culminating assessments for certification in various applied func-tions in the Microsoft Office Suite (Microsoft Word, Excel, Access, PowerPoint, etc.) Technology Integration within general classrooms can be observed when students engage in research and present their findings, when science students engage in hands on experiments using PASCO software, or when reading students log onto the Weaver reading skills program within the com-puter labs.

Describe the type and amount of computer courses and technology proficiency required of your students for graduation. Enter N/A if not applicable.

The Greenville Area School District offers a comprehensive public school set-ting for students. Equipped with the school district's motto, "Every Student is a Candidate for Greatness," the mission of every teacher is to provide all stu-dents with the knowledge, competencies, and desire to face the challenges necessary to achieve fulfillment in a global society.

The use of educational technology has been a distinct initiative within Greenville schools for many years. Greenville High School offers advanced placement (AP) courses through distance learning in calculus and physics. Daily science lessons, state-of-the-art equipment, and facilities for per-formance-based learning activities through simulated laboratory experi-ences. A full range of special education programs are offered including district programs for the gifted, learning disabled, and multi-handicapped. Student-to-student tutorial programs are available through cross-age assistance opportunities. Since 2002 Greenville High School has provided opportunities for students to enroll in Latin, German, and physics online through daily long distance satellite broadcasts. In lieu of a study hall, interested students watch and listen to broadcasts on a TV, complete assigned coursework, and correspond with a college professor through email. Tapes are available if students would like to view the broadcasts at home. This is an excellent way for students to extend their learning beyond the school day to include worthwhile instructional topics.

At the elementary level, the Every Day Mathematics Program is an activity-based curriculum offered in kindergarten through 6th grade. All students receive additional time learning mathematical skills through scheduled visits to the computer lab where interactive software is available. In addition, Greenville elementary schools offer a strong phonetic and literature based reading program for kindergarten through 6th grade. Accelerated Reader software provides incentives for students to read beyond daily assignments. An interactive science curriculum provides hands-on discovery-based programs for kindergarten through third grade and supplemental laboratory opportunities during the remaining years. Computer labs are housed within each elementary school and are complemented by mini-labs within each classroom.

Students attending Greenville High School are required to enroll in two computer education courses while in junior high school, Computer 7 and Computer 8. Computer 7 is designed as an introductory exploration of how applied technology can enrich their lives and as a refresher for students already proficient and aware of the potential learning opportunities technology offers to students. Computer 8 provides a leveled experience in word processing, spreadsheet applications, and peripheral devices vital to using technology. In grades 9–12 students utilize technology in an integrated fashion within each of the content areas.

Describe other resources and partnerships that support effective use of technology in your classrooms and school. Enter N/A if not applicable.

Greenville High School will ultimately measure the success of this project by evaluating PSSA reading and mathematics scores. Multiple data collection systems will be used to gather and disaggregate the data. This information will be used to analyze reports generated by the Cognitive Tutor, Weaver Reading, and Compass Learning software. School personnel will also use the Pennsylvania's Online Technology Assessment Survey to determine levels of technology literacy and the degree of integration of technology with the classroom.

PROJECT PLAN

Provide goals from your current district strategic plan. Goals should reflect an overarching purpose and desired end result of action or ability.

Create aligned research-based strategies for all aspects of Classrooms for the Future implementation. Strategies should reflect changes in organizational and educational practices that promote progress toward your identified goals and the project rollout. Then create aligned activities to ensure that each strategy is implemented and progress is made toward identified goals. Activities should indicate specifically what will happen when and who will be accountable.

Provide performance indicators and a timeline for all strategies. A performance indicator, or benchmark, will show how acquisition of the targeted strategy will be determined basically what measures and standards will be used. The timeline should span at least the funded course of the project with the expectation that the performance goal be met by the end of that span. (See FAQs on PDE Web site for examples).

Goal (500 char)	Strategy (500 char)	Activity (500 char)	Performance Indicator (500 char)	Timeline (30 char)
Graduate rate will meet an 80% threshold and/or show growth.	Each year, implement interventions to develop "soft skills", monitor student performance year to month to define corrective actions, and evaluate the effectiveness of interventions such as graduation rates.	Increase parent involvement using technology by allowing them to monitor student progress and grades.	Success will be with the number of parents involved in using the software and the increased grades of students because of this monitoring.	Monthly for 3 years
At least 45% of all students will be proficient in mathematics, as measured by the annual state-wide PSSA assessments.	Continue to meet the mandates of No Child Left Behind and the Pennsylvania Accountability system with expectations for performatin at Proficient or Advanced levels on the PSSA.	Use mobile technology opportunities to increase opportunites for using software for practice with math concepts.	Increase in PSSA test scores.	Evaluated on a yearly basis.
Student attendance wil meet a 90% threshold and/or show growth.	Offer a personalized standardized program.	Use of Integrated Learning Systems for instruction, remediation, and enrichment.	Variety of learning will spark student learning and attendance.	Attendance is monitored daily.
At least 95% of eligible students will participate in required state-wide assessments.	Continue to meet mandates of No Child Left Behind for performance levels on the PSSA.	Monitor student performance by use of technology using pre and post PSSA pracice tests, CDA system, and PVAAS system.	Increase in student performance on state testing.	Monthly for 3 years.

(continues)

Goal (500 char)	Strategy (500 char)	Activity (500 char)	Performance Indicator (500 char)	Timeline (30 char)
At least 54% of all students will be proficient in Reading, as measured by the annual state-wide PSSA assessments	Continue to meet the mandates of No Child Left Behind and the Pennsylvania Accountability System as defined in specific expectations for performance at the Proficient or Advanced levels on the PSSA.	Use mobile technology opportunities to increase opportunites for using software for practice with reading concepts.	Increase in PSSA test scores.	Evaluated on a yearly basis.

List the project's management team members, indicating the project responsibilities for each team member and the credentials that support the selection of the member for that role. Lead management roles should be assumed by a member of the participating high school or AVTS/CTC or the LEA within whose boundaries the high school or AVTS/CTC resides.

Team Member (50 char)	Project Responsibilities (500 char)	Credentials (500 char)
J. Ziegler, S. Ross, High School Principals	Review and revise standardized assessment program; develop a system to communicate progress to all stakeholders; provide training on effective assessment practices; review all needs assessments and respond to school and community's desire for improvement in instructional technology; facilitate the process of organizing, writing, and meeting about the grant; develop partnerships with parents, teachers, and community leaders	Doctorate in Education, Master of Educational Administration, High School Principals are responsible for curriculum, instruction, and use of technology within the classroom.
Jodi Hibbard, Technology Coordinator	Implement plan to expand the current use of technology by staff to improve the effectiveness of the learning process; identify equipment/software, etc. needed to carry out the plan; enhance the district-wide curriculum through the integration of technology; and communicate grant information to the community via the district Web site.	Bachelor of Science in Computer Science, Professional experience in deployment of technology hardware, software, and professional development.

Team Member (50 char)	Project Responsibilities (500 char)	Credentials (500 char)
Patricia Homer, Superintendent	Ensure that the district provides appropriate professional development opportunities and training for all staff members in order to enhance and facilitate the deliver of learning opportunities; appropriate essential materials and designate personnel needed to keep all technology operational; and keep the school board informed of the progress of the implementation and effectiveness of the grant project.	Doctorate in Education, Superintendent of Schools for the Greenville Area School District.
Michael Downing	Coordinate awareness for the project; conduct surveys related to project to learn public opinion; attend meetings about the software, learn to read reports that will be distributed at the end of the marking periods.	Master of Business Administration, Parent, community member and Greenville Area School Board member.
Jerry Harpst	Provide feedback regarding the applicability of the program for students and the needs of the teachers to make the initiative effective; promote acceptance among peers; and attend meeting to discuss the progress of the grant implementation.	Master of Science in Education, High school mathematics teacher and cognate leader of the math department.
Scott Ellis	Provide feedback regarding the applicability of the program for students and the needs of the teachers to make the initiative effective; promote acceptance among peers; and attend meeting to discuss the progress of the grant implementation.	Master of Science in Education, High school science teacher and cognate leader of the high school science department.
Rick Zilla	Provide feedback regarding the applicability of the program for students and the needs of the teachers to make the initiative effective; promote acceptance among peers; and attend meeting to discuss the progress of the grant implementation.	Master of Science in Education, Technology Education teacher, mentor for teachers for using technology, and cognate leader of the high school technology department.

(continues)

Team Member (50 char)	Project Responsibilities (500 char)	Credentials (500 char)
Ronald Myers	Provide feedback regarding the applicability of the program for students and the needs of the teachers to make the initiative effective; promote acceptance among peers; and attend meeting to discuss the progress of the grant implementation.	Master of Science in Education, Computer Education teacher and mentor for teachers using technology.
Jennifer Ross	Train teachers on software and assist in parent communication and meetings.	Bachelor of Science in Computer Science, expert and trainer for Allegheny Intermediate Unit III on the Comprehensive Data Analysis program that is used at Greenville High School to monitor student achievement and progress.
Judy Dennis	Train teachers on software and assist in parent communication and meetings.	Bachelor of Science in Computer Science, Systems Analyst and trainer for the Midwestern Intermediate Unit IV.

Describe briefly what will occur and when to address the technology deployment, including a breakdown of the rollout in your school (type of instructional setting such as small learning community, subject area, grade level, etc.); appropriateness of deployment strategies (rationale for deploying technology in the time and manner indicated); and steps taken to ensure interoperability with other technology deployed in instructional settings.

Technology deployment will be phased over the three-year project period. In Year One, 1) The Greenville High School Principal will participate in a mandatory pre-grant seminar. (May 2006) 2) The District Technology Coordinator will attend a Webinar recapping highlights from the principals' seminars. (June 2006) 3) Administrators, math, and science teachers will participate in 2 days of PDE Classrooms for the Future hands-on professional development opportunities. (Fall 2006) 4) Administrators, math, and science teachers will participate in 30 hours of professional development on PDE-mandated content. (Fall 2006) 5) Curriculum and technology needs assessments will occur at many levels as outlined in the school district's strategic plan. This data will serve as a base line of data. (Fall 2006) 6) A complete review of policies and procedures covering the use of technologies including technology-integrated program management practices and the current Acceptable Use Policy will occur. (Sept 2006) 7) Release time will be provided for all mathematics and science teachers. (2006–2007) 8) The Project Management Team will reconvene and present the scope of the project to the Greenville Area School District Strategic Plan's Steering Committee. (Sept 2006) 9) Professional development for administrators and teachers will take place to emphasize the need to integrate technology appropriately by adopting practices that regularly integrate technology with teaching and learning. (2006–2007) 10) Visitation to schools with technology initiatives similar to the Classrooms for the Future Project will begin. (2006–2007) 11) Consult with PDE official about the purchase of hardware and software and necessary licenses for rolling out mobile computers and related classroom technologies. (Sept 2006) 12) Provide the Classrooms for the Future coach access to classrooms in session and work with the coach to identify and address needs. (2006–2009) 13) The Teacher Induction and Mentorship program will be revised to include the principles of coaching and mentoring inherent in the Classrooms for the Future Project. Release time will be provided as needed to reach all involved parties (Fall 2006) 14) Acquire the necessary hardware and software for Year One of the project, install network security settings and software onto the laptops, configure computers to use teacher productivity software and integrated learning system software, and install peripheral devices and software. (Fall 2006) 15) Deployment of hardware and software from the Classrooms for the Future Project will take place during a well planned training sessions for all mathematics and science teachers under the direction of the high school administration and with assistance from the Classrooms for the Future Coach, and members of the Project Management Team. (Fall 2006) 16) Schedule training sessions. The first several training session will be devoted to becoming familiar with the hardware and software's functionality and capability of peripheral devices. (Fall 2006) 17) Mathematics and science teachers begin classroom activities and direct instruction using the technology provided by the Classrooms for the Future Project. (Fall 2006) 18) Conduct a Family Night Parent Awareness Workshop to familiarize parents with the project and benefit of the mobile computers and related classroom technologies. (Fall 2006) 19) Identify and submit for consideration a candidate for Keystone Technology Integrator if one does not exist in the school. (Feb 2007) 20) Evaluative activities will include monitoring, reviewing, and summarizing the project's status. Summative evaluations and formative evaluations will occur through the life of the project. (2006–2007) 21) Participate in the annual Pennsylvania Technology Inventory (PaTI) survey. (Spring 2007) In Year Two, 1) Reconvene members of the Project Management Team to review Year Two accomplishments and discuss necessary adjustments for Year Three. (June 2007) 2) Conduct the annual curriculum and technology needs assessment as outlined in the school district's strategic plan. (July 2007) 3) Project Management Team representatives will provide a status report of the project for the Greenville Area School District Strategic Plan's Steering Committee. (August 2007) 4) English and social studies teachers will participate in 2 days of PDE professional development opportunities. (Fall 2007) 5) English and social studies teachers will participate in 30 hours of professional development on PDE-mandated content. (Fall 2007) 6) Release time will be provided for all English and social studies teachers. (2007–2008) 7) English and social teachers begin classroom activities and direct instruction using the technology provided by the Classrooms for the Future Project. (Fall 2007) 8) Acquire the necessary hardware and software for Year One of the project, install network security settings and software onto the laptops, configure computers to use teacher productivity software and integrated learning system software, and install peripheral devices and software. (Fall 2007) 9) Deployment of hardware and software for the Classrooms for the Future Project will occur during activity periods for all students in grades 9–12 under the direction of the high school administration with assistance from the Classrooms for the Future Coach, and members of the Project Management Team. (Fall 2007) 10) Administrators and classroom teachers will continue to refine the use of technology and new instructional activities to match Pennsylvania's academic standards in math, science, English, and social teachers with local curriculum objectives. (2007–2008) 11) English and social studies teachers begin while math and science teachers continue classroom activities and direct instruction using the technology provided by the Classrooms for the Future Project. (Fall 2007) 12) Create a student program for coaching and mentorship. (Fall 2007) 13) A Family Night Parent Awareness Workshop will be held to familiarize new parents with Compass Learning software. (Fall 2007) 14) Parent/teacher conferences will be scheduled to share the status of project goals and activities. (Fall 2007) 15) Additional Families Nights will be held featuring students demonstrations that will highlight the advantages of the interactive technologies and the benefits to school achievement. (2007) 16) Promote student participation in programs that showcase technology skills such as the statewide Student Computer Fair. (2007–2008) 17) Continued staff development will occur throughout Year Two providing reinforcement for teachers and expanding introductory training to other grade levels. (2007–2008) 18) Evaluative activities will include monitoring, reviewing, and summarizing the project's status. Summative evaluations will occur at the conclusion of each year. Formative evaluations will occur through the life of the project. (Spring 2008) In Year Three, 1) Reconvene members of the Project Management Team to review Year Two accomplishments and discuss necessary adjustments for Year Three. (June 2008) 2) Conduct the annual curriculum and technology needs assessment as outlined in the school district's strategic plan. This includes a comprehensive analysis of the PSSA assessment scores and other pertinent data. (July 2008) 3) Project Management Team representatives will provide a status report of the project for the Greenville Area School District Strategic Plan's Steering Committee. (August 2008) 4) Acquire the necessary hardware and software for Year One of the project, install network security settings and software onto the laptops, configure computers to use teacher productivity software and integrated learning system software, and install peripheral devices and software. (Fall 2008) 5) Deployment of hardware and software for the Classrooms for the Future Project will occur during activity periods for all students in grades 7–9 under the direction of the high school administration and with assistance from the Classrooms for the Future Coach, and members of the Project Management Team. (Fall 2008) 6) Administrators and mathematics and science teachers will continue to refine the use of technology and new instructional activities to clearly match Pennsylvania's academic standards with local curriculum objectives. (2008–2009) 7) Continue to refine and generate stimulating classroom activities and direct instruction using technology. (Fall 2008) 8) Continue the student program for coaching and mentorship. (Fall 2008) 9) A Family Night Parent Awareness Workshop will be held to familiarize new parents with Compass Learning software. (Fall 2008) 10) Parents/guardians will again be invited to participate in the use of technology with the laboratories and classrooms. (Fall 2008) 11) Promote student participation in programs that showcase technology skills such as the statewide Student Computer Fair. (2008–2009) 12) Continued staff development will occur throughout Year three providing reinforcement for teachers and expanding introductory training to other grade levels. (2008–2009) 13) Evaluative activities will include monitoring, reviewing, and summarizing the project's status. Summative evaluations and formative evaluations will occur through the life of the project. (Spring 2009) 14) Seek partnerships and opportunities to support 21st century education beyond Classrooms for the Future. (2009 & beyond)

Describe briefly how you will support the Classrooms for the Future coach, Keystone teachers, and other mentors, and how the benefits derived from using peer coaches and mentors may be leveraged across the school.

Successful mentoring at Greenville High School has shown the importance of adequate training for peer coaches and mentors. Mentoring takes place during the entire school year when veteran teachers are matched with teachers new to the school district. Training and supportive resources are first allocated during the summer prior to each school year but can be used throughout the school year. Mentor teachers receive a stipend for attending the summer training and mentoring the new teacher through out the school year. It is recognized that both coaching and mentoring require additional skills beyond those used in teaching, among them are knowing how to work with adults, observe, conference, problem solve, and be an effective change agent. Conducting successful collaboration at Greenville High School has proven to be much like promoting other elements of school reform; without a careful assessment of needs and resources, and without supportive attitudes by teachers, the program is likely to fail. However, a well designed effort, one that has been planned and implemented with extensive teacher input and administrative support, have brought positive results.

Mentors for the Classrooms for the Future Project will be found without requiring mandatory participation from individuals. Mentoring at Greenville High School usually involves (but is not limited to) observing teachers, demonstrating motivational lessons, creating instructional frameworks, and modeling organizational and classroom management skills.

Administrative support is critical to a mentoring or coaching relationship. In regard to the Classrooms for the Future Project support will be provided in terms of time for initial training, support group/meetings, collaboration and observation, and the monies to allocate the training, cover classrooms, and evaluate everyone's efforts. In addition to the practical application of time the school administration will work toward establing an environment featuring consulation, collaboration, respect, and encouragement where expected outcomes ocurr spontaneously. User-freindly technical support will be available onsite where teacher's needs and just-in-time expertise is shared openly.

If applicable, describe briefly other local professional development activities that complement Classrooms for the Future.

The Greenville Area School District is in the process of completing submission of their six-year Technology Plan. During the past several years, the school district has maintained a committee of administrators, teachers, and community members that initiated a framework of annual goals and objectives to serve as guidelines for the acquisition and utilization of technology within the district. Implementing the goals within the Technology Plan and meeting on a regular basis has provided a solid foundation for the project management team.

Supportive professional development activities that complement the Classrooms for the Futures Project are rooted in the annual needs assessment which include meetings of staff, parents, and community members, results of local and state assessments, professional visits to schools with similar goals, and vendor workshops that feature innovative technologies.

The Greenville Area School District coordinates integrated staff development activities with additonal school realted groups and in the following ways: staff from Head Start, Even Start, and other preschool program work with the district personnel to align and coordinate their programs to provide a seamless curriculum and to supplement the school district's personalized standards-based program. The vocational education staff works with the district personnel to provide smooth transitions from school to work programs. Efforts to help children with disabilities are coordinated and aligned with the prescribed program of studies to provide the necessary remediation. Delinquent Youth and youth at risk of dropping out receive appropriate services in conjunction with Title I services. Services for LEP, homeless, immigrant, and migratory children are provided when needed. The Read to Succeed grant at the primary level has provided funds to implement an ILS system in the primary grades with much success. The financial impact of these programs are reviewed annually and consolidated whenever possible to create a seamless system Pre-K-12. The Greenville Area School District has made great strides by prioritizing the need for technology and providing funds each year from the school district budget. Financial assistance from other sources has been limited to Title I, Title II, and Read to Succeed funding. The district will continue to support these initiatives through the district budget and additional funding opportunities to move the use of technology toward reaching an improvement in student achievement.

MONITORING AND LOCAL EVALUATION

Describe the activities that will occur at your school or district, and when they will occur, to ensure that technology deployment, professional development, and appropriate technology integration with instructional and learning practices is occurring at the levels and within the timeframe proposed. Indicate what you will do if the implementation does not meet the proposed targets.

The educational goals of the Classrooms for the Future Project are to a) improve student achievement in content area reading, mathematics, and science; b) create a comprehensive system of student and teacher laptop acquisition; c) initiate a program of staff development that promotes a working knowledge of classroom technology; and d) provide opportunities for parents to gain greater awareness of student achievement as it relates to involvement in technology related activities.

In and effort to improve student achievement in reading area reading, mathematics, and science, a comprehensive analysis will occur of PSSA results achieved during the project years and compared with results earned in previous years. Periodic data analysis will occur throughout the school year/s to ensure that students are making progress toward project goals. By querying the databases inherent within the Greenville School Districts Pennsylvania Value Added Assessment System and the Comprehensive Database Anaylsis system, the Greenville High School staff will continually disaggregate the data to refine the procurement of laptops and re-adjust procedures if and when necessary.

Indicators of student achievement will include documentation of student progress using the Cognitive Tutor and Compass Learning software in addition to semester examinations, journal writing, projects, and technology supported activities. Successful implementation of the Cognitive Tutor, Weaver Reading, and Compass Learning software will include the monitoring of student's time on task as well as achievement data. All data will be centralized to track the percentage of annual improvement and the progress being made toward achieving Pennsylvania's state academic standards. Data collected from this process will be used to help the School District Curriculum Council meet its goal of improving school achievement.

If project implementation does not meet proposed goals, immediate and swift adjustments will ocurr. These adjustments may include increased professional development activities, increased direct instruction, reassessed time-on-task, or software revisions. In light of any outcome, the emphasis will remain on continuous and overabundant training. Technolgy advances so rapidly that faculty skills can quickly become obsolete as new hardware and/or software is introduced. The Greenville Area School District remains committed to technology-based teaching and learning and understand that success may falter unless teachers are routinely helped with the process of learning new skills.

Following a review of student achievement data and professional development surveys the Greenville Area School District has planned a series of activities that will a) improve student achievement in content area reading, mathematics, and science; b) create a comprehensive system of student and teacher laptop acquisition; c) initiate a program of staff development that promotes a working knowledge of classroom technology; and d) provide opportunities for parents to gain greater awareness of student achievement as it relates to involvement in technology related activities.

The activities call for a series of specific training sessions to gain an acute understanding of digitized learning and an applied knowledge of the advantages of mobile computing and integrated technology in the classroom. The acquisition of laptop computers and related peripherals will provide the necessary portability to take full advantage of the school's desire to create a personalized learning experience for its students. For example, the Cognitive

Tutor, Weaver Reading, and Compass Learning software programs used in high school reading and mathematics classes were chosen for their level of technological sophistication, capability to adjust for individualized needs, and inclusion of the Pennsylvania's Academic Standards. Several learning principles have guided our preliminary planning. One principle states, "One size does not fit all". This principle reminds educators that instruction must account for the learner's internal motivation, a suitable learning style, and the level of understanding. The second principle states, "More time, more gain". Research has shown that the more time students invest in developmentally appropriate integrated learning systems, the more gains in achievement will occur.

The Cognitive Tutor, Weaver Reading, and Compass software programs are individualized, interactive, and provide frequent assessment creating the chance to affect a positive change in student achievement. Learning needs are first ascertained during the initial placement sessions. During these sessions, the instructional software analyzes student proficiencies, adjusts the level of difficulty, and recommends an appropriate starting point and creates an individualized learning path. The electronic delivery system of the Cognitive Tutor, Weaver Reading, and Compass Learning software utilize full motion video, engaging interactive animation, multimedia simulations and specialized intervention to provide for the individual needs of student. Students engage in 20-minute sessions three to four times each week. Research clearly indicates that instructional technology can foster growth in mathematics skills when the instruction is individualized. Student achievement increases when time on-task is maintained over extended periods. Both software programs have an extensive data gathering and assessment component. Teachers can retrieve student data individually or by classes to address learner or curricular needs. In addition, student data can be retrieved during marking periods to share with parents.

Describe the activities that will occur at your school or district, and when they will occur, to ensure that the professional development activities and the integrated instruction and learning are appropriate and support the local educational goals. Indicate what you will do if the implementation does not meet the proposed benchmarks.

Accurately analyzing student data is important to the success of this project. Providing on-going professional development is equally important. The U.S. Department of Education's Planning has published a 2000 report and Evaluation Service entitled "Does Professional Development Change Teaching Practice? Results from a Three-Year Study" concludes that professional development is a key contributor to school performance. The study identifies six factors that contribute to high-quality professional development.

Activities will be: 1) Based on integrating technology rather than more traditional professional development activities. The Cognitive Tutor and Compass Learning software packages provide teachers with the tools they need to meet individualized learning needs and align mathematics instruction with Pennsylvania's Academic Standards. With more than 25 years of experience in the field, software programs such as Cognitive Tutor, Weaver Reading, and Compass Learning deliver innovative, state of the art educational management and assessment tools and curriculum aligned to state and national standards. 2) Sustained over time: Three years of funding will allow the Greenville Area School District to fully integrate the use of technology into all mathematics and science classrooms. Instead of an isolated one-time event of professional development, Greenville's train-the-trainer model includes activities that are connected and build upon acquired skills and prior knowledge. The school district's Technology Plan calls for training of teachers who will support others as they integrate technology within their classrooms. 3) Structured to involve teachers from the same school, grade and subject: the building principal of Greenville High School will coordinate in-service training. Teachers in grades 7–12 will meet in focus groups to discuss staff development options and make recommendations for specific training needs. 4) Inclusive opportunities for active learning: as part of their fact-finding efforts, the Technology Planning Team polled teachers concerning how they would like to be taught about the advantages of using technology in the class-room. Seventy-eight percent of the respondents indicated that they would like more help to integrate technology within their classrooms. 5) Coherent with other initiatives: all professional development activities will be focused on raising student achievement and aligning instructional to Pennsylvania's Academic Standards. Cognitive Tutor, Weaver Reading, and Compass Learning, endorsed by the Pennsylvania Department of Education as standards-based, embraces many of the same approaches as used in the school district's mathematics and science programs. It incorporates a hands-on approach to learning, emphasizes written communication; and encourages cooperative learning strategies. 6) Focused on specific content and teaching strategies: the main goal of Cognitive Tutor, Weaver Reading, and Compass Learning is to equip teachers with technology-based strategies to link instruction, curriculum, standards, and assessment.

Professional Development data will include documentation of participation in professional development activities and opportunities for active learning. This will include information regarding the impact of professional development on classroom instruction and assessment via teacher surveys and/or focus groups. The Pennsylvania State Online Technology Inventory (PaTI) will be used as well to measure the teachers' progress toward technology integration and literacy skills.

The minutes from meetings, feedback provided, and documentation of various school meetings will measure parental and community involvement. This will include information regarding the impact of these meetings and type of involvement by parents and community members in the learning environments via surveys and/or focus groups.

The chronological timeline that follows offers a quick reference of evaluative activities for year one and year two of the project. In Year 1, formative evaluative activities will include monitoring, reviewing, and summarizing the project's status to create a baseline of data for the future. 1) Formative evaluations of expectations will occur throughout the life of the project with quarterly reports submitted to the Superintendent of Schools by the Project Coordinator. 2) Data will be gathered from questionnaires, surveys, project comments, participation logs and budget summary information. 3) The Online Pennsylvania Technology Inventory sponsored by the Pennsylvania

Department of Education will be completed by the professional staff to determine levels of technology literacy and the degree of integration of technology with the classroom. 4) Summative evaluations will occur at the conclusion of each year and reflect progress toward the five project goals. 5) Progress reports through newsletters, newspapers, and information accessible from the school district's Web site will be available to the school community.

In Year Two and Three, evaluative activities will again include monitoring, reviewing, and summarizing the project's status. 1) Formative evaluations of project expectations will occur again throughout the life of the project with quarterly reports submitted to the Superintendent of Schools by the Project Coordinator. 2) Data will be gathered from questionnaires, surveys, project comments, participation logs and budget summary information. 3) The Online Pennsylvania Technology Inventory will be completed by the professional staff to determine levels of technology literacy and the degree of integration of technology with the classroom. 4) Summative evaluations will occur at the conclusion of each year. 5) Progress reports through newsletters, newspapers, and information accessible from the school district's Web site will be available to the school community.

PARTNERSHIPS AND LOCAL SUPPORT

List any business, community, or organization partners, including other local education agencies such as IUs and higher education institutions, providing a brief description of their roles and contributions to the success of the project. This narrative should also address those partners whose involvement is instrumental to the delivery of professional development, project implementation, or growth of Classrooms for the Future Project beyond the initial scope.

Partner (50 char)	Role (500 char)	Contribution (1000 char)
Compass Learning	Provides software that aligns with curriculum and PSSA. Provide professional development to the teaching staff on use and monitoring of the software.	Trains teachers to more use technology to enhance instruction. Provides students with more core curriculum learning opportunities.
Carnegie Learning	Provides software and support for mathematics curriculum and technology usage.	Trains teachers to use technology to enhance instruction. Provides students more curriculum learning opportunities.
Midwester Intermediate Unit 4	Provides support of hardware, software and networking.	Midwestern Intermediate Unit IV will continue to provide support for all hardware (including networking devices) to ensure maximum efficiency in the delivery of instruction using technology.
Reynolds School District	Distance Learning partner.	Provides opportunities for students in other schools to participate in classes at Greenville High School.

Partner (50 char)	Role (500 char)	Contribution (1000 char)
Allegheny Intermediate Unit	Provides professional support and software for a Comprehensive Data Analysis tool to be used by Greenville School District for student evaluation.	AIU3 will continue to support the upload of local and state assessments into a database (CDA) maintained by them so that we will be better able to produce reports of disaggregate groups to determine curricular changes or remediation.
Pennsylvania Value Added Assessment	Provides system to show growth in PSSA testing areas by using a comprehensive database that produces reports.	Provides professional development and guidance to Greenville staff and teachers on interpreting reports using the PSSA testing results to show student growth over years.
Smarter Ed Corporation	Provides Smartboards to classrooms to enhance instruction using technology.	Provides professional development to staff on using Smartboards and creating meaningful lessons for the curricular areas by taking advantage of interactive technology.
Thiel College	Serves as an example of a local four-year undergraduate college that currently requires and supplies mobile computers to incoming students.	Provides consultation, professional development, and guidance concerning procedures for the deployment of mobile technologies.
Weaver Reading	Provides software aligned with local curriculum and PSSA. Provides students' level of content area reading skills via computer assisted instruction.	Trains teachers to use technology to enhance instruction. Provides students more core curriculum learning opportunities.

Provide a summary narrative of the activities that the LEA conducted to ensure the acceptance of this program and the steps that will be taken to ensure the funded project's viability. Indicate how the local educational community, including superintendent, school board, curriculum and technology directors, and principal, will support the program.

The Greenville Area School Distirct is in an excellent position to ensure acceptance and vitality of the Classrooms for the Future Project. In 1999, renovations for the Greenville High School were completed. The renovations included preparation for the 21st century. The building's infrustructure was rewired with a CAT 5 and fiber optic backbone. In 2003, fiber was extended to connect all buidings with the high school complex. Internal remodling included providing seven network drops within each classroom. Advancement using technology has continued to play a large part in planning meetings whenever plans for the future are discussed. Creating a wireless environment, with assistance from the Classrooms for the Future Project, is the next logical step.

Greenville Area School District will continue to ensure that the project is funded in several ways. Every year, the district allocates money in the budget for additional equipment, repairs, and new technology devices. On purchase of hardware, Greenville has and will continue to purchase extended warranties to ensure that equipment in need of repair gets the attention necessary. Greenville also employs a trained group of support staff to sustain technology and provide professional development. Beyond the district employees, we continue to purchase contracted services such as support for the curriculum software and high level support for the network. In addition to budgeting money for technology, the administration and staff are always looking for future grant opportunities using technology to help with sustainability and cost.

To ensure the project's viability, the project management team has representation from the school board, the superintendent, the high school principal, technology department, teachers, and community.

SUSTAINABILITY

Provide a detailed plan to sustain the proposed project beyond the initial grant funding period. The plan should address maintenance and growth for all project-related resources and activities, including technology refreshment, upgrades, and enhancements, as well as ongoing professional development.

The Greenville School District is committed to integrate and supplement the entire school curriculum with the use of educational technology. This commitment began several years ago when a District Technology Technician and Assistant District Technology Technician were hired. The school district has coopertively trained an Intermediate Unit employee in an effort to continue supportive professional development efforts. In addition, a percentage of the local school budget was designated for technology on an annual basis. The school district will continue to support these initiatives through future budgets. For example, during the 2005–06 the school district allocated over $250,000 for technology alone. Budgeting for professional development and ongoing maintenance contracts associated with hardware and software programs have become a mainstay within each year's budetary process. Greenville Area School District will also provide for the continued costs associated with hardware and software upgrades by including these as line items in annual budgets.

The long-term vision for this project extends well beyond the first three years of the project. The Greenville Area School District fully intends to continue project activities with possible adjustments in format and delivery. Improving student achievement will remain a priority supported by the use of technology to maintain and analyze data. An accurate assessment of data will serve as the driving force for instruction, professional development, and on going curriculum evaluation

ASSURANCES

Administrators and teachers involved in or impacted by Classrooms for the Future will:

Participate in a minimum of 2 days of PDE Classrooms for the Future hands-on professional development opportunities.	Yes
Participate in a minimum of 30 hours of additional professional development on PDE-mandated content through a combination of offline and online training.	Yes

Use their professional development experiences to integrate the technology appropriately by adopting practices that regularly integrate technology with teaching and learning, adopting technology-integrated program management practices where appropriate, and ensuring the commitment and endorsement of all Classrooms for the Future teachers.	Yes
For teachers, commit to adopting practices that regularly integrate technology with teaching and learning.	Yes
For administrators, commit to participating in a mandatory pre-grant seminar on the leadership and support necessary to implement and sustain systemic change in instructional practices expected from all Classrooms for the Future schools.	Yes
For administrators, commit to adopting technology-integrated program management practices where appropriate.	Yes
For administrators, commit to ensuring the commitment and endorsement of all Classrooms for the Future teachers.	Yes
Provide the Classrooms for the Future coach frequent access to classrooms in session and work with the coach to identify and address needs.	Yes
Serve as Classrooms for the Future models and champion technology-enabled reform.	Yes
Participate in program evaluations.	Yes

The high school or AVTS/CTC will:

Identify and submit for consideration a candidate for Keystone: Technology Integrator if one does not exist in the school.	Yes
Promote student participation in programs that showcase technology skills such as the statewide Student Computer Fair.	Yes
Create a student program for coaching and mentorship or technical assistance if one does not exist.	Yes
Create a teacher program for coaching and mentorship if one does not exist.	Yes
Support Classrooms for the Future technology.	Yes
Participate in annual Pennsylvania Technology Inventory (PaTI) survey.	Yes
Participate in program evaluations.	Yes

The local education agency will:

Facilitate professional development opportunities supporting 21st century teaching and learning.	Yes
Provide release time for all relevant professional development opportunities.	Yes
Work with a Classrooms for the Future coach.	Yes
Support Classrooms for the Future technology.	Yes
Maintain policies and procedures that support Classrooms for the Future, including an Acceptable Use Policy.	Yes
Maintain a PDE-approved technology plan.	Yes
Participate in the annual Pennsylvania Technology Inventory (PaTI) survey.	Yes
Participate in program evaluation.	Yes
Seek partnerships and opportunities to support 21st century education beyond Classrooms for the Future.	Yes

BUDGET NARRATIVE

Grant award amounts will be based upon technology costs established through a statewide contract, which is currently in the bid process. Therefore, you will not enter any data in the Budget Detail section for this RFGA. You will simply mark it and the Budget Summary section complete. If you receive a Year One grant award, we will reopen your application for you to complete the Budget Detail section based on your awarded amount.

I have read the preceding instruction. I understand that I am to mark the Budget Detail and Summary sections complete without entering any data at this time.	Yes

SUMMARY BUDGET
FISCAL YEAR 2006–2007

ENTITY NAME: Greenville Area SD

Original

Refer to fiscal guidelines and grants manual for explanation of budget categories. ALL AMOUNTS MUST BE ROUNDED TO THE NEAREST DOLLAR. AN ACCOMPANYING DETAILED BUDGET MAY BE REQUIRED.

Cost Function	Description Of Functions	100 Salaries	200 Benefits	300 Purchased Professional & Technical Services	400 Purchased Property Services	500 Other Purchased Services	600 Supplies	700 Property	800 Dues Fees	Total
1000	Instruction	0.00	0.00	0.00	0.00	0.00	0.00	0.00	0.00	0.00
1692	Tutor Training	0.00	0.00	0.00	0.00	0.00	0.00	0.00	0.00	0.00
2100	Pupil Personnel Services	0.00	0.00	0.00	0.00	0.00	0.00	0.00	0.00	0.00
2200	Staff Support Services	0.00	0.00	0.00	0.00	0.00	0.00	0.00	0.00	0.00
2300	Administrative Support/Services	0.00	0.00	0.00	0.00	0.00	0.00	0.00	0.00	0.00
2400	Health Support Services	0.00	0.00	0.00	0.00	0.00	0.00	0.00	0.00	0.00
2500	Business Support Services	0.00	0.00	0.00	0.00	0.00	0.00	0.00	0.00	0.00
2600	Operation Maintenance	0.00	0.00	0.00	0.00	0.00	0.00	0.00	0.00	0.00
2700	Student Transportation	0.00	0.00	0.00	0.00	0.00	0.00	0.00	0.00	0.00

(continues)

235

Cost Function	Description Of Functions	100 Salaries	200 Benefits	300 Purchased Professional & Technical Services	400 Purchased Property Services	500 Other Purchased Services	600 Supplies	700 Property	800 Dues Fees	Total
2800	Central Support Services	0.00	0.00	0.00	0.00	0.00	0.00	0.00	0.00	0.00
2900	Other Support Services	0.00	0.00	0.00	0.00	0.00	0.00	0.00	0.00	0.00
3100	Food Services	0.00	0.00	0.00	0.00	0.00	0.00	0.00	0.00	0.00
3300	Community Services	0.00	0.00	0.00	0.00	0.00	0.00	0.00	0.00	0.00
	Column Totals	$0.00	$0.00	$0.00	$0.00	$0.00	$0.00	$0.00	$0.00	Sub Total $0.00

Approved Indirect Cost/Operational Rate: 0.0180 (CF 5000:OBJ 900) 0.00

Pass Through Funds (If Applicable) (CF 2990: OBJ 899) $0.00

Local Matching Funds (Not applicable to Special Education programs.)

Object Code	100	200	300	400	500	600	700	800	Total
LOCAL MATCH	$0	$0	$0	$0	$0	$0	$0	$0	$0

APPENDIX 9.3

A Module on Modules

OBJECTIVE(S)

The purpose of this module is to enable the student (teacher) to write and understand the component parts of a module by being able to do the following:

1. Write one or more behavioral objectives on a topic of the student's choice.
2. Write a rationale that supports the objectives.
3. Write a module guide that provides a step-by-step procedure for working through the modules.
4. Identify any preassessment measures that will allow the pupil to test out of the module.
5. Design appropriate instructional activities that will enable the pupil to realize the objectives.
6. Write the evaluation procedures in objective terms.
7. Provide for any necessary remediation.

Evaluation of the prepared module will be based on the assessment of the module resources person(s) using the evaluation checklist at the end of this appendix.

The prepared learning package may be used in the classroom, but such activity is not required for this module.

RATIONALE

Modules can be defined as a type of teacher-learning packet that includes the following:

1. A list of competencies that a student (teacher) is expected to have at the end of a unit
2. An explanation of any teacher-learning activities that are designed to help the individual to achieve what is expected of him/her
3. Statements of how each student's performance and progress is to be evaluated
4. Standards each student must meet in order to complete or master those things expected of him/her

The nature of teaching is determined by what the pupil to be taught needs to learn and how he or she best may learn it. The nature of the acquisition process by which teaching competency is acquired is determined by what the teacher is to learn and how he or she may best learn it. The rationale for competency-based teacher education pertains to the latter. The former determines its content.

The rationale for competency-based programs derives from concepts about the nature of what is to be learned (in this case, teaching competency) and from a model of the system most likely to enhance this acquisition.

Learning modules are becoming popular educational tools in schools today. This module designed to help a student (teacher) learn about modules by going through a self-instructional module on the concept of modules.

MODULE GUIDE

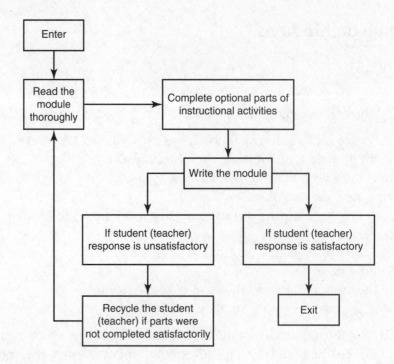

PREASSESSMENT

None

INSTRUCTIONAL ACTIVITIES

The following activities are optional but are designed to help the student (teacher) complete the module satisfactorily:

1. Read *Preparing Behavioral Objectives* by Robert Mager.
2. Study other modules in Project ESCAPE to learn types of content—the component parts.
3. Study the categories on the postassessment checklist.
4. Read *Measuring Instructional Intent* by Robert Mager.

EVALUATIVE CHECKLIST FOR LEARNING MODULES

Name of Evaluator _____

	Yes	Not Sure	No	If Not Sure or No, Please Comment
I. Objective(s)				
1. Specifies what is to be done	____	____	____	_____
2. Identifies condition	____	____	____	_____
3. States how it is to be done	____	____	____	_____
4. Provides criteria for completion	____	____	____	_____
II. Rationale				
1. Identifies relevant research	____	____	____	_____
2. Shows relationship to topic	____	____	____	_____
3. Is consistent with objective(s)	____	____	____	_____
4. Shows importance of objective(s)	____	____	____	_____
III. Module Guide				
1. Identifies prerequisites	____	____	____	_____
2. Identifies procedures for completing module	____	____	____	_____
IV. Preassessment				
1. Is consistent with objective(s)	____	____	____	_____
2. Allows student to test out of module	____	____	____	_____
V. Instructional Activities				
1. Is consistent with stated objective(s)	____	____	____	_____
2. Reasonable amount of time required	____	____	____	_____
VI. Remediation				
1. Procedure to be followed in event of unsatisfactory progress	____	____	____	_____

Suggestions for improvements (additional prerequisites, instructional activities, etc.)

_____

_____

_____

_____

_____

REFERENCE

Mager, R. F. (1984). *Preparing instructional objectives.* 2nd ed. Belmont, CA: Pitman Management and Training.

APPENDIX 9.4

Project ESCAPE Module List

I. Organizing and Teaching Subject Matter
  A. Planning
    101. **Curriculum**—fitting the curriculum of a subject or grade level into the total academic program
    102. **Planning and Teaching a Unit**—developing, executing, and evaluating plans with a central theme
    103. **A Daily Lesson Plan**—developing, executing, and evaluating a daily lesson plan
    104. **Conference Planning**—familiarizing the student (teacher) with procedures and organization of conference planning for an entire class
  B. Techniques for Teaching Subject Matter
    111. **Principles of Reinforcement**—identifying and applying various reinforcement methods in the classroom
    112. **Asking Questions**—asking higher order questions
    113. **A Module on Modules**—identifying parts of a module
II. Human Dynamics of Teaching
  A. Teacher–Pupil Interaction
    201. **Motivation**—using Maslow's Hierarchy of Human Basic Needs to assist motivational learning activities
    202. **Consistency**—demonstrating using consistency with pupils in and out of the classroom
    203. **Classroom Management**—demonstrating skills and techniques utilizing the democratic process in the classroom
    204. **Reinforcement Techniques in Written Work**—using written reinforcement techniques on written work
    205. **Handling Discipline Problems Objectively**—recognizing and handling discipline problems
    206. **Humor in Education**—demonstrating a sense of humor in the classroom
  B. Diagnosing Classroom Climate
    211. **The Sociogram: Social Isolates**—using the sociogram to identify social isolates and prescribing a suitable remedy
    212. **Learning Difficulties**—diagnosing learning difficulties and prescribing appropriate teaching-learning strategies
    213. **Children's Misbehavior Goals**—identifying and dealing with children's misbehavior goals as described by Adler
  C. Teacher–Pupil Relationships
    221. **Empathetic Responses**—aiding and developing empathetic responses
    222. **Group Structure and Dynamics**—reviewing group processes and their effects on dynamics and task achievement
    223. **Attitude Feedback**—measuring and finding a means to a positive attitude
    224. **Value Clarification**—defining values and related behavioral problems

225. **Recognizing Enthusiasm**—identifying verbal and nonverbal behaviors that demonstrate enthusiastic teaching and assessing the consequences of those behaviors

III. Developing Teaching Skills

   A. Technical Skills of Teaching

      301. **Handwriting**—demonstrating the ability to form letters according to the curriculum guide of the student's (teacher's) school

      302. **Use of Instructional Media**—developing and executing an instructional presentation demonstrating the proper operational techniques of audiovisual media

      303. **Plan Book/Grade Book: Development and Utilization**—developing and using a plan book and a grade book to meet the needs of a student's (teacher's) teaching situation

      304. **Utilizing and Supplementing Cumulative Records**—familiarizing the student (teacher) with ten pupils through cumulative records, observations, and interviews

      305. **Parent Conferences**—conducting a parent–teacher conference

      306. **Field Trips**—planning or executing a field trip

   B. Varied Approaches to Teaching

      311. **Individualizing Instruction**—demonstrating techniques of individualizing instruction

      312. **Guided Discovery**—using the guided discovery technique

      313. **Problem Solving**—using the problem-solving technique

      314. **Performance-Based Education in the Classroom**—preparing and implementing a performance-based lesson plan identifying specified skills or competencies

      315. **Creativity**—describing and demonstrating the humanistic teaching technique of creativity

      316. **Individual Needs**—using activities for meeting individual performance levels

   C. Verbal Communication in Teaching

      321. **Enunciation**—focusing attention on and corrective measures for commonly mispronounced words

      322. **Communicating on the Pupil's Level**—restating a school directive at the pupil's level of understanding

      323. **Voice Simulation**—using voice simulations in storytelling, story reading, and role playing

      324. **Listening Skills**—using listening variables and reacting to pupil comments to facilitate better pupil understanding

      325. **Lecture and Demonstration**—describing and practicing lecture and demonstration techniques

IV. Professional Responsibilities

   A. Policies and Regulations for the Classroom

      401. **Rules and Regulations**—familiarizing the student (teacher) with state and local regulations, requirements, and curriculum policies

      402. **Emergency Preparedness**—demonstrating knowledge of and developing a plan for federal, state, and local emergency preparedness plans

403. **School Policy**—demonstrating knowledge of local policies and procedures as presented in policy handbooks
404. **Good Health**—demonstrating the importance of a working knowledge of health factors in education

B. Professional Contributions of the Classroom Teacher

411. **Professional Organizations**—learning about professional educational organizations
412. **Code of Ethics**—demonstrating a knowledge of ethical behavior
413. **Legal Responsibility of the Teacher**—demonstrating legal responsibility
414. **School Communication and the Community**—demonstrating the ability to communicate with the community through various media
415. **Co-Curricular Activities**—identifying common problems of and participating in activities that are not part of the regular academic program
416. **Professional Growth**—demonstrating a knowledge of professionalism, an awareness of impedances to it, opportunities and resources for growth, and professional responsibilities

BOOK OVERVIEW (SUMMARY)

This book is written for school leaders at all levels. It assists department chairs to help teachers write small, single-authored grants to improve their classrooms, and it helps school administrators and central office administrators use large team-written grants to meet important district needs such as raising scores on state and national tests.

Many teachers will never write a grant; however, with encouragement and support, others will amaze you with their eagerness and ability to write small grants to improve their classrooms. With experience, these teachers will become strong grant-writing team members, committed to improving their schools.

Chapter 1

Writing multipage grants should begin with a three-ring binder. Up front, put a clear, succinct statement of your school or school district's mission statement. Follow with a bulleted list of your district's strengths and your community's strengths. Include a section that briefly describes unique strengths of teachers, administrators, and community members (including local CEOs and parents) who are willing to help write grants. Include a brief section on your district's needs, but don't permit it to overshadow its strengths. Once identified, these strengths can be reported on many future proposals. Keep the team focused on the district's mission and on your stated expectations.

Chapter 2

Grant writing is all about dreaming and creatively devising plans for turning those dreams into reality. This requires making every grant *the best it can be*—good enough to communicate your dreams so clearly and passionately that potential funders will want to be part of your dream. Remember the sign on the Savannah principal's door: "Our business is learning, and we are getting better every day." Your grant writers must live out their dreams every day. It's all about dreams, and grants are just tools to make those dreams come true.

Chapter 3

Because grant writing is clothed in a mask of acronyms and jargon that make it mysterious and threatening to novice grant writers, and sometimes confusing and frustrating to experienced ones, your three-ring binder should contain a glossary of grant terms. Follow with a section of terms and trends in education, and conclude with a section of political buzzwords. By using the politicians' language, you can directly address the issues that are perceived to be our schools' greatest needs. Help your teachers keep this list updated by providing current journals, either online or in hard copy. They can use these journals to capture quotable quotes and important data. These persuasive tools can be used repeatedly in many future proposals. Remind teachers that in grant writing, less is more, and numbers are far better than words.

Requests for proposals (RFPs) are the grant writer's best guide; they should be used as a blueprint, responding to every sentence. To improve your aim, phone the potential funder's office and ask for the rating form that will be used to rate your proposal. Listen for funder goals that are not in the RFP.

Remind your writers that the job is to devise a plan to reach your district's goals and the funder's goals, always giving the funder's goals top priority. Put copies of the RFP and the rating form in your three-ring binder.

Chapter 4

Include a copy of your targeted funder's mission statement and goals. Encourage your writers to respond to RFPs, as opposed to writing each grant and then seeking a funder. Put a copy of the source map in your binder to prevent wasting time by sending your proposals to funders for which you are not qualified.

Chapter 5

Check the RFP and include all parts mentioned. This refers to the following parts, even if they are not required: (1) Abstract, being careful not to exceed the maximum word limit; (2) a one-page Table of Contents; (3) a plan for sustaining the program beyond its funding period; and (4) a plan for having your program assessed by an evaluator outside your school district.

Chapter 6

List the budget parts in the same order that they appear in the RFP. For unlisted parts, put Personnel at the top. List the expendable items at the bottom. Be careful to ask for enough money to do a good job, but no more. You can do this by obtaining the cost of all equipment, materials, and services, and by using exact dollar amounts instead of words. Remind your writers that the goal is to make the budget clear, not just to yourself but to the funder.

To ensure that all details are included, some grant writers recommend preparing the budget as you write the narrative, as opposed to waiting until the narrative is finished. Write a short summary using only two or three sentences to explain each budget item. Unless the RFP says otherwise, limit the budget to one short page. To make your proposal more appealing, include plenty of in-kind contributions. Prepare to negotiate by including an expendable part. When your proposal draft is completed, edit it and then ask a colleague to read it. Then give it a mirror test by ensuring that every budget item is mentioned in the narrative, and vice versa.

Chapter 7

Put clarity above everything else by avoiding the use of jargon and unnecessarily long words, paragraphs, and sentences. Put the subject at the beginning of the sentence, followed immediately by an active verb written in the present tense. Include only one idea per paragraph. Replace bulky terms with single words, and replace two-dollar words with twenty-five-cent words.

Chapter 8

Department chairs should advise all who are initiating new grants to immediately notify their district office. Keep a list of potential funders in your three-ring binder and study their missions. Involve community members, listening carefully to their suggestions and making each a full partner in your grant-writing program. Align each proposal with your district's mission and goals. Meet the CEOs and the directors of local institutions, getting to know each personally. Partner with other school districts and local agencies with missions similar to yours. Make a list of willing grant writers along with their areas of expertise.

Chapter 9

Correctly written, every funded grant is a treasure chest of secrets for getting the next proposal funded if you are careful to document each accomplishment, use grant money wisely, and account for all spending. Looking for business connections with your district can increase your chances of being funded. Having a plan to disseminate your program to benefit as many as possible is always advantageous.

Chapter 10

Getting grants *re*funded is much easier than getting the original funding. You should start your efforts to get each grant refunded before it is approved by making the original proposal as good as it can be. Document everything, always looking for ways to raise the level of this documentation. Keep all documentation in your three-ring binder.

Create a Publication section in your binder, and use it to inform others of your program's progress, along with the team's individual and group achievements. A one-page, carefully drafted questionnaire can gather data needed to reflect your district's needs and also to show progress after the program gets underway. Try to use more numbers and percentages than words. Precede the mailing of the questionnaire with a short letter explaining how completing the questionnaire will benefit the recipient.

Use simple and clear language. When drafted, edit the proposal several times, and then ask a colleague to read it and give you some feedback. Remind your grant writers that some rejections are unavoidable; they can be steps to progress, and the only failure is not to write them in the first place.

INDEX

A

Abstract, 23, 47, 149
  Classrooms for the Future project,
    213–215
  Emergency Response and Crisis
    Management grant, 115, 116
  Reach for the Stars, 194
Action research, 139–142
AFT. *see* American Federation of
    Teachers (AFT)
American Federation of Teachers
    (AFT), 100
American Speech-Language Hearing
    Association (ASHA), 105
Annual partnership evaluations, 210
Anthony Trollop's Time-saving Tip, 15
Apostrophes, 170–171, 176–177
ARAS report. *see* At-Risk Alert System
    (ARAS) report
ASHA. *see* American Speech-Language
    Hearing Association (ASHA)
Assurances, Classrooms for the
    Future, 232–234
At-Risk Alert System (ARAS) report, 152
At-Risk Student Innovative Grant
    West Ashley High School, 151–164
Awards, school district, 39, 42

B

Bean counters, grant evaluators as, 26
Beating to a Different Drum project,
    188–193
  budget, 192–193
  design/plan, 189–191
  goals of, 189
  phases of, 190–191
  proposal narrative, 188–191
  summary, 188
Beineke, John, Dr., 58, 100
Bell curve, 77
Best, Charles, 83
Bijou Community School
  TWI program at, 165–168
Bilingual grant, 65
Block grants, 23, 33, 149
Boilerplate, 149
Books
  and grant writing, 24
  for TWI classes, 167
BP grant proposal, 63–64
Brevity, of grant proposal budget, 55–56
Brooks, Sandy, 123–129
Brown, Cindy, 82
Budget, grant proposal, 51

Beating to a Different Drum project,
    192–193
  briefness, 55–56
  clarity about, 55
  defined, 54
  Emergency Response and Crisis
    Management Grant, 59, 116–118
  errors, 58
  evaluation/sustainability, 63–65
  fringe benefits, 57
  indirect costs, 57–58
  negotiation, 63
  parts of, 58–65
  Personnel, 56–57
  personnel expenses, 58–62
  preparation of, 54–65
  principles, 59–60
  purpose of, 54
  Reach for the Stars, 196
  for TWI classroom, 167–168
  West Ashley High School, 163–164
Budget justification, 149
Budget narrative, 116, 118
  Classrooms for the Future, 234–236
Buffalo Colorado's Strategy, 39
Buzz words, 131

C

Cadwallader-Staub's Tip, 10
Cataloging process, 25
CATS. *see* Continuous Advancement
    Toward Success (CATS)
CCSD. *see* Charleston County School
    District (CCSD)
CEO. *see* Chief Executive Officer (CEO)
Charleston County School District
    (CCSD), 153
Checklist
  Emergency Response and Crisis
    Management grant, 114–115
  for grant proposal, 51–52
Chief Executive Officer (CEO), 23, 149
Child Advocacy Center, Cullman
    County, 212
Clarity
  about budget, 55
  in grant writing, 70, 72
Classrooms
  funding sources to improve, 82–93
Classrooms for the Future, 121–122,
    213–236
  assurances, 232–234
  budget narrative, 234–236
  goals of, 213, 226

  local evaluation, 226–230
  mentors for, 225
  monitoring, 226–230
  needs assessment, 215–218
  project plan, 218–222
  sustainability, 232
  technology deployment for, 222–225
Cognitive Tutor, 227–229
Collaboration, 6, 23, 99, 149
  advantages, 18
  disadvantages, 20
  with other districts, 99–104
  tips, 18–20
Collaborative proposals, timeline for, 17
Commas, 169, 174
Community Awareness/Emergency
    Response Partnership, Cullman
    County's, 201–212
  crisis planning, phases of, 205–206
  design, quality of, 207–210
  evaluation, quality of, 210–211
  management plan, quality of,
    211–212
  need for, 201–204
  significance, 204–206
Compass Learning, 224–225,
    227–229
Competitive priorities
  CATS/WRAP initiatives, 163
Conferences, educational
  and ideas for grants, 102
Connections. *see* Interpersonal
    relationships, and grant writing
Connors, Peggy, 41
Continuous Advancement Toward
    Success (CATS)
  budget, 163–164
  competitive priorities, 163
  dissemination, 163
  evaluation, 162–163
  management, 160–162
  need statement, 151–154
  project design, 154–160
  sustainability, 162
  timeline, 159
Costs
  direct, 149
  indirect, 57–58, 149
Cost sharing, 149
County Commission, Cullman
    County, 212
Cover letter, 149
  questionnaire, 145–147
Credit Union of America, 86–87

Cullman County, Alabama, 114–121
   Child Advocacy Center, 212
   Community Awareness/Emergency
     Response Partnership, 201–212
   County Commission, 212
   Emergency Management Agency, 221
   Health Department, 212
   safety issues in, 201
   Sheriff's Department, 211

D

Data collection, of funding agencies, 34
Deadline, 33–34
   and high-quality proposal, 5–6
   tips for handling, 16–18
Dickens, Charles, 72
Direct costs, 149
Discouragement, tips for handling,
   9–10
Dissemination
   CATS/WRAP initiatives, 163
Documentation, grant, 138–139
Dollar-for-dollar match, 23, 149
DonorsChoose, 83–85
   writing process, steps of, 83–85
DUNS Number, 23, 149
Dykstra, Craig, 102

E

Editing, step-by-step process, 74–75
Educational conferences
   and ideas for grants, 102
Educational Improvement Act (EIA)
   grants, 105, 108
Educational terms, grammar and,
   172–173, 179–180
EIA grants. *see* Educational
   Improvement Act (EIA) grants
Elegant approach, for evaluation, 50
Eleventh-hour proposal, 5
EMA. *see* Emergency Management
   Agency (EMA)
Emergency Management Agency
   (EMA), 211
Emergency Response and Crisis
   Management Grant, 114–121
   application checklist, 114–115
   Budget, 59, 116–118
   Executive Summary Report for, 118,
     119–121
   lessons learned from, 118
   proposal abstract, 115–116
   table of contents, 115–116
Emergency response reviews, 211
ESCAPE. *see* Project Elementary
   and Secondary Competency
   Approach to Performance
   Education (ESCAPE)

Evaluation
   CATS/WRAP initiatives, 162–163
   Classrooms for the Future, 226–230
   Community Awareness/Emergency
     Response Partnership, 210–211
   external, 63, 149
   formative, 149
   grant proposal, 50–51
   as part of budget, 63–65
   of Reach for the Stars, 195
Evaluators. *see* Grant evaluators
Every Day Mathematics Program, 218
Executive Summary Report
   for Emergency Response and Crisis
     Management grant, 118, 119–121
Expenses
   other, 61–62
   personnel, 58–62
External evaluation, 63, 149

F

Facilities, school/school district's, 39
Family Night Parent Awareness
   Workshop, 223–224
Federal Register, 23, 34, 36, 81, 107, 149
Adams, Myra, 40
Flow chart
   Project Elementary and Secondary
     Competency Approach to
     Performance Education, 128
Flow charts, 77
   grant proposal, 49–50
   sample, 78
Follow-up letter, questionnaire, 145–146
Formative evaluation, 149
Foundation grants, 99–104
Foundations, 23, 149
Franklin, Ben, 26
Freund, Gerald, 100
Fringe benefits, 57
Front-end loading, 55
Fuel Up to Play 60, 97–98
Funder, 23, 149
Funding
   amount, availability of, 34
   cycle, 23, 149
   guidelines, 23, 149
   resources, unavailability of (*see*
     Funding sources)
   role of luck in proposal, 4–5
Funding agency
   goals, and grant writer's strengths,
     34–35
   mission statement of, 36–37
Funding cycle, 23, 149
Funding sources
   Credit Union of America, 86–87
   DonorsChoose, 83–85

Home Depot, 95
   to improve classrooms, 82–93
   to improve schools/school districts,
     94–111
   Kappa Delta Pi, 87–88
   New England Dairy & Food
     Council, 96
   parents as, 89–90
   Phi Delta Kappa International, 91,
     92–93
   Principal's proven strategy for
     identifying, 94–99
   searching for, 81–111
   Target Field Trip Grant, 88
   unavailability of, 2–3
   United Way, 95
   United Way of the Midlands, 95

G

Gender, and grant writing, 76
Glossary, 23–24
Goals
   funding agency, and grant writer's
     strengths, 34–35
   grant proposals, 48–49
Grammar, 169–180
   apostrophes, 170–171, 176–177
   commas, 169, 174
   education terms and, 172–173,
     179–180
   hyphens, 171, 177–178
   its, usage of, 170, 175–176
   number agreement, 169–170, 175
   technology terminology and,
     171–172, 178–179
Grantee, 23, 149
Grant evaluators, 4, 55
   as bean counters, 26
   instructions to, 27
Grantor, 23, 149
Grant proposals. *see* Proposals, grant
Grants, 23, 149
Grants administrator, 23, 149
Grant writers
   and forcefully writing, 70, 72
   ideas and, 101–102
   integrity as quality of, 58
   source map, 33
   strengths, and funding agencies
     goals, 34–35
   success of, role of luck in, 4–5
   tips for (*see* Tips)
   tools for, 22–31
   as voracious readers, 101–102
Grant writing, 101
   clarity in, 70, 72
   commitment toward, 137–138
   forcefully, 70, 72

Grant writing (*continued*)
 funding for (*see* Funding)
 gender bias and, 76
 interpersonal relationships and, 3
 myths about, 2–6
 overview, 1–2
 partners, selection of, 19
 paths, selection of, 32–42
 personal library and, 24–25
 politics and, 134–135
 precaution against using
  unnecessary jargon, 68–69
 simple structure for, usage of, 70
 style, 67–79
 teachers and, 1
 time for, 3–4
 timeline, 17
 tips for (*see* Tips)
 Uncle Daniel approach, 6
 usage of graphics in, 76–79
 vocabulary, 22–31
Graphic organizer, 77
Graphics
 usage, in grant writing, 76–79
Graphs, and grant writing, 77
Greenville Area School District, 213–236
 needs assessment, 215–218
 Strategic Plan's Steering Committee,
  223–224
 Teacher Induction Plan, 216
Greenville High School, 213–236
 mentoring at, 225
 renovations for, 231
 staff development, 215
 technology deployment in, 222–225
Guarantee letter. *see* Transmittal letter

H

Hands-On Universe, 195
Haven, Kathy, 65
 TWI Bilingual grant, 165–168
Hayes, Karen, 94–99
Head Start, 104
Health Department, Cullman
 County, 212
Hemmingway's lesson, 74
Home Depot, 95
Human resources
 schools/school districts, 39
Hyphens, 171, 177–178

I

Ideas, and grant writers, 101–102
Indirect costs, budget, 57–58, 149
In-kind contributions, 23, 58–59, 61, 149
 Reach for the Stars, 196–197
Input goals, 149
Integrity, as quality of grant writer, 58

Intergenerational Tutorial Grant, 94, 95
Internet
 and search for funding sources, 81
Interpersonal relationships, and grant
  writing
 lack of, 3
 tips for making, 11–13
IRS Form 990, 150
Its, usage of, in grammatical
  construction, 170, 175–176

J

Jargon-free proposal, 23, 68–69, 150
Jefferson Elementary School, 105
 funded project titles/focus, 106–107
Johnson, Samuel, 74
Journals, and grant writing, 24–25

K

Kappa Delta Pi, 87–88, 91
 state-wise list of awards, 181–182
Kellogg Foundation, 100–101
Kurt Vonnegut's Tip, 13

L

Lake Tahoe Unified School District
 (LTUSD), 165
 budget, 168
Language, and grant writing, 22–24
 grammar exercises, 169–173
Learning modules, 237–239
 defined, 237
 evaluative checklist for, 239
 guide, 238
 instructional activities, 238
 list, Project ESCAPE, 240–242
 objectives, 237
"Less Fortunate Us" syndrome
 tips to overcome, 10–11
Letter of inquiry, 150
Letter of intent, 150
 Fuel Up to Play Wellness Activation
  Grant Programs, 97–98
Letter of support, 23, 150
Library, personal
 and grant writing, 24–25
LTUSD. *see* Lake Tahoe Unified
  School District (LTUSD)
Luck
 role, in proposal funding, 4–5

M

Matching budget/grant, 150
McKenzie, Paul, 10
McWilliams, Christie, 92–93
Memorandum of agreement (MOA), 150
Mentoring, at Greenville High
 School, 225

Mescher, Brenda, 87–89
 tips from, 88–89
Mirror test, 61, 65, 150
Mission statement, 23, 150
 of funding agency, 36–37
 school district's, 26–27, 38
MOA. *see* Memorandum of agreement
 (MOA)
Modules. *see* Learning modules
Money
 distribution, inequality in, 3
Monitoring
 Classrooms for the Future,
  226–230
My listening ears, 29
Myths, about grant writing, 2–6

N

National Board Certified Teachers
 (NBCT), 39
National Council of Teachers of
 Mathematics (NCTM), 88
National Education Association
 (NEA), 99
National Radio Astronomy
 Observatory (NRAO), Green
 Bank, 194–195
National School Age Care Alliance
 (NSACA), 189
Naysayers, 9
NBCT. *see* National Board Certified
 Teachers (NBCT)
NCLB. *see* No Child Left Behind
 (NCLB)
NCTM. *see* National Council of
 Teachers of Mathematics (NCTM)
NEA. *see* National Education
 Association (NEA)
Needs assessment
 Classrooms for the Future, 215–218
Need statements, 23, 150
 West Ashley High School, 151–154
Negotiation, budget, 63
New England Dairy & Food
 Council, 96
Nielsen, Waldemeir, 100
Nighttime approach, *see* Shotgun
 approach
No Child Left Behind (NCLB),
 113, 154
NRAO, Green Bank. *see* National
 Radio Astronomy Observatory
 (NRAO), Green Bank
NSACA. *see* National School Age Care
 Alliance (NSACA)
Number agreement, in grammar,
 169–170, 175
Numbers, and grant writing, 76–77

O

Online Pennsylvania Technology Inventory, 230
Order of budget items, 55
Orlich's 20-Day Rule, 6
Output goals, 150

P

Parent
  as funding sources, 89–90
Parental safety survey, 211
Parent power, 65
Parent Teacher Organization (PTO), 105
Partners, grant writing
  selection of, 19
Partnership grants, 113–135
  Classrooms for the Future grant, 121–122
  Emergency Response and Crisis Management grant, 114–121
  Project Elementary and Secondary Competency Approach to Performance Education, 123–129
  Summer Physics Institute grant, 129–133
  technology grants, 133–135
Partnerships, 23, 150
  and local support, 230–232
Passion, 13
Paths, grant writing
  selection of, 32–42
PaTI survey. *see* Pennsylvania Technology Inventory (PaTI) survey
PDK. *see* Phi Delta Kappa International (PDK)
Pennsylvania System of School Assessment, 213
Pennsylvania Technology Inventory (PaTI) survey, 223
Personnel, expense category, 56–57
Personnel expenses, as part of budget, 58–62
Petersburg Elementary School
  Reach for the Stars and, 194–197
Phelps, Connie, 69, 86–87
Phi Delta Kappa International (PDK), 91, 92–93
  Regional Project Application, 183–187
Phi Delta Kappan, 142
Phillips, Bill, Dr., 98–99
Phrases
  replacement, with single words, 70, 71
Politics, and grant writing, 134–135
Ponder Heart, The, 6
Powerful writing, by grant writers, 72–74
Principal investigator, 23, 150

Project Coordinators, Reach for the Stars, 197
Project Elementary and Secondary Competency Approach to Performance Education (ESCAPE), 123–129, 138
  flow chart, 128
  lessons learned from, 128–129
  module list, 240–242
  purpose of, 124–128
Project Management Team, 223–224
Project summary statement, 150
Proposal rating form, 24, 28–29, 150
Proposals, grant. *see also* Requests for Proposals (RFP)
  abstract, 47
  budget of, 51
  checklist for, 51–52
  eleventh-hour, 5
  evaluation, 50–51
  flow chart, 49–50
  funding for, luck and, 4–5
  gender bias and, 76
  goals, 48–49
  importance of meeting deadline, 5–6
  jargon-free, 23, 68–69, 150
  negative words, removal of, 74–75
  objectives, 49–50
  parts of, 44–52, 109–110
  purposes, 48
  questionnaires and, 18
  simple structure for, 70
  sustainability, 50
  table of contents, 47–48
  timetables/timeline, 49
  title page, 45–46
  transmittal letter, 44–45
  usage of graphics in, 76–79
  vocabulary for, using simple, 68–69
PTO. *see* Parent Teacher Organization (PTO)

Q

Query letter, 150
Questionnaires, 18, 139, 142
  cover letter, 145–147
  developing, 142–144
  follow-up letter, 145–146
  length of, 147
  one-page, 140–141
  preliminary letter, 144
  sending, 144–145
  testing, 144
  types of questions in, 143–144
Questions
  arrangement of, 143–144
  types, in questionnaires, 143
Quotable quote, 24, 26, 150

R

Ragu story, 122
Rating forms, 27–31
Reach for the Stars, 194–197
  budget, 196
  evaluation of, 195
  goals/objectives, 194–195
  implementation methods, 195
  in-kind support, 196–197
  NRAO, 196
  project coordinators, 197
  timeline, 196
Redlhammer, Ann, 133–135
Requests for proposals (RFPs), 3, 10, 24, 27, 36, 43, 55–56, 65, 81, 150. *see also* Proposals, grant
  defined, 30
  graphic organizer and, 77
  outline, classrooms for future, 30
  specifications, 34
  table of contents, 47–48
Reviewers. *see* Grant evaluators
Review of literature, 24, 150
RFPs. *see* Requests for proposals (RFPs)
Rhodes, Jack, 129–133
Rifle approach, 32–34
RMHC. *see* Ronald McDonald House Charities (RMHC)
Robert Wood Johnson Foundation, 100
Ronald McDonald House Charities (RMHC), 96
  Grant Application Form, 198–200

S

Safety needs assessment, 210
Savage, Hanna, 40–41
School districts
  awards, 39, 42
  collaboration with other, 94–104
  facilities/space of, 39
  funding sources to improve, 94–111
  human resources, 39
  mission statement of, 26–27, 38
Schools
  facilities/space of, 39
  funding sources to improve, 94–111
  human resources, 39
  mission statement of, 38
Science, Technology, Engineering, and Mathematics (STEM)
  grant, budget summary for, 55–56
SCSHA. *see* Speech Language and Hearing Conference (SCSHA)
SCVHS. *see* SC Virtual High School (SCVHS)
SC Virtual High School (SCVHS), 153
Sheriff's Department, Cullman County, 211

Shotgun approach, 32, 34
Single-authored proposals, timeline for, 17
SLP. *see* Speech Language Pathologist (SLP)
Smokestack theory, 24, 150
Source map, 24, 33, 150
SPAs. *see* Specialty Professional Associations (SPAs)
Special education grants, 104–111
Specialty Professional Associations (SPAs), 103–104
  list of, 103
Speech Language and Hearing Conference (SCSHA), 110
Speech Language Pathologist (SLP), 105, 110
STARLAB, 195
STEM. *see* Science, Technology, Engineering, and Mathematics (STEM)
Stevenson, Robert Louis, 25–26
Student incident reports, 211
Summer Physics Institute grant, 129–133
  lessons learned from, 132–133
Sustainability, 39
  CATS/WRAP, 162
  Classrooms for the Future, 232
  grant proposals, 50
  as part of budget, 63–65
  plan, 24, 150

T
Table of contents, grant proposal, 47–48
  Emergency Response and Crisis Management grant, 115–116
Table of specifications, and grant writing, 77, 79
Tables, and grant writing, 77
Tale of Two Cities, A, 72
Target audience, and block grants, 33
Target Field Trip Grant, 88
Teacher Induction Plan, Greenville Area School District, 216
Teachers
  collaboration, with colleagues, 6
  and grant writing, 1
  tips for, 9–20

Technology
  Classrooms for the Future project and, 213, 222–225
  terminology, and grammar, 171–172, 178–179
Technology grants, 133–135
  enhancing education through, 151–164
  lessons learned from, 135
Third Circle, The, 188–189
Three-ring binder, 25–26, 37–38
Time, for grant writing, 3–4
  tips for having more, 13–16
Time-finding strategies, 16
Timeline, 17, 24, 150
  grant proposal, 49
  Reach for the Stars, 196
Tips, 9–20
  for collaboration, 18–20
  for handling deadlines, 16–18
  for handling discouragement, 9–10
  for having more time, 13–16
  for making connections, 11–13
  to overcome "Less Fortunate Us" syndrome, 10–11
  Wendy Wingard-Gay's, 108
Title page, grant proposal, 45–46
Transmittal letter, 44–45
Triangular model, 24, 35–36, 150
TWI program. *see* Two-Way Bilingual Immersion (TWI) program
Two-Way Bilingual Immersion (TWI) program
  benefits of, 166
  at Bijou Community School, 165–168
  budget, 167–168

U
Uncle Daniel approach, 6
Union Alternative Model, 154
United Way, 95
United Way of Metropolitan Atlanta, 188–189
  goals, 188
  strengths, 188–189
United Way of the Midlands, 95

V
Vocabulary, grant writing, 22–31
  usage of simple, 68–69

W
WAHS. *see* West Ashley High School (WAHS)
Wally, Barbara, Dr., 41
Weaver Reading, 227–229
We hate grant writing, 10
Weighted rating form, 24
Welty, Eudora, 6
West Ashley High School (WAHS)
  At-Risk Student Innovative Grant, 151–164
  budget, 163–164
  CATS model (*see* Continuous Advancement Toward Success (CATS))
  goals, 158
  need statements, 151–154
  objectives, 158
  project design, 154–160
  WRAP initiative (*see* Wildcats Redirection and Prevention (WRAP))
Wildcats Redirection and Prevention (WRAP)
  budget, 163–164
  competitive priorities, 163
  dissemination, 163
  evaluation, 162–163
  key elements of, 157
  management, 160–162
  need statement, 151–154
  project design, 154–160
  sustainability, 162
  timeline, 159–160
Wilde, Oscar, 137
Wingard-Gay, Wendy, 60, 69, 104–110
  tips on grant writing, 108
WRAP. *see* Wildcats Redirection and Prevention (WRAP)
Writers, grant. *see* Grant writers

Y
York School District One, 105

Z
Zadravec, Steve, 99
Ziegler, John, 121–122